Hiking the Gulf Coast

HELP US KEEP THIS GUIDE UP TO DATE

Every effort has been made by the author and editors to make this guide as accurate and useful as possible. However, many things can change after a guide is published—trails are rerouted, regulations change, facilities come under new management, and so forth.

We welcome your comments concerning your experiences with this guide and how you feel it could be improved and kept up to date. While we may not be able to respond to all comments and suggestions, we'll take them to heart, and we'll also make certain to share them with the author. Please send your comments and suggestions to the following address:

FalconGuides
Reader Response/Editorial Department
246 Goose Lane
Guilford, CT 06437

Or you may e-mail us at: editorial@falcon.com

Thanks for your input, and happy trails!

Hiking
the Gulf Coast

A Guide to the Area's Greatest Hiking Adventures

Joe Cuhaj

FALCONGUIDES

GUILFORD, CONNECTICUT
HELENA, MONTANA

FALCONGUIDES®

An imprint of Rowman & Littlefield
Falcon, FalconGuides, and Outfit Your Mind are registered trademarks of Rowman & Littlefield.

Distributed by NATIONAL BOOK NETWORK

Copyright © 2016 by Rowman & Littlefield
Photos: Joe Cuhaj
Maps: Alena Joy Pearce © Rowman & Littlefield

British Library Cataloguing-in-Publication Information available

Library of Congress Cataloging-in-Publication Data
Cuhaj, Joe.
  Hiking the Gulf Coast : a guide to the area's greatest hiking adventures / Joe Cuhaj.
    pages cm
  "Distributed by NATIONAL BOOK NETWORK"—T.p. verso.
  Includes index.
  ISBN 978-1-4930-0812-4 (paperback : alk. paper) — ISBN 978-1-4930-1450-7 (electronic) 1. Hiking—Florida—Guidebooks. 2. Hiking—Alabama—Guidebooks. 3. Hiking—Mississippi—Guidebooks. 4. Hiking—Louisiana—Guidebooks. 5. Hiking—Texas—Guidebooks. 6. Natural resources—Florida—Guidebooks. 7. Natural resources—Alabama—Guidebooks. 8. Natural resources—Mississippi—Guidebooks. 9. Natural resources—Louisiana—Guidebooks. 10. Natural resources—Texas—Guidebooks. 11. Florida—Guidebooks. 12. Alabama—Guidebooks. 13. Mississippi—Guidebooks. 14. Louisiana—Guidebooks. 15. Texas—Guidebooks. I. Title.
  GV199.42.F6C84 2015
  796.510976—dc23
                        2015023077

∞™ The paper used in this publication meets the minimum requirements of American National Standard for Information Sciences—Permanence of Paper for Printed Library Materials, ANSI/NISO Z39.48-1992.

Contents

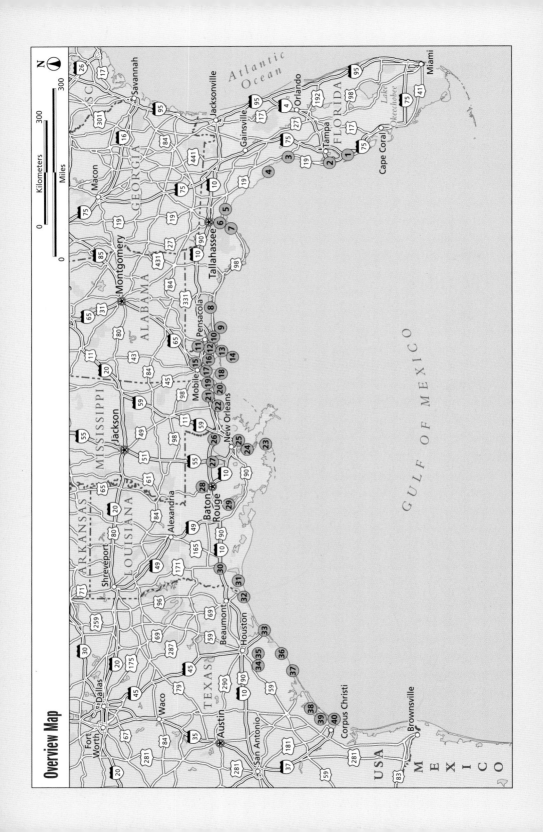

Overview Map

Texas Honorable Mentions

Acknowledgments

It would be impossible for me to thank all of the hikers, clubs, organizations, agencies, and land managers for their help putting this book together. Just know that I am very grateful for all of your support and input.

There are two groups that I need to specifically thank for their help and guidance. A big thank-you to the members of the Florida Trail Association and Alabama Hiking Trail Society for their help in suggesting trails to be included in this guide.

I also send my thanks to the rangers and staff of the US Fish and Wildlife Service and National Park Service and all of their volunteers working at the national wildlife refuges and parks I visited during my research. I have never met a group of people so dedicated, friendly, helpful, and knowledgeable. Thank you!

There is one person I need to single out and thank, my wife, Maggie, who once again hiked every mile of trail with me for this book along with our rescue Labrador, Archer. I seriously couldn't have done it without her and couldn't have had better company.

Introduction

Some people call it the "Big Crescent," others call it the "Third Coast," but most everyone calls it paradise: Shimmering emerald green waters, brilliant pristine white beaches, calming black-water rivers, salt marshes, and tidal flats—they all make up the Gulf Coast.

The Gulf Coast can truly be called a paradise for the lovers of the outdoors. With its subtropical climate, you can lose yourself in an endless variety of activities virtually year-round. Oh, there are some bumps in the road that I'll discuss in a minute, but for the most part, it's a great place to live and visit any time of year.

Since moving to the Gulf Coast some thirty years ago, it has always been a dream of mine to drive the crescent from one side to the other, not on the interstates but the back roads through the small towns and villages that dot the coast. Little did I know that one day I would not only get that opportunity, but also do it while partaking in my favorite sport—hiking. When FalconGuides and I partnered to do this book, I knew I was in for an adventure and one that I wanted to share with all of you.

There are five states that form the rim of the coast: from east to west—Florida, Alabama, Mississippi, Louisiana, and Texas. The goal of this guide is to provide you with information on the forty best coastal hikes across these states. Of course, the word *best* is subjective. What's best for one person may not be for you. I have tried to make this book as diverse as possible so that everyone will find a trail to their liking and then will want to go out and try the others.

In this guide we will be covering hikes that fall between Tampa, Florida, and Corpus Christi, Texas—about 90 percent of the entire Gulf Coast. The treks within these pages are by no means all there is to hike on the Gulf Coast. I have also included "Honorable Mentions" at the end of each state's section. These are other hikes along that state's coastal area that I think you might like to check out. In the end I hope that this guide will inspire you to find the many other hiking adventures along the Gulf Coast.

When talking about this area with locals and tourist officials, you may hear them refer to it as the "Third Coast." That rubs some Chicagoans the wrong way, since up there many call the shores of the Great Lakes the "Third Coast." But come on, really? A lake coast versus an ocean coast? I rest my case. (Sorry, just had to add a little friendly fuel to the fire of this ongoing rivalry.)

The ecosystems of the Gulf are quite diverse. In south Texas we'll hike through salt marshes and tidal flats; in north Texas and Louisiana, it's marshes, wetlands, and cedar and tupelo swamps; in Mississippi and Alabama, slow-moving black-water rivers, expansive deltas, and transitional forests; and in Florida we'll hike through scrub pine over ancient sand dunes and visit amazing sinkholes in what is known as a karst topography. Plus we will hike on some of the Gulf's famous barrier islands. These great long stretches of sand hold all of this fascinating ecosystem together like a picture frame by protecting the mainland from the battering of ocean waves and storms and providing habitat for thousands of different species of birds and wildlife.

An expansive view of the wetland from an observation deck along the Sabine Wetland Walkway (hike 31)

History

The history of the Gulf Coast is a long one—over 180 million years long. That is when the supercontinent called Pangea began breaking apart. By the time this colossal jigsaw puzzle was finished rearranging itself, the Gulf was much larger than it is today. The first Gulf of Mexico would have stretched from Oklahoma all the way north to Arkansas, and Georgia would have had Gulf Coast beaches. (Florida was underwater at the time.)

When it comes to the history of the region, all five states share a common thread. Each was inhabited thousands of years ago by Native Americans who first discovered the bounty this ocean had to offer. Europeans began exploring and settling the coast in the late 1400s, with the Spanish leading the parade. One of the first landings in Texas happened quite by accident. Ángel de Villafañe was sailing to Mexico but was shipwrecked on an island which we now know as Padre Island.

A great blue heron waits patiently for his photo to be taken along the Estuary Trail at Big Lagoon State Park, Florida.

Following a series of similar shipwrecks along the south Texas coast, Spain decided to look for a place where they could protect their fleet and shipping while being able to provide quicker assistance to shipwrecked sailors. Tristán de Luna y Arellano led an expedition to the north-central Gulf Coast looking for that safe harbor and landed in Pensacola Bay in 1559.

It wasn't long after that the French began to move in. Explorers like Pierre Le Moyne d'Iberville and Jean-Baptiste Le Moyne helped the French create settlements and forts along the coast on Dauphin Island, Alabama, and in Ocean Springs, Mississippi.

Through subsequent wars and treaties, the land of the north-central and east Gulf Coast passed through the hands of the Spanish, French, British, and then to the United States following the War of 1812. Most of the major cities that line the coast can claim to be a city of "Five Flags" (the Confederacy is counted as one of those flags). In Texas their allegiance was a bit different: Spain, France, Mexico, the Republic of Texas, the United States, and the Confederacy—six flags.

The Gulf Coast has been in the news over the last few years, making new history. In the last ten years, the coast saw some of the deadliest and costliest hurricanes in US history come ashore (see the sidebar "5 'n' 10" in hike 22, Pirate's Alley Nature Trail).

More recently, and one I'm often asked about, is the Deepwater Horizon Oil Spill, better known to all of us on the coast as the BP Oil Spill, which is recognized as the worst such spill in US history.

On April 20, 2010, an oil rig located 42 miles off the coast of Louisiana, the Deepwater Horizon, exploded, killing eleven rig workers. Deep below the surface in the cold darkness, cameras discovered that the drill and pipe were leaking oil and gas. The well wasn't capped until July 15, eighty-seven days later. By then 4.9 billion barrels of oil had leaked into the Gulf.

The results were devastating, both on the environment and on area businesses. Oyster beds were destroyed, fragile wetlands and marshlands were overtaken, birds covered in oil, nesting sea turtles threatened, fishing fleets closed. The cleanup was monumental, but today there is very little evidence that the spill occurred. Scientists from universities around the world, however, are keeping a close precautionary eye on the health of these waters.

The Gulf and its people are resilient and have fought back from these setbacks, and I'm here to tell you, the Gulf Coast is back, better than ever, and open for business.

Flora and Fauna

The ecosystem of the Gulf Coast is extremely diverse and often fragile. Many species of endangered or threatened animals and birds call the beaches and back bays of the Gulf home.

Along the thousands of miles of barrier islands, the loggerhead and Kemp's ridley sea turtles come to nest. Baby turtles have a hard enough time making a go of it without losing their habitat to condominiums and beach houses. The turtles lay their eggs high above the tide level on the white Gulf beaches. When they hatch it's a mad dash to the Gulf where, if they're lucky, they will make it through the gauntlet of predator fish who love to feast on the young hatchlings. Combine this with the disappearance of their nesting grounds and it's clear why the turtles are endangered. Thankfully local towns and volunteers, as well as state and federal agencies, are teaming up to protect the nesting grounds and help the sea turtle make a comeback.

A couple other reptiles that are endangered who call the Gulf region home are strange bedfellows: the gopher tortoise and the eastern indigo snake. Both thrive in longleaf pine forests, but the destruction of these forests for lumber has left the duo without a place to go. The gopher tortoise burrows into the soft sandy ground to make its home. The indigo snake actually lives in the burrow with the tortoise. There is a good chance you will see the gopher tortoise at some time during your hikes through the pines. The indigo, not so much. Their numbers are small. Many people mistake black racers for the indigo but there is a difference—the racer has scaly skin, the indigo smooth skin.

A couple of birds that are trying to make a comeback that you may be able to see along these trails are the Florida scrub-jay and the whooping crane. The crane frequents the south Texas area and Aransas National Wildlife Refuge. Their numbers

The red berries of yaupon holly brighten the Jeff Friend / Centennial Trail (hike 14).

are few, with only just over 400 remaining, but the good news is that population is slowly, ever so slowly, trying to come back (see hike 38, Heron Flats Loop).

The Florida scrub-jay is the state's only endemic bird and is completely reliant on scrub forests to survive. A scrub forest is one of Florida's most unique ecosystems and is found in the state's coastal regions and along the tops of sand ridges. The forest is characterized by dwarf and scrub oak trees such as the sand live oak, myrtle oak, and Chapman's oak, with large patches of barren white sand interspersed with a few pines, palms, and saw palmetto.

Of course, from Texas to Florida there is an abundance of white-tailed deer, armadillo, raccoon, marsh and cottontail rabbits, bobcat, coyote, and, well, you get the picture. There are some wildlife you'll find from one end of the Gulf to the other you don't want to mess with—ticks, mosquitoes, and yellow flies. Remember, many of the trails in this book travel along water features, and you are bound to get eaten alive at some point or another by mosquitoes and have a few ticks tag along for the ride. You will encounter these mainly in summer, but with our damp, mild falls and winters, they can pop out at any time. Carry the insect repellant and you will be fine.

Yellow flies, on the other hand, are a real bother. These large, yellow, biting flies are ferocious in the heat of summer, leaving large welts on your skin, and to make matters worse, they swarm. There isn't anything I've found to stop these bugs from biting. Most of the time I would rather reschedule a hike when it's yellow fly season.

An animal that everyone wants to see is the American alligator. You will have plenty of opportunities to view one up close and personal on many of these hikes. Just remember, alligators are naturally afraid of humans and will for the most part slide out of the way. Now if people have been feeding them, that changes the rules. They may seem slow at first, but an alligator has remarkable speed on land for a short distance so don't underestimate them. And please, heed the warnings posted at the parks and refuges and in the hike descriptions within, especially concerning the safety of your children and pets.

What amazes people most when they hike the trails of the Gulf Coast is that only the slightest change in elevation, from a few inches to a few feet, changes the habitat. Great examples of this can be seen along the Rocky Bayou Double Loop (hike 8), where along the banks of a stream you will descend down to the stream and wetland and in a few feet go from a scrub pine forest to a coastal flatwood forest, or on the Pine Beach Trail in Alabama (hike 13), where you start the hike in a maritime forest, transition to a wetland, then wind up on the dunes of the Gulf of Mexico, all in less than a mile.

You will see a lot of shrubbery with red or purple berries as you walk from state to state. The American beautyberry is prevalent along the trails, with its distinctive clusters of glossy, iridescent purple berries hugging its branches. Same with yaupon holly and its ever-present bright red berries.

In the marshes and wetlands there is plenty of flowering prickly pear cactus, some sharp Spanish dagger plants, and glasswort. A glasswort looks a lot like asparagus, only shorter, and grows in salt marshes. The plant is unique in that it can actually convert saltwater from its brackish environment into freshwater, then stores it in its stems.

My advice is to get yourself a good wildflower and plant guide. There literally isn't enough room here to tell you about all of the wonderful plants you will see as you hike the Gulf Coast.

Weather

The entire Gulf Coast from Corpus Christi to Tampa is located in the subtropics. Summertime temperatures average a high of 90° to 95°F, with lows between 70° and 75°F. Wintertime temperatures average daytime highs between 65° and 70°F and lows in the low 40s. That is not to say the coast doesn't get cold. Temperatures do on occasion drop below freezing—even into single digits—but those days are few and far between.

That sounds all nice and, well, tropical, but with it comes some weather extremes. Now please, don't let this discourage you from hiking the Gulf Coast. These are just some of the weather issues you need to be aware of to have a safe hike.

Of course, there is the heat. You will notice that most of the hikes in this book suggest the best time to hike them is from fall to spring. That is not to say you can't hike them in the summer, but be aware that temperatures often cruise to 100°F. Combine that with high humidity and the heat index is off the scale. Many of these trails, especially in Florida and Texas, have little to no cover, so take precautions by wearing something to protect your head, use sunscreen, and drink plenty of fluids. And if the heat index does get that high, remember, the trail will be there another day so reschedule.

The one thing most people are concerned with is hurricanes. Hurricane season generally runs from June 1 to November 30—generally. Some pretty significant storms have hit the coast before and after those dates.

Over the last ten years, the Gulf Coast has experienced five of the costliest and deadliest storms on record. But don't let that frighten you off. With a few exceptions, storms begin off the coast of Africa and take a week or so to cross before we even know if they will enter the Gulf or not, so you have plenty of time to make plans. Once a hurricane is in the Gulf, it's time to keep your eyes and ears open and be ready at a moment's notice to evacuate.

The Gulf Coast is also known for its severe summer thunderstorms that can dump inches of rain in a matter of hours. These storms pop up frequently in the heat of the afternoon, with dangerous lightning and strong winds. Again, just be prepared, keep up with the weather forecast and the weather radio, and enjoy the trails!

Restrictions and Regulations

Considering how fragile the coastal environment can be, it's fair to say that local, state, and federal officials do a pretty good job of protecting it while still giving visitors ample recreational opportunity to explore. While I have listed specific regulations for each hike within each listing, things do change. Please do your part and pick up a park regulation brochure when you arrive at your destination and review it for any changes.

The trails in this book are all day hikes, but some of those do allow trailside or backcountry camping where you can pack your gear in and spend the night in a fascinating swamp or along a bayou. Those that do are noted in the trail descriptions.

All state parks have primitive camping areas for tents and what are called "improved campsites" that have their own water spigot and electrical outlets. Reservations are not required for primitive campsites but are highly recommended for improved or ocean-side sites. Reservations are usually accepted up to twelve months in advance. Generally speaking, up to eight people are allowed per site. Fees and additional regulations may apply, so be sure to check at the ranger station of each park for details or the website noted in the text.

There are a few national wildlife refuges and national parks that allow camping, such as Davis Bayou (hike 21) and Fort Pickens (hike 9). Once again, these sites are noted in the text.

Small day-use fees are required at all state parks. One national park, Fort Pickens, charges a per person fee; however, that fee allows you access to the park for seven days.

A palmetto pathway along the Ochlockonee River Loop (hike 7)

With only a few exceptions, dogs are welcomed on the trails described here, and those that do not allow pets are noted in each hike. All pets must be on a leash no longer than 6 feet at all times. And for those trails where dogs are permitted, consider your environment before bringing them. Pets and alligators don't mix, and if you're walking a narrow trail along a bayou, they could be in danger. I have noted these warnings in the text where they apply.

For the most part, hunting is not a problem for the trails described in this book. Hunting is allowed on some wildlife refuges in Texas, but the trails are not within hunt areas. Hunting is allowed in two Texas state parks, Sea Rim and Brazos Bend (hikes 32, 34, and 35); Cedar Key Scrub State Preserve in Florida (hike 4); and the Perdido River Trail (hike 11) in Alabama. Check dates for closings online. For Texas visit tpwd.texas.gov/state-parks/parks/things-to-do/hunting; Florida, myfwc.com/hunting/season-dates; and Alabama, outdooralabama.com.

How to Use This Guide

This guide contains just about everything you'll ever need to choose, plan for, enjoy, and survive any hike along the Gulf Coast. To assist in your hiking choices, the coast has been divided into the states covered—Florida, Alabama, Mississippi, Louisiana, and Texas. To aid in quick decision-making, we start each hike chapter with a short summary to give you a taste of the hiking adventure to follow. You'll learn about the trail terrain and what surprises the route has to offer. If your interest is piqued, read on; if it isn't, skip to the next hike.

The hike specifications that follow are fairly self-explanatory. Here you'll find the quick, nitty-gritty details of the hike: where the trailhead is located, hike distance, hiking time, difficulty rating, type of trail terrain, best seasons to hike, what other trail users you may encounter, canine compatibility, land status, nearest town, whether fees or permits are required, trail schedule, available maps, and trail contacts where you can get updates on trail conditions. "Finding the trailhead" provides dependable directions from a nearby city right down to where you'll want to park and includes GPS coordinates.

"The Hike" is the meat of the chapter. Detailed and honest, it has been carefully researched and my impression of the trail is noted here. While it's impossible to cover everything, you can rest assured that we won't miss what's important. "Miles and Directions" provide mileage cues to identify turns and trail name changes, as well as points of interest.

The "Hike Information" section at the end of each hike is a hodgepodge of information. Here we'll tell you where to stay, where to eat, and what else to see while you're hiking in the area.

The Honorable Mentions are hikes that didn't make the cut. In many cases it's not because they aren't great hikes, but they may be overcrowded or environmentally sensitive to heavy traffic. Be sure to read through these. A jewel might be lurking among them.

How to Use the Maps

Overview Map

This map shows the location of all the hikes described in this book, so you can choose a hike based on geography or see which hikes are nearby. You can find your way to the start of the hike from the nearest sizable town or city. Coupled with the detailed directions provided in the "Finding the trailhead" entries, these maps should visually lead you to where you need to be for each hike.

Route Map

This is your primary guide to each hike. It shows all the accessible roads and trails, points of interest, water, towns, landmarks, and geographical features. It also distinguishes trails from roads. The selected route is highlighted, and directional arrows point the way.

Trail Finder

Best Hikes for Backpacking

11 Perdido River Trail

27 River / Bottomland Hardwood Trail

29 Trail C

Best Hikes for Beach Lovers

2 Osprey-Pelican Loop

9 Fort Pickens Seashore Trail

11 Perdido River Trail

13 Pine Beach Trail

Best Hikes for Birding

2 Osprey-Pelican Loop

18 Audubon Bird Sanctuary

34 Lake Loop

38 Heron Flats Loop

40 Salt Island Marsh Trail

Best Hikes for Families with Children

22 Pirate's Alley Nature Trail

24 Barataria Preserve Trail (short segments)

25 Bayou Segnette Nature Trail

31 Sabine Wetland Walkway

Best Hikes for Geology Lovers

6 Leon Sinks Loop

Best Hikes for History Buffs

9 Fort Pickens Seashore Trail

15 Historic Blakeley State Park

16 Village Point Park Preserve

28 Port Hudson Historic Site

Best Hikes for Views

1 Robinson Preserve Loop

10 Estuary Trail

40 Salt Island Marsh Trail

Best Hikes for Wildflowers

23 Fiddler's Loop

34 Lake Loop

Best Hikes for Dogs

2 Osprey–Pelican Loop

8 Rocky Bayou Double Loop

19 Escatawpa Trail

35 White Oak–Red Buckeye Loop

Map Legend

95	Interstate Highway	⬛	Bench
98	US Highway	⬛	Boat Ramp
24	State Highway	⏝	Bridge
762	County Road	▪	Building/Point of Interest
	Local Road	▲	Campground
	Unpaved Road	▲	Campsite
	Railroad	⊛	Capitol
	Utility/Power Line	†	Cemetery
	Featured Trail	▥	Dining
	Trail	⬯	Gate
	Boardwalk	⚟	Lighthouse
	International Line	℗	Parking
	State Line	⊞	Picnic Area
	Small River/Creek	⬛	Ranger Station
	Intermittent Stream	⬛	Restroom
	Body of Water	⬛	Scenic View/Viewpoint
	Marsh/Swamp	◣	Shelter
	Sand	⬛	Tower
	National/State Forest	○	Town
	National Wilderness/ Preserve/Reserve	10	Trailhead
	State/County Park	❓	Visitor/Information Center
	Wildlife Refuge/ Miscellaneous Park	⬛	Water
	Miscellaneous Area		

Florida

They don't call it the Sunshine State for nothing. Hiking and outdoor recreation of any kind is a pleasure in Florida most any time of the year anywhere you travel. Of course, there are caveats to that statement that I'll discuss in a moment.

The Florida Gulf Coast is divvied up into "sub-coasts" mainly for tourist purposes, but the trails we will explore in this guide fit neatly into each "coast." The hikes are scattered about Florida's Gulf Coast from Tampa to Pensacola. That takes in a lot of different environments to explore and discover.

The Tampa Bay area is on what is called the "Cultural Coast," having been recognized as the cultural center of the state since the early 1920s. This area is a large 400-square-mile estuary. Red, black, and white mangroves cling to the banks of saltwater bays and marshes, shoring up the coastline from erosion and providing nesting for birds. Salt marshes and mudflats provide additional shoreline protection from severe Gulf storms and is prime habitat for clams, crabs, and thousands of migratory, wading, and shore birds. Some of the hikes we'll explore in this region include Robinson Preserve (hike 1) and the Osprey-Pelican Loop (hike 2).

The "Nature Coast," or what used to be called the "Big Bend," is aptly named. This is the place for outdoor recreation, with an abundance of paddling, biking, snorkeling, and hiking opportunities. For hiking this area from Citrus to Wakulla Counties is characterized to the south by scrub forests, one of Florida's most unique ecosystems, with dwarf and scrub oak trees and large patches of barren white sand interspersed with a few pines, palms, and saw palmettos. To the north, coastal marshes and tidal creeks provide a thriving habitat for birds and wildlife. One of those is the endangered Florida scrub-jay that needs a scrub environment to survive.

Just a little farther away from the coast to the north is an amazing natural wonder called the Woodville Karst. This is a series of watery sinkholes and caves created by a process called *karst* where surface water erodes the soft limestone underground, forming this intricate series of underground, and watery, passages.

We'll explore the environments of the Nature Coast along the Cedar Key Scrub Nature Trail (hike 4), Lighthouse Levee (hike 5), and Leon Sinks (hike 6).

Finally there is the "Emerald Coast," again an aptly named area from Pensacola to Apalachicola where the Gulf waters are an amazing shade of emerald green, which is only enhanced and deepened by the brilliant white beaches. The sand contains Appalachian quartz that has washed down from the mountains far to the north. This gives the beaches that beautiful sugary appearance, and many say that they are most stunningly beautiful beaches in the world. Chances to experience life as a beach-comber come with the Estuary Trail at Big Lagoon State Park (hike 10) and Fort Pickens (hike 9).

The Emerald Coast is also home to the extreme eastern edge of the Gulf Islands National Seashore, a 160-mile stretch of barrier islands that begin in Mississippi on Cat Island and end here just east of Pensacola. These fragile islands protect the main-land from the ferocious Gulf storms that would otherwise destroy the coastline and provide habitat for hundreds of species of wildlife.

As I said, the weather along Florida's Gulf Coast is nearly perfect. In the Tampa area at the easternmost end of our excursions, the temperatures range from a high of 70°F and a low of 52°F in January to a high of 90°F and low of 75°F in July. The heaviest rain usually comes in August, when the hot, humid Gulf air kicks up those famous Gulf Coast afternoon rainstorms.

To the north from Pensacola to Apalachicola, temperatures run a little cooler, just a little, from a high of 63°F and a low of 41°F in January to a high of 90°F and low of 73°F in July. Again the heaviest rainfall comes in August, averaging around 8 inches a year. Just remember that the humidity can rise dangerously high in the summertime throughout the state, causing the heat index to rise over 100°F.

Now there are the extremes. First, those pesky hurricanes. From listening to the news, you would think that Florida is a magnet for hurricanes, but consider how large the state is and that it is bordered by the Atlantic Ocean on the east coast, the Gulf of Mexico on the west coast, and the Caribbean to the south. It's just in a bad place.

Hurricane season generally runs from June to November, but hurricanes can pop up outside of that window. Just check the local weather wherever you hike to keep up with any tropical depressions or hurricanes that have formed and heed the advice of local emergency officials, and you will be fine.

1 Robinson Preserve Loop

The Robinson Preserve Loop is an amazing walk over dirt and gravel footpaths and elevated boardwalks through wetlands teeming with birds like great blue heron, egret, wood stork, dowitcher, and the beautiful red-hued roseate spoonbill. The walk is highlighted by a bird's-eye view of the wetlands from atop a five-story observation tower.

Start: Robinson Preserve trailhead on northwest side of parking lot
Distance: 3.3-mile loop
Hiking time: About 2 hours
Difficulty: Easy over level terrain
Trail surface: Gravel path, boardwalk, pavement
Best seasons: Year-round
Other trail users: Joggers, cyclists
Canine compatibility: Leashed dogs permitted
Land status: City preserve

Nearest town: Bradenton
Fees and permits: None
Schedule: Year-round; summer hours 6:30 a.m. to sunset, fall–spring 8 a.m. to sunset
Maps: USGS Anna Maria, FL
Trail contact: Manatee Board of County Commissioners, PO Box 1000, 1112 Manatee Ave., Bradenton, FL 34205; (941) 748-4501; mymanatee.org/home/government/departments/parks-and-recreation/natural-resources/preserves/robinson-preserve.html

Finding the trailhead: From the intersection of FL 64 and 75th Street SW in Bradenton, take 75th Street W north 0.7 mile. Turn left onto 9th Avenue NW. Travel 1.5 miles and turn right onto 99th Street NW. Travel 0.5 mile. The entrance gate will be on the left. Continue straight through the gate about 0.25 mile to the parking lot. The trailhead is on the northwest side of the parking lot. GPS: N27 30.846' / W82 39.711'

The Hike

Along the banks of Tampa Bay is a 487-acre tract of land that at one time was nothing more than "disturbed farmland." There was nothing here except acres of invasive species of plants like Australian pine and Brazilian pepper trees. But in 2008 that all changed.

The owners of the property, the Robinson family, had plans to convert the land into an eighteen-hole golf course and subdivision, but being conservationists at heart, they decided at the last minute to change their mind. With funding in part by Manatee County, the Florida Forever program, Florida Fish and Wildlife, the US Army Corps of Engineers, and the US Environmental Protection Agency, and a lot of back-breaking work by what Manatee County officials call "legions of volunteers," the land went through a miraculous transformation and became known as Robinson Preserve.

Today the preserve boasts over 3 miles of paddling trails that take kayakers to the Manatee River and Perico and Palma Sola Bays; 3 miles of paved walking, biking, and fitness trails; and over 5 miles of hiking trails over a shell footpath with six boardwalks. The Robinson Preserve Loop described here is only a subset of the trails in the preserve, and you are encouraged to wander about and take in the sights and sounds—and there's plenty to take in.

This 3.3-mile loop winds its way through a salt marsh and saltern ecosystem. A saltern is a series of saltwater ponds that gradually evaporate, leaving only salt. Ponds like these were the source of salt for humans in prehistoric times, and even today salterns are still used in parts of the world. Hiking this trail on a sunny day with deep blue skies and puffy white clouds is a photographers dream as they shine down on the many reflective surfaces.

Walking along the banks of the ponds and marshes, you will be treated to beautiful wildflowers like black-eyed Susan, Indian blanket, and a tunnel of butterfly-loving sea myrtle through a mangrove stand and swamp. Walk quietly and you'll see many shore- and seabirds including black-bellied plover, willet, wood stork, least tern, Florida scrub-jay, and the roseate spoonbill with its beautiful pink plumage. Osprey nests dot the horizon. As the trail makes its way to the banks of Tampa Bay, you will be sharing the path with fiddler crabs and there is a good chance that you'll cross paths with black racer snakes and a gopher tortoise or two.

Two highlights of the trail include a 0.1-mile-long boardwalk with remarkable views of one of the ponds and bayou, and a 54-foot-tall observation tower. From atop the tower you will get an expansive view of the preserve plus four counties and Tampa Bay with the Sunshine Skyway Bridge on the horizon.

The last leg of the trail uses a section of the paved fitness trail. Along this route you will pass exercise shelters where you can do pull-ups, chin-ups, and any number of exercises—or just sit in the shade and relax. Each station has an informational sign that tells you how to correctly do the exercise at that station.

Robinson Preserve is a very popular park, so most of the time you won't be alone when you walk. The best time to hit the trail is first thing in the morning when the park opens.

Oh, and don't forget to stop by the Valentine House during your visit. This is a 125-year-old house that was moved onto the property and is now the preserve's visitor center. The many volunteers who staff the center and keep the trails clean are extremely friendly and helpful. It shows that they truly love Robinson Preserve, as I'm sure you will.

A walk high above a bayou, the park's observation tower in the distance

Miles and Directions

0.0   Start at the parking lot and head northwest. In 300 feet arrive at the trailhead kiosk. If you have your dog with you, pick up a dog waste bag at the station to pack out any mess. The trail is paved here. Two ponds flank the trail on either side.

0.2   A wide dirt/gravel path comes in from the right (north). This is part of the Osprey Trail. Turn right here off the paved route onto the Osprey Trail and head north.

0.4   Come to a Y. The right fork goes to a campground. Take the left fork (north). A sign here says "Tower .2 Mile."

0.5   Come to a Y with a trailside shelter and benches. The right fork skips the tower and rejoins the tower section of the trail at 0.9 mile. Take the left fork to head to the tower.

0.6   Arrive at a boardwalk that takes you to the observation tower. In less than 0.1 mile, arrive at the tower. When you're finished viewing, return to the boardwalk and at the end turn left (northeast) onto the gravel path.

0.9   Arrive back at the main trail. Turn left (north). In a few yards cross a bayou over a long boardwalk. After the boardwalk the trail ducks into a forest of mangroves, palms, and palmettos.

1.1   Cross a 0.1-mile-long boardwalk over a bayou next to the park's canoe trail. You will pass a canoe landing on your left (south) and have great views of the tower reflecting in the water as well as paddlers plying the water and many species of birds.

1.2   As the trail bends to the west, pass a picnic table on your right (north). Along this section expect nice views of the bayou to your left (south) and the Manatee River and Tampa Bay on your right (north).

1.3   Pass a short side trail to the right (north). The trail leads to a small beach on the bay, and you'll have a view of the Sunshine Skyway Bridge in the distance. There are signs along the canoe trail that is on your left warning paddlers of strong currents.

1.4   After crossing a boardwalk, pass through a cave of mangrove trees and sea myrtle.

1.5   Cross a short boardwalk. The trail is much more enclosed and shady here.

1.6   Cross an inlet from the bay over a long boardwalk.

1.8   Come to an intersection. Straight is a primitive trail; to the right (north) is a 100-foot side trail to the bay with some nice views at the end. When done, return to the intersection and head south.

2.2   Pass a trail on the left (east); continue straight to the south.

2.5   Cross over a bridge and pass a side trail to the left (east) that leads to a fishing pier. There is also a shelter with a bench and information sign on doing crunches. In less than 0.1 mile, the gravel path intersects with the paved preserve road. A sign here reads "To main entrance" and points to the left (northeast). Turn left onto the paved road.

2.7   Pass another shelter with a bench and pull-up bar with information on how to do pull-ups. There is a nice view of the lake here as well.

2.9   Pass another shelter with an information sign on how to warm up for exercising.

3.2   Pass the turnoff you made at mile 0.2. Continue straight (east).

3.3   Arrive back at the trailhead.

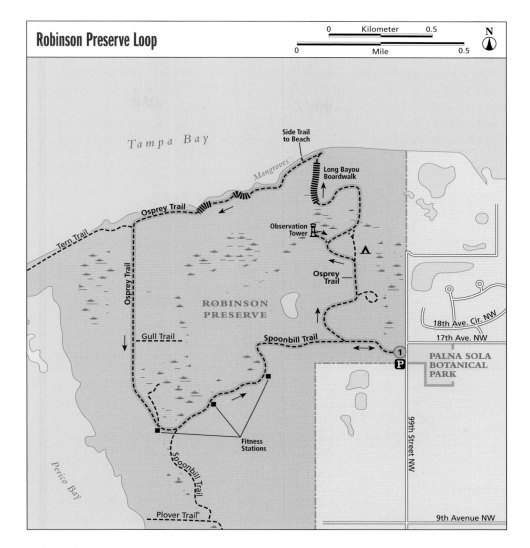

Hike Information

Local Information: City of Bradenton, 101 Old Main St. W, Bradenton, FL 34205-7865; (941) 932-9400; cityofbradenton.com

Local Events/Attractions: Boo Fest, 8100 Lakewood Branch Blvd., Bradenton; lwrcac.com. Held the Friday before Halloween, Boo Fest transform Main Street Bradenton into a family-friendly "spooktacular" with scarecrows, haunted houses, graveyards, and plenty of treats.

Restaurants: Sage Biscuit Cafe, 6656 Cortez Rd., Bradenton; (941) 792-3970; sagebiscuit cafebradenton.com

Other Resources: Audio tour of Robinson Preserve: (941) 926-6813. Pick up a brochure at the Valentine House and punch in the number of the stop along the route to hear a description.

2 Osprey-Pelican Loop

The Osprey-Pelican Loop combines two trails at Honeymoon Island State Park: the Pelican Trail, which winds its way along the banks of Pelican Cove with beautiful ocean views, small white sand beaches, and sea oats lining the path waving in the breeze, and the Osprey Trail. It's easy to see where the Osprey gets its name. Along the route you will find yourself encircled by dozens of osprey nests and the parents of young chicks putting on an aerial show as they vie for dinner.

Start: Parking lot near picnic area and playground
Distance: 2.6-mile loop
Hiking time: About 1.5 to 2 hours
Difficulty: Easy on level terrain
Trail surface: Grass, beach sand
Best seasons: Sept to May
Other trail users: None
Canine compatibility: Leashed dogs permitted
Land status: State park

Nearest town: Dunedin
Fees and permits: Admission fee
Schedule: Year-round, 8 a.m.–sunset
Maps: USGS Dunedin, FL; maps available at entrance station
Trail contact: Honeymoon Island State Park, #1 Causeway Blvd., Dunedin, FL 34698; (727) 469-5942; floridastateparks.org/honeymoonisland

Finding the trailhead: From the intersection of US 19 and Curlew Drive / FL 586 in Dunedin, take Curlew Drive 2.6 miles. Curlew Drive / FL 586 becomes Causeway Drive. Continue straight 3.2 miles, crossing St. Joseph Sound and arriving at the Honeymoon Island State Park entrance. After paying your admission fee, continue straight 0.3 mile and make a right turn toward the picnic area. In 0.2 mile come to the picnic and playground area parking loop. Park here. The trailhead is at the north end of the parking area. GPS: N28 04.085' / W82 49.827'

The Hike

On a small barrier island that forms the western boundary of St. Joseph Sound is a beautiful little state park that is aptly nicknamed "a barrier island paradise," Honeymoon Island. Native Americans called this island home thousands of years ago, with Europeans, namely the Spanish, arriving in 1530. It wasn't until the 1830s when settlers began flocking to west Florida that the island had a name, Sand Island.

In 1848 a hurricane blasted through the island, pushing over 5 feet of water over it. One of the only surviving businesses on the island was a small hog farm, and with that the island received a name change—Hog Island.

The island finally became known as Honeymoon Island in 1939 when a New York City land developer, Clinton Washburn, purchased it. Fifty thatched bungalows were constructed, and with the help of *LIFE* magazine, a contest was held where newly married couples could win a two-week "honeymoon" in one of the cottages. Ever since, the island has been known as Honeymoon Island.

One of the Osprey Trail's namesakes keeping an eye on us hikers

Since that time this wonderful state park was built among the mangrove swamps, tidal flats, and salt marshes of the island. In all there are just over 9 miles of hiking and nature trails in the park along with concession stands where you can get a drink, snacks, and souvenirs or rent a kayak to paddle around in.

The Osprey-Pelican Loop is actually made up of two trails, the Osprey Trail and Pelican Trail. The Osprey Trail winds its way through one of the last virgin slash pine forests in the state, interspersed with the ubiquitous palm tree, and is described by the park as its premier hiking trail. The trail is so named because of the dozens of osprey nests that line the wide grassy path, so don't forget your binoculars.

At the northern most end of the loop near the intersection with the Pelican Trail, you will come to an area that is clearly marked as the location of an eagle nest. During mating and nesting season, which is generally early spring, this area of the trail is closed to the public but an observation area is set up so you can view the majestic birds.

Besides these birds of prey, there are plenty of other animals and plants to experience along the hike. You will likely catch glimpses of great horned owls, roseate spoonbills, snowy egrets, great blue herons, and least terns. You may also encounter armadillo and gopher tortoise. The park estimates that there are over 300 tortoises living on the island.

While not blazed, the path is very easy to follow. There are 4-by-4-inch posts with mile markers on them every quarter mile.

The Osprey Trail is actually an elongated loop that travels up the east side of the island then loops back to the south along a parallel path. For this hike we skip the southbound side and instead join up with the Pelican Trail, which is named for the bay it's nestled beside. The trail skirts the banks of the bay through lines of mangroves. Sea oats wave in the breeze while fiddler crabs busily go about their business. The view here is magnificent, especially of the sunsets over Pelican Bay and the Gulf of Mexico in the distance. The best view is at the very northern end of the trail just after its intersection with the Osprey Trail, where there are benches overlooking the bay. Be patient and you may see a dolphin or manatee.

Keep in mind that much of the footing on the Pelican Trail is fine "sugar" sand that can make walking more of a chore. Sections of the Pelican Trail sometimes flood after a good Southern soaker and may be closed, as it was when I hiked the path. If that's the case, use one of the many side connectors to take you back to the Osprey Trail to finish the hike; otherwise, continue straight south another 0.2 mile to the end of the trail, where it will once again connect with the Osprey.

One additional note about Honeymoon Island State Park is that it is very dog-friendly. Attendants at the entrance station greet your dog when you pay your entrance fee with a biscuit. The park is one of the few that allow dogs on the beach, provided they are on leashes, of course. They even have a special shower to rinse Fido off after he takes a dip in the saltwater. And the Osprey Trail goes a step further and has a station with biodegradable waste bags at the trailhead so you can clean up after your pet. Park rangers will warn you, though, to keep your pet on a leash not only for the safety of others on the trail, but for your dog as well. There are eastern diamond-back rattlesnakes hidden away in the brush.

If you do bring your dog, remember that they are not allowed on the Pelican Trail. Instead you should opt to simply do the complete Osprey Trail, forgoing the Pelican Trail.

Miles and Directions

0.0 Start at the parking lot next to the playground and picnic area. Follow the paved road to the north. In a few hundred feet, arrive at the trailhead kiosk that has information and a "Kids Corner" where children draw pictures of the things they see on the trail and post them here. There is also a station where you can pick up bags for your dog's waste.

0.2 Pass a bench and the first informational signs about the great horned owl and eastern diamondback rattlesnake. In less than 0.1 mile, pass a bench.

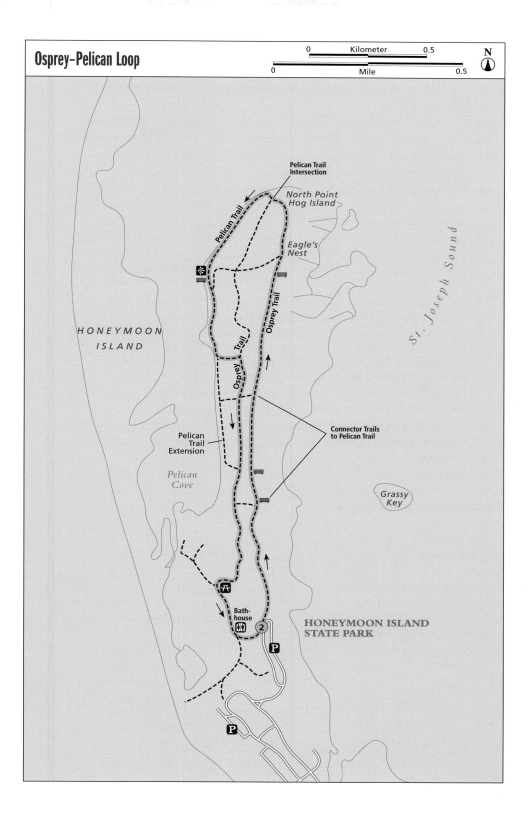

Osprey-Pelican Loop

Kilometer
0   0.5

Mile
0   0.5

N

Pelican Trail
Intersection

North Point
Hog Island

Eagle's
Nest

St. Joseph Sound

Pelican Trail

*HONEYMOON
ISLAND*

Osprey Trail

Osprey Trail

Pelican
Trail
Extension

Connector Trails
to Pelican Trail

*Pelican
Cove*

*Grassy
Key*

Bath-
house

2

P

**HONEYMOON ISLAND
STATE PARK**

P

0.3 Begin seeing a series of osprey nests to the right (east) and soon on both sides. In less than 0.1 mile, pass a trail coming in from the left (west). This is a connector to the Pelican Trail. There's another dog waste bag station here and a bench. Continue straight (north).

0.4 Pass a bench.

0.5 Pass a bench at the half-mile marker. Trail turns from a dirt road into a grassier path.

0.6 Another side trail to the Pelican Trail comes in from the left (west). Continue straight (north).

0.7 Another side trail to the Pelican Trail comes in from the left (west). Continue straight (north). In less than 0.1 mile, pass a bench.

0.9 Pass a bench. There are now many osprey nests around you.

1.0 Come to the "Eagle's Nest" on your right (east), which is marked with an information sign. Another side trail to the Pelican Trail comes in from the left (west). Continue straight.

1.2 The trail swings to the west and is now the Pelican Trail. From this point on pets are not allowed. The trail follows the banks of St. Joseph Sound and Pelican Cove. There are benches here and it is a great place to watch the sunset. The path is now deep beach sand.

1.5 Best view of St. Joseph Sound. In a few feet the sand path gives way to a grassy path.

1.6 Arrive at an area that could be underwater after heavy rains. A sign pointing to the left (east) reads "Osprey Trail." Turn left here (east) to head back to the Osprey Trail. Ospreys surround you. The trail is wide and grassy. In less than 0.1 mile, turn right (south) onto the west side of the Osprey Trail. *Option:* If the Pelican Trail is open, continue straight to return to the intersection with the Osprey Trail farther south.

2.1 Pass a forest restoration sign and a path to the left that takes you back to the north side of the Osprey Trail, which you were just on. Continue straight (south).

2.3 Come to a Y. A sign here reads "Picnic Area" and points to the left. Take the left fork (south). In a few feet come to another Y at a sign that reads "Exit." Take the left fork (southeast).

2.5 Walk around a chain gate. In a few yards you will see a bathhouse to your left. Walk around the bathhouse to the east and follow the cement sidewalk over a wooden bridge.

2.6 Arrive back at the parking lot.

Hike Information

Local Information: City of Dunedin, 542 Main St., Dunedin, FL 34698; (727) 928-3007; dunedin gov.com

Local Events/Attractions: Orange Festival, Edgewater Park, 51 Main St., Dunedin; (727) 736-1176; dunedinorangefestival.com. Celebrate the Florida orange at this annual festival held the middle of July. The festival features the Mojo Cook-off, Duck Derby races, food, music, and a special "Orange Fest after Dark" for the grown-ups.

Restaurants: Dunedin Brewery, 937 Douglas Ave., Dunedin; (727) 736-0606; dunedinbrewery.com

3 Churchhouse Hammock Trail

Just across the highway from the Crystal River Mall, a beautiful thick palm and cedar hammock awaits you on the Churchhouse Hammock Trail as it winds its way to a saw grass marsh. Along the route you will most likely see gopher tortoises and evidence of the region's karst limestone topography. A portion of the trail is boardwalk and ADA-accessible.

Start: Parking area / trailhead
Distance: 1.4-mile loop with out-and-back
Hiking time: About 1.5 hours
Difficulty: Easy over boardwalk, moderate along Primitive Trail
Trail surface: Sand, dirt, boardwalk
Best seasons: Sept to May
Other trail users: None
Canine compatibility: Leashed dogs permitted

Land status: State park preserve
Nearest town: Crystal River
Fees and permits: None
Schedule: Year-round, 8 a.m.–sunset
Maps: USGS Red Level, FL
Trail contact: Crystal River Preserve State Park, 3266 N. Sailboat Ave., Crystal River, FL 34428; (352) 563-0450; floridastateparks.org/crystalriverpreserve

Finding the trailhead: From the intersection of FL 44 and US 19, take US 19 north 1.8 miles, passing the Crystal River Mall on the right. Make a U-turn and head south on US 19 for 0.1 mile. The entrance and parking lot is on the right. The trailhead is on the south side of the parking lot. GPS: N28 54.699' / W82 36.449'

The Hike

It's called Florida's "Nature Coast," a section of the state that is world-renowned for its outdoor adventure. Along what used to be called the "Big Bend" between Wakulla County and Pasco County, there is an amazing array of outdoor recreational opportunities waiting for you: Snorkeling, scuba diving, scalloping, swimming with manatees—if you love the outdoors, this is the happenin' place.

Then, of course, there is the hiking, and one of the popular trails to visit is the beautiful, tropical-like setting of the Churchhouse Hammock Trail at Crystal River Preserve State Park. The park is tucked away inconspicuously off US 19 right across the highway from the Crystal River Mall.

The preserve protects 20 miles of Gulf coastline encompassing over 30,000 acres of salt marsh, scrub, and hydric hammock. A hydric hammock is described as a well-developed pine or palm forest. The understory of this hammock is typically dominated by ferns and palms and occurs in areas of moist soil with a limestone base. That is the perfect description of the habitat this hike will take you through.

A tropical feel envelops you along the Churchhouse Hammock Trail.

The Churchhouse Hammock Trail was named for the old Church House Hammock Baptist Church that stood nearby in 1844. The trail begins at the circular gravel parking lot that has plenty of room for a good thirty cars. There is also a composting toilet here.

The trail itself starts out on an ADA-accessible boardwalk and is a good 0.3-mile loop. We'll come back to the boardwalk in a moment, but for right now, in about 300 feet from the trailhead, you move off the boardwalk and hit a traditional footpath called the "Primitive Trail" on the map at the kiosk but referred to as the "Path to the Past" in state park postings. This section of trail winds its way through a dense forest that is classified as a mesic hammock, or closed canopy forest. The dominant trees and shrubs found here are live and laurel oak, magnolia, cabbage palm, palmetto, and southern red cedar. The state is currently working to convert this environment back to its natural long-leaf pine setting.

Strolling down the dirt path, red cardinals and black-and-white warblers dart through the brush, a reminder that this trail is part of the Great Florida Birding and Wildlife Trail. There's also a good chance you'll scare up a white-tailed deer, quail, or wild turkey along the way.

The footing is unique in that it is studded with limestone rocks, evidence of the area's karst topography. The term *karst* describes the dissolution of soluble rocks by surface or ground water. As you walk, it's not only the rocks you have to watch for, but also gopher tortoises.

At the far end of the trail, the canopy lightens up a bit. Through the trees you catch a glimpse of an estuary, and then you arrive at an elevated boardwalk. The next 0.1 mile is called the Marsh Boardwalk / Birding Trail and takes you right out into the estuary for a great view of the water feature. The boardwalk ends at an island but it is closed off, so this is where you turn around and retrace your steps back to the boardwalk near the trailhead.

As I said, the boardwalk portion of this hike is ADA-accessible as it winds around the forest. Wildflowers like the yellow leafcup and morning glory brighten the path, and benches are scattered along the route so you can sit and take in the scenery.

When you're finished hiking the Churchhouse Hammock Trail, Crystal River has four more trails nearby that you can hike: Dixie Shores, Redfish Hole, Eco-Walk, and 7-Mile Loop. Visit the Crystal River Preserve State Park website for more information.

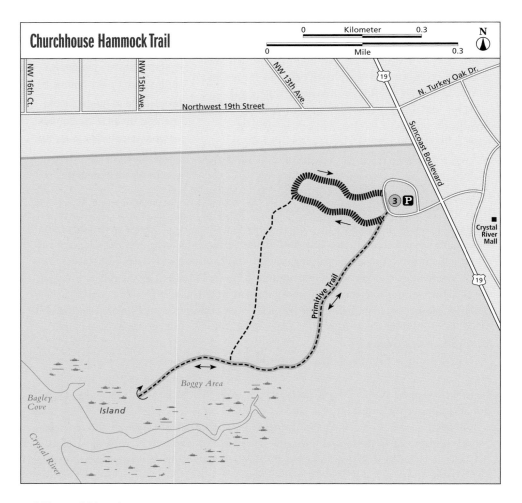

Churchhouse Hammock Trail

Miles and Directions

0.0 Start at the kiosk on the south side of the parking lot. In a few feet come to a boardwalk at a Y intersection. Take the boardwalk to the south. In less than 0.1 mile, leave the boardwalk and the trail becomes a dirt footpath.

0.4 Cross over a boggy area that could be very wet after rain. In less than 0.1 mile, the trail is sometimes overgrown and even underwater. If it isn't, continue straight ahead to the west as the trail winds through the forest.

0.5 The canopy thins a bit as you arrive at a bridge over a bayou, a feeder of Bagley Cove. There's a nice view from the bridge and well worth the effort to get here. The island is inaccessible, so turn around here and retrace your steps to the boardwalk.

1.0 Arriving back at the boardwalk, turn left (west) onto the boardwalk. You will be walking intermittently over boardwalk and dirt path. There are benches here. Soon the trail will be a mix of boardwalk and hard-packed dirt/gravel about 6 feet wide in places.

1.1 Cross a long boardwalk. In less than 0.1 mile, come to a Y. You can go either left or right because each fork rejoins in a few yards.

1.3 Come to the end of the boardwalk. In less than 0.1 mile, cross another boardwalk with a bench.

1.4 Arrive back at the parking lot.

Hike Information

Local Information: Visit Citrus County, 9225 W. Fishbowl Ave., Homosassa, FL 34448; (800) 587-6667; visitcitrus.com

Local Events/Attractions: Ellie Schiller Homosassa Springs Wildlife State Park, 4150 S. Suncoast Blvd., Homosassa; (352) 628-5343; floridastateparks.org/homosassasprings. Like their ad says, "Get nose-to-nose with a manatee." View West Indian manatees every day of the year through the park's underwater observatory. The park also features other animals native to the area.

Restaurants: Grannie's Country Cooking, 1712 SE US 19, Crystal River; (392) 795-8884

4 Cedar Key Scrub Nature Trail

The Cedar Key Scrub Nature Trail on the east side of Cedar Key Scrub State Reserve is a fascinating walk through an endangered Florida scrub forest. The trail is characterized by a few wetlands and dwarf oak trees and shrubs, the perfect habitat for the rare Florida scrub-jay, the state's only endemic bird, as well as pileated woodpeckers and the endangered eastern indigo snake and gopher tortoise.

Start: Trailhead on north side of parking lot
Distance: 3.2-mile lollipop
Hiking time: About 2 hours
Difficulty: Moderate over deep sand, no shade
Trail surface: Sand
Best seasons: Sept to May
Other trail users: Equestrians, cyclists
Canine compatibility: Leashed dogs permitted
Land status: State park reserve
Nearest town: Cedar Key
Fees and permits: None
Schedule: Year-round, sunrise–sunset

Maps: USGS Cedar Keys, FL, and Ocala, FL; maps available at trailhead kiosk
Trail contact: Cedar Key Scrub State Reserve, 8312 SW 125th Ct., Cedar Key, FL 32625; (352) 543-5567; floridastateparks.org/cedarkeyscrub
Special considerations: Limited hunting is allowed in the reserve generally from Sept through Nov. Visit the Florida Fish and Wildlife Conservation Commission website for exact dates at myfwc.com/viewing/recreation/wmas/cooperative/cedar-key-scrub.

Finding the trailhead: From the intersection of US 19/98 and FL 24 in Otter Creek, take FL 24 west 15.5 miles. The parking lot and trailhead will be on the right and well-marked. GPS: N29 12.309'/W82 59.292'

The Hike

The Cedar Key Scrub Nature Trail is located on the east side of Cedar Key Scrub State Reserve, a 5,028-acre tract that sports a diverse ecosystem ranging from salt marsh to pine flatwoods to sand pine scrub as it slopes down to the Gulf of Mexico.

In all there is a total of 12 miles of multiuse trail within the reserve, which is split nearly down the middle by CR 37. There are 8 miles of trail on the west side and 4 miles on the east side. The Cedar Key Scrub Nature Trail described here uses the trails of the east side to wind around several seasonal wetlands and through a scrub forest.

The scrub forest is one of Florida's most unique ecosystems and is found in the state's coastal regions and along the tops of sand ridges. The forest is characterized by dwarf and scrub oak trees such as the sand live oak, myrtle oak, and Chapman's oak, with large patches of barren white sand interspersed with a few pines, palms, and saw palmettos. The sand, a combination of Orsino and Myakka sands, can be up to 7 feet deep, which means that it drains quickly after a rain. Myakka, by the way, is an Indian word that means "big waters"; it is the official soil of Florida, and it is only found here. Being deep, fine sand means only one thing for hikers—a workout when walking.

The trails are well-marked at Cedar Key, with a challenging deep, fine sand base.

The scrub forest is the perfect environment for such animals and birds as the gopher tortoise, pileated woodpecker, Florida mouse, and two rare and endangered species: the Florida scrub-jay and eastern indigo snake. The Florida scrub-jay is the state's only endemic bird and is completely reliant on this type of forest. The jay is omnivorous, meaning that it not only eats acorns and nuts, but also lizards, crickets, and small frogs. The eastern indigo is a black snake that makes its home in the burrow of the gopher tortoise. Black racers are often mistaken for the indigo, the difference being that the racer has scales while the indigo has smooth skin. The eastern indigo is quite shy and nonvenomous.

The hike begins at the trailhead kiosk just off FL 24. There is a picnic table here under a shelter for shade and a composting toilet. Informational brochures and a trail map are also available here.

The trail is either marked with 4-by-4-inch posts that have the color of the trail painted around them or 4-by-4-inch posts with the trail color and an engraved brown and white sign with the trail number. This loop is blazed in white and uses four separate trails: Trail 2, Trail 5, Trail 4, and Trail 3. There is one exception with the blazing. At mile 2.1 you will come to a T intersection with Trail 3. To the right is a sign indicating what trail this is but it is blazed orange. To the left the trail is blazed in white. You will turn left to continue on the white-blazed loop. ***FYI:*** If you were to take the trail to the right, you could walk to CR 347 and over to the trails on the western half of the preserve.

As mentioned earlier, this is a scrub forest with fine deep sand. The footing on the entire loop is made up of this sand and will make this hike a workout. All trails in the reserve are multiuse and are also used by equestrians and cyclists, although I would think cyclists would have a tough time of it in the deep sand.

Shade is nonexistent on this hike, so be sure to wear something to protect your head, put on sunscreen, and drink plenty of fluids to stay hydrated, especially when hiking this trail in the summer.

The trail passes by a few seasonal wetlands, meaning that between the hot intense sun and the percolation of water through the sandy soil, they may not be visible. Your best chance to visit them is after a good rain.

Finally, remember that limited hunting is allowed generally from September through November. Visit the Florida Fish and Wildlife Conservation Commission website for exact dates (see "Special considerations").

Miles and Directions

0.0 Start at the trailhead on the north end of the parking lot and head north. There is an information kiosk here and brochures. If the gate is closed, pass through the hiker entrance on the left side of the wooden gate. The trail is a wide, sand service road with very little shade, so bring along a hat and plenty of water in the summer. The trail is blazed with 4-by-4-inch posts; the number of the trail is engraved on a sign attached to the posts and a band of paint indicates the color of the trail. You are on Trail 2. The entire loop is blazed white. In 300 feet pass a sign telling equestrians that they need proof of Coggins to ride the trail. You will pass your first trail marker, a sign showing you're on Trail 2.

0.2 Cross Trail 3 (Orange Trail). You will be returning on this trail from the west. Right now continue straight to the north.

0.5 Pass Trail 1 (Blue Trail) on your right (east). Trail 2 ends here and Trail 5 continues straight to the west. In a few yards the path parallels private property on your right (north). You will see houses, heavy equipment, and a Quonset hut on the other side of a metal fence.

0.8 Pass a dirt road to the north with a handwritten "No Trespassing" sign. Continue on Trail 5 to the southwest.

1.1 Pass a seasonal wetland to the right (north).

1.2 Pass a barbwire fence along a private property line to the right (north).

1.3 Come to an intersection. The right path to the northwest is private property. The path straight ahead to the west is an old service road. Turn left (south) and continue on Trail 5 (you will see the sign just after turning). There are nice palm trees through here, and a small stand of trees provides a little shade.

1.6 Come to an intersection. Turn left onto Trail 4. You will see the trail sign after making the turn. The path is very deep sand at this point. You may want to stay to the sides.

1.8 Pass a side service road on your right (west).

2.1 Pass a side service road on your left (east). A nice wetland is here during the rainy seasons. In less than 0.1 mile, come to a T intersection. Turn left (northeast) onto Trail 3.

2.4 Pass a service road on the right (south). Continue straight (northeast).

2.7 The path is lined with yellow low hop clover.

2.8 Pass a bench on the left (north).

3.0 Arrive back at the intersection of Trail 3 and Trail 2. Turn right (south) onto Trail 2.

3.2 Arrive back at the trailhead.

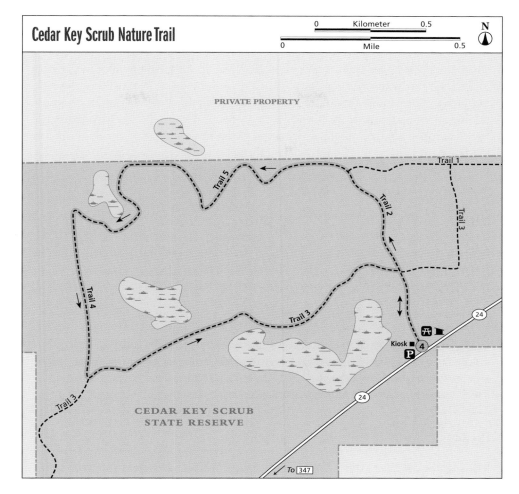

Cedar Key Scrub Nature Trail

0 | Kilometer | 0.5
0 | Mile | 0.5

N

PRIVATE PROPERTY

Trail 1

Trail 5

Trail 2

Trail 3

Trail 4

Trail 3

24

Kiosk

P

4

CEDAR KEY SCRUB
STATE RESERVE

24

To 347

Hike Information

Local Information: Cedar Key Chamber of Commerce, 450 Second St., Cedar Key, FL 32625; (352) 543-5600; cedarkey.org

Local Events/Attractions: Cedar Key Museum State Park, 12231 SW 166th Ct., Cedar Key; (352) 543-5350; floridastateparks.org/park/Cedar-Key-Museum. An interesting museum that chronicles the history of this Gulf Coast town from its earliest days as a thriving seaport in the 19th century to the present. Open Thurs–Mon, 8 a.m.–5 p.m. Small admission fee; children under 5 free.

Restaurants: Blue Desert Cafe, 12518 FL 24, Cedar Key; (352) 543-9111; facebook.com/pages/Blue-Desert-Cafe-Inc/92784302331?ref=ts. Unique calzones and pizzas, including seafood pizza.

Organizations: Friends of the Lower Suwanee & Cedar Key National Wildlife Refuges, PO Box 532, Cedar Key, FL 32625; friendsofrefuges.org

5 Lighthouse Levee Trail

The Lighthouse Levee Trail is a short and easy hike but one that provides an amazing experience for young and old alike. Walking atop the levee, you will have sweeping views of Apalachee Bay, Gulf and marsh impoundments, and one of the most photographed lighthouses in Florida. Not to mention you will also be surrounded by wildlife. You may see dolphins plying the waters in the bay, view a wide variety of butterflies, or be surprised by the bellow of a mama alligator only yards from the trail.

Start: Parking area / trailhead across from lighthouse
Distance: 1-mile out-and-back
Hiking time: About 1 hour
Difficulty: Easy over flat levee
Trail surface: Grass, sand levee
Best seasons: Sept to June
Other trail users: None
Canine compatibility: Leashed dogs permitted

Land status: National wildlife refuge
Nearest town: Crawfordville
Fees and permits: Day-use fee
Schedule: Year-round, sunrise–sunset
Maps: USGS Tallahassee, FL; maps available at visitor center
Trail contact: St. Marks National Wildlife Refuge, 1255 Lighthouse Rd., St. Marks, FL 32355; (850) 925-6121; fws.gov/saintmarks

Finding the trailhead: From the intersection of FL 267 and US 98 in Crawfordville, take US 98 east 0.5 mile. Turn right onto Lighthouse Road. Travel 3.7 miles and arrive at the visitor center. After paying your admission, continue 6.5 miles south on Lighthouse Road. The road will end at the lighthouse parking lot and trailhead. GPS: N30 04.451' / W84 10.806'

The Hike

The Lighthouse Levee Trail at St. Marks National Wildlife Refuge is a short hike but oh so sweet. There is so much packed into this 1-mile out-and-back that kids of all ages will enjoy it. It's just short enough for the young ones and has enough to keep even the fussy kids engaged—and parents, too.

Before we get to the trail, we need to tend to a little history about the feature that stands out the most at the very beginning of the hike, the St. Marks Lighthouse.

There are actually four lighthouses within the refuge, but St. Marks is the oldest. Construction began on the tower in 1829 and was finally finished in 1831. The lighthouse has seen its share of war and could have been taken down on numerous occasions, but it survived them all, beginning with the second Seminole War of 1835 and the Civil War when the Confederate army tried to blow up the tower so that the Union army couldn't use it as a lookout. Their plan was unsuccessful, but it did cause significant damage. The tower was repaired with 4-foot-thick walls in the caretaker's residence and 2-foot-thick walls in the tower itself. It was also heightened to 82 feet tall.

The St. Marks Lighthouse is seen from the trail.

The lighthouse has also withstood nature, having survived over a hundred hurricanes over its history. The light was eventually automated in 1960 and is still in operation today. Visitors can explore the tower with guides the first Saturday of each month from 1 to 4 p.m.

The refuge itself is no spring chicken either. St. Marks National Wildlife Refuge was established in 1931 to provide an important wintering habitat for migratory birds. The refuge now encompasses over 70,000 acres and 43 miles of Gulf Coast shoreline and is one of the oldest in the refuge system. Wildlife abounds in this coastal refuge, with 38 species of amphibians, 69 species of reptiles, 44 species of mammals, and 300 species of birds calling this land home.

The refuge has a wonderful visitor center that is open Monday through Friday from 8 a.m. to 4 p.m. and Saturday and Sunday from 10 a.m. to 5 p.m. (closed Thanksgiving and Christmas). The center is staffed by knowledgeable and friendly rangers and volunteers who love to talk about the history, plants, and wildlife found here. The

Nature Store, which is located in the visitor center, carries items that highlight the animals and plants of the refuge, with all profits going to support refuge programs and projects.

The Lighthouse Levee Trail follows, as its name implies, along the top of a levee that was built in 1930 by the Civilian Conservation Corps (CCC). These levees form ponds or impoundments that are important habitat for wintering and migratory birds. As you begin your walk, you will notice a sign to your right next to the south end of one of those impoundments warning you about the presence of American alligators. Keep an eye peeled for a gator or two swimming in the water or sunning on one of the banks. Don't be surprised as you walk to hear the bellow of a mama gator at her nest just a few yards away or a loud splash or two. Alligators are naturally wary of humans and they would rather make themselves scarce, but remember, don't feed them! Feeding alligators changes the rules.

For the first 0.3 mile you will be walking with Apalachee Bay and the Gulf of Mexico to your left. It's not uncommon to see bottlenose dolphins plying the waters, and you might catch a glimpse of a Florida manatee.

Plant lovers won't be disappointed on this hike. Of course, the plants here have to deal with a harsh environment, everything from extreme wind and heat to saltwater and even freezing temperatures. The hardy plants that thrive here include prickly pear cactus, salt bush, wax myrtle, dotted horsemint, yaupon holly, sabal palm, and yucca, to name only a few. The refuge has a complete guide to the plants you will see, available at the trailhead or online (see "Other Resources").

Butterflies are quite at home in the refuge, including monarch, viceroy (which are often mistaken for monarch), and spicebush swallow. And, of course, there are plenty of birds to see—red-cockaded woodpeckers, bald eagles, ospreys, loons, and brown pelicans are common residents. Again, the refuge has a brochure to help you track your birding activities (see "Other Resources").

At the 0.3-mile mark, the trail will turn right and head to the northeast. Here you will find a picnic table with a shelter and a kiosk that tells the story of the St. Marks Lighthouse, the Spanish Hole "mystery shipwreck," and nearby Fort Williams. From here to the turnaround you will be walking along the northern end of the impoundment and the banks of a narrow bayou. The turnaround is at a parking lot and boat launch at the 0.5-mile mark. Turn around here and retrace your steps back to the car, but don't think you've seen everything there is to see. The trip back offers amazing views of the lighthouse from a couple of different angles.

Here are a couple of things to keep in mind when hiking this trail. First, if you hike the trail in mid- to late summer through early fall, be ready for yellow flies, and they are ferocious. My black Lab turned yellow as he stepped out of the car getting ready for our hike, and that's only a slight exaggeration.

And speaking of dogs, and children, remember that there are alligators nearby. Keep children close at hand and away from the brush, and make sure your dogs are on a leash.

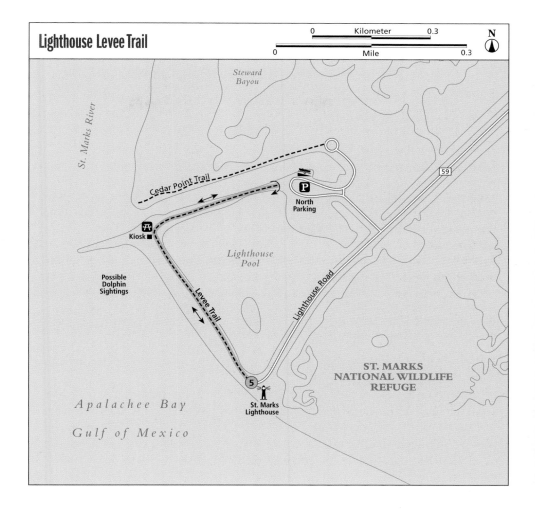

Miles and Directions

0.0 Start from the parking lot at the end of Lighthouse Road. The St. Marks Lighthouse will be to your left (south). The actual trailhead is well-marked with a "Lighthouse Levee Trail" sign and is only a few yards to the north. Other signs here remind you not to go crabbing in the pools and to beware of alligators. Along this straight section of the trail, be watchful for dolphins swimming in Apalachee Bay / Gulf of Mexico to your left (west), the many butterflies and wildflowers, and the bellow—and large splash—of alligators next to the trail just a few feet away.

0.3 The trail makes a right turn to the northeast. At the bend there is an informational kiosk and picnic table. You're now walking along the south bank of a bayou that's a little brushier and not as open as the first part.

0.5   Come to a parking lot. This is your turnaround to head back to your car. There is a great view of the lighthouse here across the pool to your south. As you walk back, there are many more wonderful views of the lighthouse. (***Option:*** At the parking lot, access the Cedar Point Trail, which will take you along the north bank of the bayou for an additional 0.5 mile. The trail ends at a beach on the Gulf of Mexico. This trail is more brushy than the Lighthouse Levee and yellow flies can be a big problem from summer to early fall.)

1.0   Arrive back at the trailhead.

Hike Information

Local Information: Wakulla County Tourist Development, 1505 Coastal Hwy., Panacea, FL 32346; (850) 984-3966; visitwakulla.org

Local Events/Attractions: St. Marks Stone Crab Festival, 788 Port Leon Dr., St. Marks; (850) 984-3966; stmarksstonecrabfest.com. Held annually the weekend before Halloween, this festival celebrates local fishermen and their stone crab harvest. Of course, there's lots of music, arts and crafts, and delicious stone crab.

Restaurants: Ouzt's Too Oyster Bar and Grill, 7968 Coastal Hwy., Newport; (850) 925-6448; ouztstoo.com. BBQ and fresh seafood.

Tours: St. Marks National Wildlife Refuge, 1255 Lighthouse Rd., St Marks; (850) 925-6121; fws.gov/saintmarks. Lighthouse tours are held the first Saturday of each month from 1 to 4 p.m.

Other Resources: St. Marks National Wildlife Refuge brochures, bird and plant checklists, and more are available at fws.gov/refuge/St_Marks/brochures.html.

6 Leon Sinks Loop

The area just south of Tallahassee is known for its karst topography, a layer of limestone that has been weathered and carved over the centuries by the elements to form a system of caves, holes, and tunnels. The Leon Sinks Loop allows hikers to explore this geology with excellent examples of wet sinkholes, natural bridges, depressions, and disappearing streams.

Start: Parking area / trailhead next to restrooms
Distance: 3.1-mile loop
Hiking time: About 2 hours
Difficulty: Moderate with hills
Trail surface: Dirt, sand
Best seasons: Year-round
Other trail users: None
Canine compatibility: Leashed dogs permitted

Land status: National forest
Nearest town: Crawfordville
Fees and permits: Day-use fee
Schedule: Year-round, 8 a.m.–8 p.m.
Maps: USGS Tallahassee, FL; maps available at entrance station
Trail contact: Apalachicola Ranger District, 11152 NW SR 20, Bristol, FL 32321; (850) 643-2282; fs.usda.gov/apalachicola

Finding the trailhead: From the intersection of FL 267 and US 319 in Crawfordville, take US 319 north 3.2 miles. Turn left onto Crawfordville Road / US 319 and travel 0.2 mile to arrive at the entrance gate and fee box. After paying your fee, continue about 0.1 mile to the parking lot. The trailhead is on the north side of the paved parking lot and is well-marked. There is a nice restroom here as well. GPS: N30 18.573' / W84 20.752'

The Hike

The Leon Sinks Geological Area within the Apalachicola National Forest is a remarkable landscape. The area is literally littered with dozens of sinkholes, which are all part of what is known as the Woodville Karst Plain, and the best way for us to see these marvelous sinkholes is by hiking the Leon Sinks Loop.

The Woodville Karst Plain is an area of limestone from just south of Tallahassee that slopes to the Gulf of Mexico. Because of the porous nature of the limestone, water is allowed to flow freely through, causing erosion or what is known as *karst*. This erosion causes a Swiss cheese–like effect with the rock and has created an amazing network of caves and caverns throughout the region, the largest being the Leon Sinks Cave System.

It is in this cave system that divers had a difficult challenge—to chart the system. What made it more difficult is that depths ranged to as much as 300 feet. In all the divers charted over 28 miles of passageways, making this the longest mapped

Dark waters fill Big Dismal Sink, which is 100 feet deep and has myriad underwater caves.

underwater cave system in the United States and fourth-longest in the world. A world record was set here in 2007 for the longest cave dive between two entrances.

The Leon Sinks Loop consists of two trails, the Sinkhole and Crossover. The Sinkhole Trail loops around from east to west and highlights several impressive sinkholes. The Crossover Trail cuts through the beautiful cypress and tupelo Center Swamp over a long boardwalk. An option would be to extend this hike an additional 1.7 miles by skipping the Crossover Trail and using the Gum Swamp Trail instead, which connects with the Sinkhole Trail at mile 2.3 and 2.8 of the hike described here. The extension takes you through Bear Scratch and Shadows Swamps. Either way, you're in for a picturesque journey.

The trail is marked with 4-by-4-inch posts that have directional arrows posted on them and blue paint blazes. Sinkholes are well-marked with 6-by-6-inch posts and the sink's name carved into a sign. The trail has plenty of interpretive signs that teach you about the karst topography, the particular sink you're at, or the plants or wildlife of the area. Service road crossings have signs on the opposite side that show you the way so you don't make a wrong turn, and when the trail makes a sharp turn, there are "dit-dot" paint blazes. These are two paint blazes stacked one on top of the other. The two blazes mean there is a turn; the top blaze is offset to either the left or right, which indicates the direction of the turn.

The footpath is a wide dirt and sand trail, about 5 to 6 feet wide. This is one trail that you will definitely notice the transition in environments from pine forest to hardwoods as you make your way down into the sink area. It's not a big elevation change, but just enough for you to get winded if you're not in shape. But never fear, numerous composite benches line the trail throughout the route for you to take a break.

You will experience two types of sinkholes on this hike, wet sinks and dry sinks. Dry sinks are just what you would expect: dry depressions in the ground where undoubtedly underground streams and springs caused the surface to collapse.

The other and more striking type are the wet sinks. In all you will pass eight wet sinks, with the most impressive being Hammock, Big Dismal, and Black Sink. Hammock and Big Dismal each have their own long boardwalk that leads down to the sinkhole for closer examination. Normally the water is crystal clear, but sometimes, like after a good rainstorm, the water turns brown and tealike. This is from the tannin in the surrounding plants.

As you visit Big Dismal Sink, sit quietly and listen. You may hear the sound of groundwater dripping into the hole, showing that this is still a work in progress. By the way, Big Dismal is 130 feet deep.

Black Sink is another impressive wet sinkhole, but rather difficult to see through the trees until the leaves are down in the fall and winter. You may be tempted to climb down but don't. As rangers will remind you, as we just did, this karst topography is constantly changing and the banks of a sinkhole can collapse at any time. And remember, while the cool, clear water looks inviting, swimming is not allowed.

As you round the bend at mile 2.3, you will come to what is called the Natural Bridge. Here, Fisher Creek flows but with a twist. Right before your eyes the stream disappears underground. It flows under this rock bridge to the north to reappear in what is known as the Fisher Creek Rise.

Besides pines and oaks, the trail is lined with reindeer moss, magnolia trees, and in some sections with saw palmettos.

▶ **A stretch of land on the Florida Gulf Coast between St. Marks and Mexico Beach is fondly called the "Forgotten Coast." It was literally forgotten during the huge development boom of the north Florida coast, but today people appreciate that the region was forgotten and the history and natural beauty still remain.**

Miles and Directions

0.0 Start from the trailhead on the west side of the parking area between the restroom. The trail is a wide dirt path with plenty of canopy.

0.1 Come to a T intersection with the Sinkhole Trail at a sign pointing the direction to the Gum Swamp and Crossover Trails to the left (southwest), and Hammock and Big Dismal to the right (northeast). Turn right (northeast) onto the Sinkhole Trail. The path has blue blazes.

0.2 The trail slowly makes its way downhill and you transition from pines into a more hardwood forest.

0.3 Come to a sign and a short side trail to Dry Sink. In less than 0.1 mile, come to a sign and a short side trail that leads to Turner Sink. After visiting, continue northeast and in a few yards pass a bench.

0.4 Cross a dirt service road to the north. The trail narrows to a 4-foot-wide path. In less than 0.1 mile, come to the Dry Palmetto Sink on the right.

0.5 Come to the Back Sink on the left.

0.6 Come to a long boardwalk side trail that leads to Hammock Sink.

0.7 Arrive at the end of the boardwalk at Hammock Sink. When done viewing, retrace your steps back to the main trail and turn left (northwest). The path widens and levels out a bit.

0.8 Pass a bench on the left. In less than 0.1 mile arrive at Tiny Sink. The main trail starts a short uphill climb and reenters the pines.

1.0 Top a short hill. The trees open up a bit with grass.

1.1 Come to the Big Dismal Sink on the right. There is a boardwalk that will take you there and an overlook. Two rough side trails are adjacent to the boardwalk entrance, but don't use them! Park officials are attempting to restore the area to its natural state, plus it's a dangerous climb.

1.2 Come to Dry Field Sink. Shortly after, there is a split in the trail. The right side is a washout; take the left upper route.

1.3 Come to the Big Eight Sink on the right.

1.4 Pass a bench on the right.

1.5 Come to the Magnolia Sink. In less than 0.1 mile, cross a dirt service road to the south.

1.9 Come to Black Sink on the left. There is a bench here and a very steep side trail to the sink. If you venture down, use extreme caution! It's a long drop.

2.1 Cross a service road to the south. In less than 0.1 mile, pass two benches on the right (west) and a sign that reads "Sinkhole Trail" and points to the right, with "Lost Stream Overlook" pointing to the left (east). Continue to the right (south).

2.3 Pass a bench on the left (north). In less than 0.1 mile, pass a sign for the Natural Bridge and climb down seven big creosote pole steps. Come to an intersection with the Crossover Trail and the Gum Swamp Trail. Take the left path on the Crossover Trail to the east. You will also be near the Natural Bridge, which is on your right (south). The trail is now blazed white.

2.4 Cross a service road to the east.

2.7 The trail veers to the right (east) while a dirt service road continues straight.

2.7 Begin crossing Center Swamp over a long boardwalk. The trail is now blazed yellow.

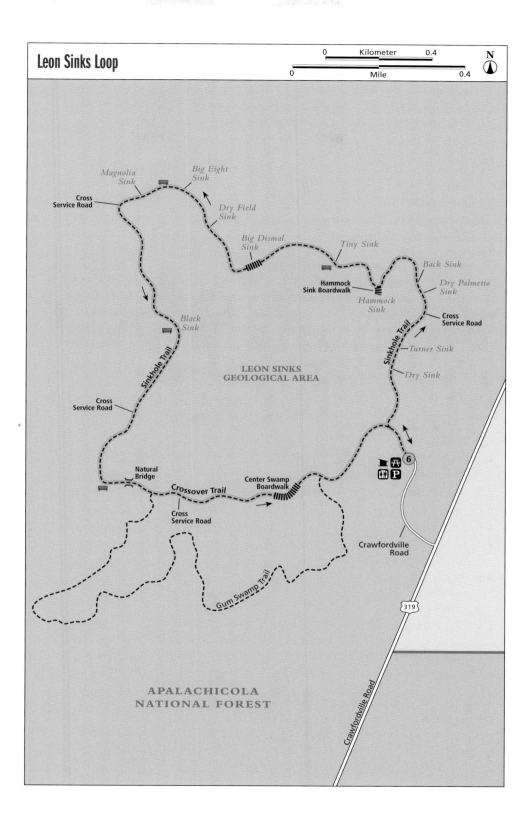

2.8 Come to the end of the swamp boardwalk. In less than 0.1 mile, come to an intersection marked with a sign showing the direction to all of the trails off the loop. Turn left (northeast) to head back to the trailhead.

2.9 Come to a trail sign pointing the direction to the Gum Swamp, Sinkhole, and Hutchinson Spur Trails to the right (east) and Sink Hole and the trailhead straight (northeast). Continue straight.

3.0 Arrive back at the intersection at mile 0.1. Turn right (southwest).

3.1 Arrive back at the trailhead.

Hike Information

Local Information: Wakulla County Tourist Development, 1505 Coastal Hwy., Panacea, FL 32346; (850) 984-3966; visitwakulla.org

Local Events/Attractions: Wakulla Wildlife Festival, Wakulla Springs State Park, 465 Wakulla Park Dr., Wakulla Springs; (850) 561-7286; wakullawildlifefestival.com. The Wakulla Wildlife Festival is an annual celebration of the area's wildlife. The family-friendly event is held the middle of April and features games, music, and a variety of nature-oriented tours. A small admission fee is charged.

Lodging: Wakulla Springs Lodge, 550 Wakulla Park Dr., Wakulla Springs; (850) 421-2000; wakullaspringslodge.com. A Florida architectural landmark with its Mediterranean revival and art deco motif, the lodge has been hosting guests since 1937 and is located at Wakulla Springs State Park.

Restaurants: Spring Creek Restaurant, 33 Ben Willis Rd., Crawfordville; (850) 926-3751; springcreekfl.com. Serving up fresh seafood dishes since 1977.

7 Ochlockonee River Loop

A fantastic little hideaway for the entire family, Ochlockonee River State Park offers up wonderful swimming on the banks of the park's namesake river where it intersects with the Dead River before heading to the Gulf of Mexico and, of course, hiking. The Ochlockonee River Loop is an easy walking path with beautiful views of the river, a reflecting pond, and a chance to view wildlife including deer, fox squirrel, and a variety of birds.

Start: Parking area / trailhead alongside river
Distance: 2.2-mile loop with tail
Hiking time: About 2 hours
Difficulty: Easy over a level grass and sand path
Trail surface: Sand, grass
Best seasons: Year-round
Other trail users: None
Canine compatibility: Leashed dogs permitted
Land status: State park

Nearest town: Sopchoppy
Fees and permits: Admission fee
Schedule: Year-round, 8 a.m.–sunset
Maps: USGS Sopchoppy, FL, and Saint Teresa, FL; maps available at entrance station
Trail contact: Ochlockonee River State Park, 429 State Park Rd., Sopchoppy, FL 32358; (850) 962-2771; floridastateparks.org/park/Ochlockonee-River

Finding the trailhead: From the intersection of Rose Street and US 319 / FL 377 in Sopchoppy, take US 319 / FL 377 south 4.3 miles. Turn left onto Ochlockonee River State Park Road. In 2.1 miles arrive at the pay station. After paying the entrance fee, continue straight on Ochlockonee River State Park Road another 0.9 mile and arrive at the parking lot. The trailhead is on the east side of the parking lot. GPS: N30 00.236' / W84 28.367'

The Hike

At the confluence of the Dead and Ochlockonee Rivers sits a beautiful little out-of-the-way park—Ochlockonee River State Park. The park is 543 acres in size and is characterized by what is called pine flatwoods. The land is extremely flat, or as the rangers call it, a monotonous terrain with a thin forest of pine trees surrounded by swaying savannah grasses and punctuated with patches of saw palmetto.

The park and the Ochlockonee River Loop hike sit atop ancient sandbars, deposited here thousands of years ago when the region was covered by the ocean. You can tell you are standing on or near one of these sand dunes by the scrub oak that grows on them.

Humans lived on this land anywhere from AD 300 to 1000 in what is known as the Weedon Island Period. This period of time was named for a Native American site that was discovered near Tampa. The people of this time period had established a broad-based economy for themselves that included hunting, fishing, and gardening.

A beautiful Southern sky is mirrored in the Reflecting Pond.

An ancient shell midden, an area where the remains of eaten shellfish lie, was discovered along the banks of the Dead River that dates back some 1,500 years.

This area was also the site of a bustling turpentine industry in the late 1700s. As you walk through the park, look for what are called "cat-face" trees. These are trees that have a large scar on them where the bark was stripped and the resin or pitch was allowed to seep from them into pails, later to be made into turpentine. This material had a number of uses, one of which was to seal the bottoms of boats.

This quiet little park was established in 1970 and has plenty of outdoor activities for all ages, including canoeing, swimming, fishing, picnicking, a playground, and, of course, hiking. The campground here is very nice and peaceful. Nestled beneath a hardwood canopy along the banks of the Ochlockonee River, the campground has thirty improved campsites with water and electricity.

The Ochlockonee River Loop uses two of the parks trails: the Pine Flatwood Nature Trail and the Ochlockonee River Nature Trail. Both trails feature interpretive signs describing the history, plants, and animals that call the park home.

The hike begins on the Pine Flatwood Nature Trail at the eastern end of the parking lot at the junction of the two rivers. The entrance is well-marked and you won't miss it. The trail is a good 5-foot-wide sand and mowed grass path. Along its entire length you will be surrounded by savannah grass pines and saw palmettos. Don't be surprised if you come across lots of white-tailed deer. Their tracks are everywhere. Other animals that call the park home include the fox squirrel, gray fox, snowy egret, and gopher tortoise. Florida black bear do live in the park, but chances are you won't come across one. Another animal you might catch a glimpse of is the white squirrel. These squirrels are almost albino in color but do not have pink eyes.

At the 1-mile mark of the trip, you will come to a beautiful grass pond called the Reflecting Pond. And it is just that—a beautiful mirrorlike surface that reflects the deep blue Florida sky and passing puffy white clouds.

Heading south the trail crosses the park road and makes its way to the banks of the Ochlockonee River. This section to the end of the trail has wonderful views of the river and recreational boats plying the water. Along the path you'll pass several landings with stairs that head down to the banks of the river for swimming. Remember, swim at your own risk. There are no lifeguards on duty.

Miles and Directions

0.0 Start from the trailhead on the east side of the parking lot.

0.1 Pass a bench on the right.

0.2 Good view of the pine savannah as you walk through a boggy area from the rutted path.

0.7 Come to a T intersection. You'll take the left turn to the southeast in a minute; right now, turn right (northwest). The trail is now a sand path.

0.9 Come to a T intersection at a service road. Turn right (northwest) onto the service road.

1.0 Arrive at the small wooden observation deck at the Reflecting Pond. When done viewing, turn around and retrace your steps to mile 0.7.

1.2 Back at the intersection at mile 0.7, continue straight to the southeast.

1.4 Cross the main park road to the south, where you'll pick up the Ochlockonee River Nature Trail. The trail is a wide grassy path again. You will see the campground to your left (east). In less than 0.1 mile, pass a side trail to your left (east) that leads to the campground. Continue straight to the south.

1.5 Come to the Ochlockonee River at a T intersection. There is a bench here. Turn left (northeast).

1.6 A side trail to the left (north) takes you to the campground. To the right (southeast) a short trail takes you to the river with a nice view. Continue straight to the northeast.

1.7 Pass the park's campfire circle with benches next to the river on the right (southeast). There's a little set of stairs that lead to the river, where you can swim. From here to the end

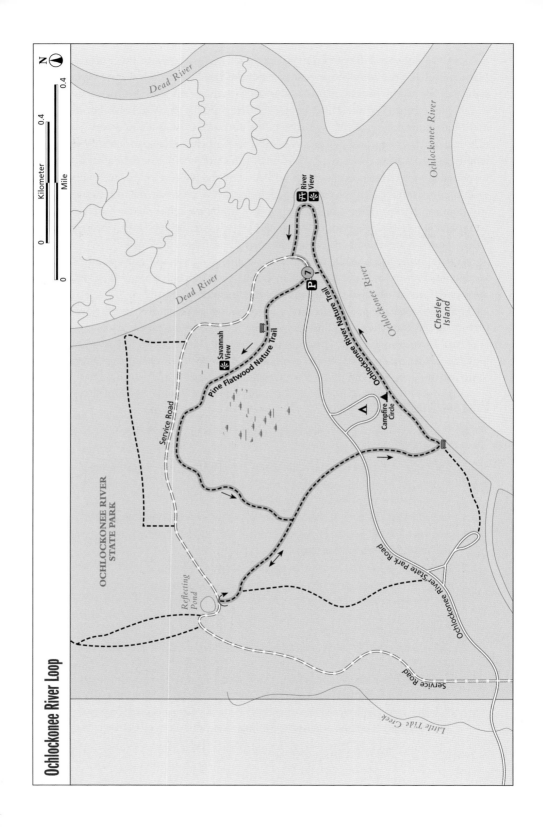

Ochlockonee River Loop

of the hike, you will be walking directly next to the river with splendid views and access to its banks. In less than 0.1 mile, pass stairs that lead to the banks of the river on the right.

2.0 A short side trail on the left (north) takes you back to the parking lot. Continue straight to wrap around the point. Several nice picnic areas are along this short section, with access to the river and swimming.

2.1 Arrive at the point with a great view of the river. The trail now swings to the left (west) to head back to the parking lot, passing a picnic pavilion and a swimming platform and fishing pier on the right, and often kayakers plying the waters.

2.2 Arrive back at the parking lot.

Hike Information

Local Information: City of Sopchoppy, 105 Municipal Ave., Sopchoppy, FL 32358; (850) 962-4611; sopchoppy.org

Local Events/Attractions: Sopchoppy Worm Gruntin' Festival, 105 Municipal Ave., Sopchoppy; (850) 962-4611; wormgruntinfestival.com. Worm gruntin' is a method to make earthworms come to the surface by vibrating the soil. This annual event features a worm gruntin' competition, music, arts and crafts, and the Worm Gruntin' Ball.

Restaurants: Hamaknockers BBQ, 2837 Coastal Hwy., Crawfordville; (850) 926-4737

8 Rocky Bayou Double Loop

Old-growth longleaf pine, some over 300 years old, are the highlight of the Rocky Bayou Loop. The trail is actually a double loop, with the first loop taking you to the lovely banks of Rocky Bayou and the second loop taking you to the freshwater bayou and wetland formerly known as Puddin' Head Lake.

Start: Parking area / trailhead at the north end of Puddin' Head Lake, unless you need to use the day-use parking area at the canoe launch (refer to "Finding the trailhead")
Distance: 2-mile double loop
Hiking time: About 1.5 hours
Difficulty: Easy to moderate with some short hills
Trail surface: Dirt, sand path
Best seasons: Year-round
Other trail users: None

Canine compatibility: Leashed dogs permitted
Land status: State park
Nearest town: Niceville
Fees and permits: Day-use fee
Schedule: Year-round, 8 a.m.–sunset
Maps: USGS Destin, FL; maps available at entrance station
Trail contact: Fred Gannon Rocky Bayou State Park, 4281 FL 20, Niceville, FL 32578; (850) 833-9144; floridastateparks.org/rockybayou

Finding the trailhead: From the intersection of FL 85 and FL 20 / E. John Sims Parkway in Niceville, take FL 20 / E. John Sims Parkway east 4.3 miles and turn left onto the unnamed state park road. Travel 0.1 mile and arrive at the entrance station. After paying your fee, continue straight another 0.1 mile and turn right onto the campground loop. The parking area and trailhead is 0.2 mile ahead on the right. During the busy summer season, the park asks that you park in the day-use parking area. To get there, just after the entrance station, turn left and follow the road around 0.6 mile. From here you will have to walk the road back the way you came about 0.4 mile to the playground area. A cutoff trail leads you from here to the campground road and the trailhead on the east side of the campground. GPS: N30 29.923' / W86 25.592'

The Hike

Nestled along the banks of Rocky Bayou is this 357-acre state park, the Fred Gannon Rocky Bayou State Park, or better known to the locals simply as Rocky Bayou. The park features just over 3 miles of hiking trails, the longest of which is this double loop, what we call the Rocky Bayou Double Loop.

The park itself was established in 1966, but its history began in 1940 when 800 acres were ceded to the US government, which quickly turned the land into a practice gunnery and bombing range. Following the attack on Pearl Harbor by the Japanese in 1941, Colonel James Doolittle and his Raiders practiced here for the first retaliatory bombing run over Japan by dropping 500-pound cement bombs. The remains of one, believed to be from the Doolittle practice runs, can be found along a short side trail on the first loop of this trip.

One of many views of Rocky Bayou along the first loop of this hike

The rapid urban development of the area following the war forced the government to cease using the property. In the late 1950s the Director of Civil Engineering at nearby Eglin Air Force Base, Fred Gannon, proposed that the area be turned into a public recreational area. Along with Eglin's civil engineers, Gannon began building Rocky Bayou State Park. The work was completed in 1966 and it became part of the Florida state park system, eventually being renamed for the man who made the park possible.

Rocky Bayou is a finger of Choctawhatchee Bay. The coastline that borders the state park is part of the Rocky Bayou Aquatic Preserve, which is an effort by state, local, and federal agencies to preserve and maintain the pure, clean, natural state of this fresh to brackish waterway. The first loop of this hike, the Rocky Bayou Trail, affords you plenty of opportunity to visit the tranquil bayou via short side trails. This is a nature trail with numbered stations along the way that tell you about the habitat you're walking through. Be sure to pick up a brochure at the kiosk at the start of the hike.

Along this loop you will be walking through a sand pine scrub forest that gives way to coastal flatwoods. Bright green deer moss lines the path, as do sparkle berry and blueberry. In the flatwoods tall slash pine and turkey oak will be found, as well as saw palmetto.

The Sand Pine Nature Trail is a 1.1-mile loop through a magnolia, pine, and hardwood forest. I just love place names, and when I saw that this loop takes you to "Puddin' Head Lake," I was excited. Well, Puddin' Head Lake ain't no more. Instead, it is now Puddin' Head Stream. The state returned the lake to its original state, a unique and rare habitat for many species of animals and reptiles such as cooter, soft shell, and box turtles; deer; and raccoon, and plants like the Florida anise and pitcher plants.

The double loop is also a birder's paradise. Local birder Charles Parkel documented 154 species of birds in the park, including red-tailed hawk, osprey, and American kestrel, to name only a few. A monument to Mr. Parkel, an informational kiosk describing the birds and a birding checklist, will be found at the start of the hike.

The trail begins at a nice pavilion with plenty of shade high above the stream that provides a good view of the wetland below. If you have a dog with you, there is a doggy waste bag station strategically located here. Take a bag or two to clean up after your pup as you walk.

The trail starts downhill at a sign with the "Prayer of the Woods" on a cement sidewalk but quickly turns into a 4- to 5-foot-wide sand and dirt path. There is a thick canopy throughout the hike, and along with the breeze from the bay, it makes summertime hiking a pleasure. In the background you will hear the occasional roar of a jet from the air base, but it's nothing distracting. There are many benches scattered all along the trails.

A note about parking: In the fall and winter, when there are fewer people here, you can park in the small lot next to the trailhead. In the summertime, however, the park asks you to use the day-use parking area about 0.4 mile from the trailhead (see "Finding the trailhead" for details).

Miles and Directions

0.0 Start from the parking lot next to the campground (see "Finding the trailhead"). There are informational kiosks here, dog waste bags, and the "Prayer of the Woods." Follow the cement sidewalk downhill to the east. In a few feet there is an elevated overlook with views of the stream, and in 300 feet come to a bridge. There are more info kiosks here. Cross the bridge to the southeast and arrive at another set of kiosks.

0.1 Come to a Y. This is the intersection between the two loops. Take the left fork to the northeast and immediately come to another Y. This is where the first loop joins together. Take the left fork to the north onto the Rocky Bayou Trail.

0.2 Come to a side trail to the left (northwest) that leads to the edge of the bayou. When done viewing, turn around and go back to the trail.

0.3 Back on the trail, turn left (northeast) onto the Rocky Bayou Trail.

0.4 Pass a bench.

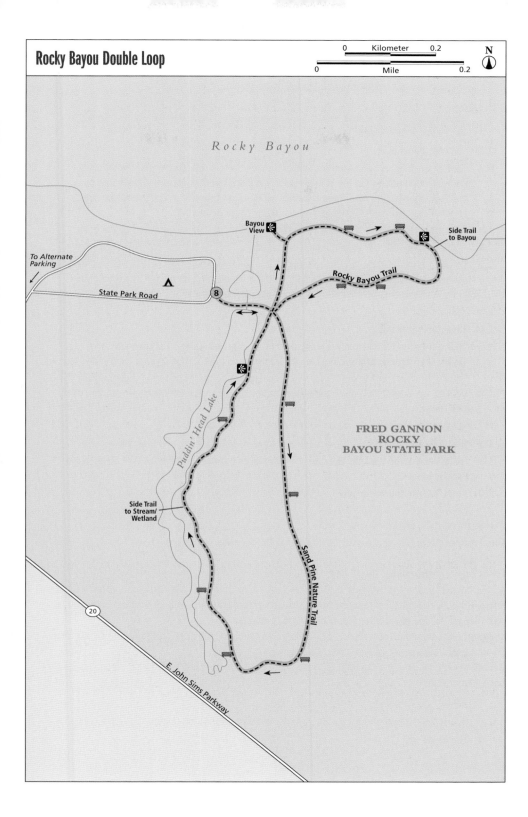

Rocky Bayou Double Loop

0   Kilometer   0.2

0   Mile   0.2

N

Rocky Bayou

Bayou View

Side Trail
to Bayou

To Alternate
Parking

State Park Road

Rocky Bayou Trail

8

Puddin' Head Lake

FRED GANNON
ROCKY
BAYOU STATE PARK

Side Trail
to Stream/
Wetland

Sand Pine Nature Trail

20

E. John Sims Parkway

0.5 Pass a bench. The trees here are draped with Spanish moss. In less than 0.1 mile, pass another side trail to the water on the left (north) and a bench. In less than 0.1 mile, pass another side trail to the water on the left and a bench.

0.6 Pass an old service road that is chained off on the left (southeast). In less than 0.1 mile, pass another bench. In less than 0.1 mile, pass a side trail on the right (north). Keep going straight to the west.

0.7 Pass two benches.

0.8 Back at the intersection of the two loops at mile 0.1, turn left (south) and immediately come to another Y. This is the connector for this loop. Take the left fork to the south onto the Sand Pine Nature Trail. There is a split-rail fence on your left. In a few yards pass a bench. The path is literally flooded with reindeer moss all around.

0.9 Pass a bench on the left. You will be walking under a nice canopy provided by the oaks.

1.0 At interpretive post 12, pass a bench on the left.

1.2 Come to what looks like a Y. The left fork is an abandoned trail. Take the right fork to the southwest (a sign says "Turkey Oak") and a big magnolia tree on the left. The trail footing turns into deeper sand for a short distance as you head downhill.

1.3 Pass a bench.

1.4 Pass another bench.

1.5 Pass a bench on the left as you walk through an impressive stretch of magnolia. The stream and wetland of what used to be Puddin' Head Lake will be on your left for the remainder of the hike.

1.6 A short side trail takes you to the wetland and stream on the left. Continue straight to the north.

1.7 Pass another bench.

1.8 Best view from the trail of the wetland and stream, with lily pads and frog song.

1.9 Arrive back at the Y at mile 0.1. Take the left fork to the west and retrace your steps to the parking lot.

2.0 Arrive back at the parking lot.

Hike Information

Local Information: City of Niceville, 208 N. Partin Dr., Niceville, FL 32578; (850) 729-4008; cityof niceville.org

Local Events/Attractions: Boggy Bayou Mullet Festival, E. College Boulevard, Niceville; (850) 729-4545; boggybayoumulletfestival.info. Described as "more than your average seafood festival," the Boggy Bayou Mullet Festival features food, arts and crafts, and performances by big names in the music business. The event is held annually in mid-October.

Lodging: Fred Gannon Rocky Bayou State Park Campground, 4281 FL 20, Niceville; (850) 833-9144; recreation.gov. Rocky Bayou has 42 improved campsites.

Restaurants: Front Porch Restaurant, 306 Bayshore Dr., Niceville; (850) 897-1027; facebook.com/pages/Front-Porch/172525716189253?rf=116240531737903

9 Fort Pickens Seashore Trail

Fort Pickens, the largest of four forts built to defend Pensacola, is steeped in history from its days during the Civil War through World War II, but why drive to the fort to experience this fascinating history when you can hike it on this wonderful trail that takes you not only to the fort but over bayous teeming with birds and the beaches of Pensacola Bay?

Start: Trailhead on south side of Battery Worth parking lot
Distance: 2.2-mile out-and-back with beach loop
Hiking time: About 1.5 hours, not including touring the fort and museum
Difficulty: Easy over level shell path, moderate on beach walk
Trail surface: Ground shell footpath, fine beach sand
Best seasons: Year-round
Other trail users: Cyclists

Canine compatibility: Leashed dogs permitted but not on beach section
Land status: National park
Nearest town: Pensacola Beach
Fees and permits: Admission fee
Schedule: Year-round, 7 a.m.–sunset
Maps: USGS Gulf Breeze, FL; maps available at entrance station
Trail contact: Gulf Islands National Seashore, 1801 Gulf Breeze Pkwy., Gulf Breeze, FL 32563; (850) 934-2600; nps.gov/guis/plan yourvisit/fort-pickens.htm

Finding the trailhead: From the intersection of Shoreline Drive and Gulf Breeze Parkway in Gulf Breeze, take the Gulf Breeze Parkway south 0.2 mile and bear right onto FL 399. Travel across Pensacola Bay on the bridge (there is a toll). Travel 2 miles and turn left onto Fort Pickens Road. In 3.4 miles arrive at the Fort Pickens pay station. After paying your entrance fee, continue straight to the west on Fort Pickens Road. In 5.2 miles turn right into the Battery Worth picnic area. Park anywhere. The trailhead is on the south side of the parking lot next to the battery. GPS: N30 19.438' / W87 16.758'

The Hike

For over 185 years Fort Pickens has stood, watching over and protecting Pensacola Bay and the city of Pensacola. The fort has a rich and storied history that dates back to its original construction in 1829, eventually being completed in 1834. Its mission was to protect Pensacola but more importantly the Navy Yard.

Fort Pickens was the largest of four forts built along the bay, with the thought being that if there was going to be an attack, it would come from the sea. How ironic that the first threat to the city and fort came from the mainland. In January 1861 Confederate forces took Forts Barrancas and McRee and demanded that the Union surrender Fort Pickens. Fort commander Lieutenant Adam Slemmer refused, and it looked like the first battle of the Civil War wouldn't be at Fort Sumter but Fort Pickens.

Your first view of Fort Pickens from the trail shows the damage from an accidental explosion in the 1800s.

Both sides met and reached an agreement that the Union could continue to man the fort as long as they didn't reinforce it with troops and arms. The battle was averted—that is until Fort Sumter went under attack and the Civil War officially began. Immediately the Union began reinforcing the fort in anticipation of an attack. What ensued came to be called the Battle of Santa Rosa Island, during which Confederate general Braxton Bragg said that the artillery barrage was the "heaviest in the history of the world." When it was over Union troops took the city of Pensacola.

After that the fort was put into use to handle other potential threats. During World War II, for example, 12-inch mortars and 6- and 3-inch rapid-fire guns were installed.

Now, you could drive down Fort Pickens Road to go visit the fort, but we're here to hike and the Fort Pickens Seashore Trail is the way to go—a beautiful 2.2-mile out-and-back with a little loop that takes you to the beaches of Pensacola Bay.

The trail is actually a subset of the Florida National Scenic Trail (or the Florida Trail, or FT). A sign at the beginning and where the trail ends near the fort proudly proclaims this fact. The kiosk near the fort is actually the western terminus of the 1,000-mile-long trail. You will see the FT's signature orange blaze at the beginning and end of the trip.

The path begins at the Battery Worth parking lot. Right at the trailhead the ominous-looking gray and black cement battery stands. You are invited to walk the

WALKING THE FLORIDA TRAIL

Imagine backpacking 1,300 miles from the buoy at Key West, Florida, to Fort Pickens on Florida's panhandle. You can on the Florida National Scenic Trail, or FT (Florida Trail).

The trail was the brainchild of Jim Kern, a Florida resident and hiker who was tired of having to travel far out of the state to go backpacking due to the lack of such trails in his home state. In 1966 Jim set out on a hike to bring awareness of this fact to the public. Government agencies like the US Forest Service thought he was joking, but overwhelming response from the public made them believers.

With that the Florida Trail Association (FTA) was born, with an initial goal of building 500 miles of continuous hiking trail. The first 26 miles were completed in the Ocala National Forest in 1969. Since that time FTA has built over 1,000 miles of linear trail with 365 miles of loops through swamps, marshes, beaches, and more. Their goal now is to increase the mileage to 1,300 miles.

While the Florida Trail is a great backpacking experience to add to your résumé, it has become an important piece of a bigger adventure—the Eastern Continental Trail (ECT). Over the last few years, dozens of hikers have begun hiking the FT at Key West, hiked north to Pensacola on the panhandle, then continued hiking north through Alabama and into Georgia, where the trail connects to the Appalachian Trail and then the International AT, eventually ending in Cape Gaspé, Canada, a hike of 5,500 miles!

Whether or not you hike the ECT, don't miss doing a day, weekend, or longer hike on the Florida Trail. Visit FTA online at floridatrail.org.

unit and explore, with a great view waiting for you from atop the tower. You can visit the battery either as you start the hike or when you return.

From here the trail heads generally to the west and with a ground shell footpath. For the most part it is a good 4- to 5-foot-wide trail. The trail is also used by cyclists, so keep your eyes and ears open for them. Along the trail are prickly pear cactus, wild rosemary, and yaupon holly. Chances are you'll notice the female of the species with its ever-present red berries.

As you make the half-mile mark, you will notice that you are walking between two bayous. Through this section be on the lookout for some winged friends including Cape May and magnolia warblers. Osprey nests dot the landscape.

Soon you'll cross the bayou over a wooden bridge with a stunning view of the canal. Tall sea oats line the banks. The water is clear but is stained brown from the tannin of the nearby plants. Look carefully and you may see turtles swimming across the still water.

A bayou courses across the trail as you near Fort Pickens.

The trail comes to an end at the parking lot just north of the fort. Follow the road around to the fort. Take your time and explore. And don't miss the museum just north of the fort. When you're done, retrace your steps back toward the trailhead.

At mile 1.4 you will come to an intersection with a service road that was passed on your trip out. Turn left here and head to the beach. (**Note:** Dogs are not allowed.) Here along the banks of Pensacola Bay, you'll have expansive views of the bay; across the way is NAS Pensacola and the black Pensacola lighthouse. You'll turn here to the southeast for a 0.5-mile beach walk. The dunes here are lined with tall, waving sea oats, seaside elder, and sea rocket, three important dune-building plants.

Remember that the trail has sparse canopy, so be prepared in the hot summer months to wear protection on your head, use sunscreen, and drink plenty of water.

Miles and Directions

0.0   Start from the trailhead on the south side of the Battery Worth parking lot right next to the battery. You can visit the battery and its tower with a view of the Gulf of Mexico and Pensacola Bay either now or when you return. The ground shell trail heads to the west. A small sign announces that this trail is part of the Florida National Scenic Trail and it is 0.7 mile to the fort.

Fort Pickens Seashore Trail

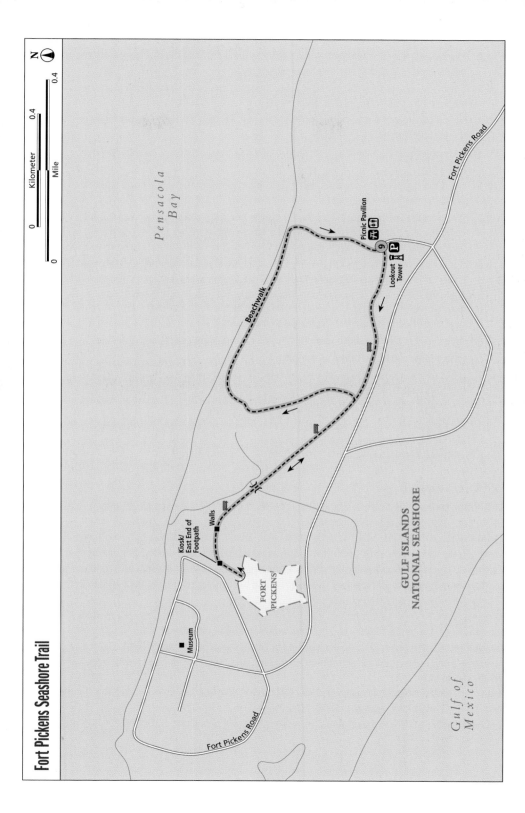

0.2 Pass an old cement foundation and a bench on the right. Ahead to the left you will see an osprey-viewing platform and nearby an osprey nest.

0.3 Cross a service road to the northwest. This shell road will be the access trail to the beach on the return trip.

0.4 Pass a bench on the right among rows of very tall sea oats. The path narrows to about 2 feet wide from here.

0.5 A very pretty little bayou is on both sides of the trail as you continue heading to the northwest.

0.6 Cross the bayou over a short wooden bridge with nice views of the water and grasses. Watch for turtles swimming in the water.

0.7 Pass a bench on the right. In less than 0.1 mile, the trail passes between two low, thick cement walls, possibly seawalls. The Florida Trail orange blaze will be seen on the left side. As you make your way through, you will get your first glimpse of the fort ahead to your left.

0.8 Come to the end of the trail at the fort parking lot. There is an informational kiosk here. Follow the road and parking lot around to the left (west) toward the fort. In less than 0.1 mile, arrive at the fort. Take your time to explore the rich history and scamper around the fort. You may also want to check out the museum to the northwest of the fort. When done, turn around and retrace your steps back to mile 0.3.

1.4 Arrive back at the intersection with the service road. Turn left (north) onto the road.

1.5 Pass a large pile of old bricks on the right.

1.7 Cross over sand dunes and arrive at the beaches of Pensacola Bay. Turn right (southeast) and do a little beach walking.

2.0 Turn right (south) and head off the beach.

2.1 Pass the picnic area and restrooms on the north side of the Battery Worth parking lot. Follow the parking lot south back to the trailhead.

2.2 Arrive back at the trailhead.

Hike Information

Local Information: Santa Rosa Island Authority, PO Drawer 1208, Pensacola Beach, FL 32562; (800) 635-4803; visitpensacolabeach.com

Local Events/Attractions: Star Gazing on Pensacola Beach, Gulfside Pavilion, Casino Beach Boulevard, Pensacola Beach; (800) 635-4803; visitpensacolabeach.com/events/star-gazing.php. The Escambia County Amateur Astronomers Association sets up over twenty telescopes for the public to use to view the wonders of the galaxy. The event is held one weekend a month from April to October. Visit the website for dates and changes due to bad weather.

Lodging: Fort Pickens Campground, 1801 Gulf Breeze Pkwy., Gulf Breeze; (877) 444-6777; recreation.gov. The campground has 200 sites with water and electricity.

Restaurants: Surf Burger, 500 Quietwater Beach Blvd., Pensacola Beach; (850) 932-1417; the surfburger.com. A great "burger and bands" restaurant featuring their popular Surf Burger, and the joint is pet-friendly.

Tours: Fort Pickens Tour, Gulf Islands National Seashore, 1801 Gulf Breeze Pkwy., Gulf Breeze; (850) 934-2600. Guided tours are given daily at 2 p.m.

Organizations: Florida Trail Association, 5414 SW 13 St., Gainesville, FL 32608; (352) 378-8823; floridatrail.org

10 Estuary Trail

Picturesque is an understatement for the Estuary Trail as it winds its way between Long Pond, Grand Lagoon, and its namesake Big Lagoon. Blue herons wade in the shallows, fishermen line the banks and piers, kayakers ply the waters as they head to the Gulf, and the sunsets are simply gorgeous. Oh, and there is the famous four-story Big Lagoon observation tower with panoramic views of the park and the lagoon.

Start: Parking area near Governor's Pavilion
Distance: 2.8-mile out-and-back with 2 small loops
Hiking time: About 2 hours
Difficulty: Moderate to difficult over thick beach sand
Trail surface: Sand, pavement, boardwalk
Best seasons: Year-round
Other trail users: None
Canine compatibility: Leashed dogs permitted

Land status: State park
Nearest town: Pensacola
Fees and permits: Admission fee
Schedule: Year-round, 8 a.m.–sunset
Maps: USGS Fort Barrancas, FL; maps available at entrance station
Trail contact: Big Lagoon State Park, 12301 Gulf Beach Hwy., Pensacola, FL 32507; (850) 492-1595; floridastateparks.org/biglagoon

Finding the trailhead: From the intersection of US 98 and FL 173 in Pensacola, take FL 173 south 3.2 miles. Turn left onto FL 292 West and travel 3 miles. Turn left onto Vincent Road. In 0.6 mile Vincent Road becomes Bauer Road. Continue straight another 1.2 miles and arrive at the park's entrance station. After paying your fee, continue straight ahead 1.5 miles. The parking area and trailhead are on the right near the Governor's Pavilion. GPS: N30 18.657'/W87 25.021'

The Hike

On the Florida panhandle just south of Pensacola, you will find Big Lagoon State Park. The aptly named park is located on the banks of Big Lagoon, a body of water that separates the mainland from Perdido Key and the Gulf of Mexico.

This 678-acre park first opened in 1978 and has been a popular panhandle attraction ever since. The park offers over 5 miles of hiking trails, camping, and swimming. The park is a birder's paradise and is recognized as the "Gateway to the Great Florida Birding Trail." The location makes it a prime destination for wintering and migrating birds and, of course, its normal yearly residents such as king rails, great blue herons, cardinals, and nuthatches. Binoculars are available for loan at the ranger station.

The Estuary Trail is a moderate to difficult, 2.8-mile out-and-back with two small loops at each end, almost a dog bone. The walk is rated difficult because of the thick, fine sand that makes up the footing of the trail. The hike begins at the parking lot near the Governor's Pavilion and gives you plenty of opportunities to experience the park's wetlands, ponds, and lagoons.

Brilliant white sand, a picnic pavilion, and reflections rippling in Long Pond make a picturesque scene.

The trek begins on the east side of the parking lot. Take the crosswalk here to the north to cross the park road and begin the sandy hike on the other side. It won't be long before you are walking a very nice ADA-accessible boardwalk near the west end of Long Pond. Interpretive signs tell you the stories of the wildlife and plants you will be seeing along the hike.

At 0.2 mile into the hike, you will leave the boardwalk at a shelter and begin the main hike between the ponds and lagoons. For the most part the trail is fine, deep sand as it meanders along the banks of Long Pond and Grand Lagoon, making walking it a chore if you're not ready for it. Don't be surprised if white-tailed deer or marsh rabbits dart across the path in front of you.

As you walk, you will have beautiful views of the water features. Fishermen and crabbers dot the banks while blue herons wait patiently to catch their next meal. The path is lined with short sand pine, needlerush, and the gnarled trunks of sand live oaks. Ospreys and their nests are scattered about. Walk quietly and watch as they dive for their breakfast then maneuver their meal in their talons so that the fish is facing forward as they fly, giving the bird less air resistance.

The trail has intermittent orange blazes and a few directional signs, which can make travel a bit confusing. Some of the blazes are painted on downed trees, some on 4-by-4-inch posts sunk into the sand, while others are painted on PVC pipes that are sunk into the sand.

At mile 0.7 you cross the park road once again to the south, cross a parking lot, and come to the park's new amphitheater. Nature presentations are given here periodically, but the view of the Intercoastal Waterway and Big Lagoon from the deck that wraps around the building is wonderful.

When done viewing you will follow the park road to the southeast; orange blazes are painted intermittently on a wood fence next to the road on the right. In 0.3 mile you will arrive at one of the park's biggest attractions, the four-story observation tower where you will have breathtaking views of the water features and, literally, a bird's-eye view of black-bellied plover, least sandpipers, and red-breasted mergansers as well as many other wintering and permanent resident birds.

A great blue heron poses for the camera.

The tower is part of a nearly half-mile boardwalk that has incredible views and provides access for swimming along the beach. On a cool foggy morning, it is an amazing place to walk as kayakers ply the waters beneath and around the structure, heading out into the lagoon. If you decide to hit the beach at the northern end of the boardwalk, there is a restroom with shower to wash the saltwater off.

From here you pick up the trail across the road to the north and return along the banks of the lake and pond. When you return to the first boardwalk, take a turn to the north to walk across the western end of Long Pond.

Bear in mind that hiking this trail in the summer can be brutal. There is very little, if any, shade along the route, so if you want to do a little summertime hiking here, be prepared with sunscreen, head protection, and plenty of water.

Miles and Directions

0.0 Start from the parking lot near the Governor's Pavilion. Head north a few yards to the park road, then turn right and head east along the road.

0.1 Cross the road to the northeast using the crosswalk and pick up the sandy footpath in front of you. In about 30 yards you will be walking on a long, wide boardwalk with interpretive signs over a marshy area surrounded by scrub.

0.2 Come to a Y. Take the right fork off the boardwalk and in a few feet come to a small shelter. A sign here reads "Trailhead—Estuary Loop 2 Miles." The trail is hugging the south bank of Long Pond on your left (north). The path is deep sand. In less than 0.1 mile, come to a Y with a post in the center. Take the right fork to the southeast.

BARRIER ISLANDS OF THE GULF

Many of the hikes covered in this book are on barrier islands. In fact, much of the Gulf of Mexico is ringed by these tiny, fragile islands. They can even be found on the eastern seaboard from New England to Miami.

Barrier islands are long, narrow deposits of sand that are separated from the mainland by a waterway such as a bay or sound. How the islands got there has been a topic of discussion among scientists for years. The latest theory is that the sand was deposited over 18,000 years ago at the end of the last ice age. As the glaciers melted and receded, the oceans began to rise and flood depressions behind ancient beach ridges. Sand from the ridges was swept up and deposited in shallows just off the newly formed coastlines. It wasn't long before vegetation found a home on these islands, and wildlife soon followed.

The islands are home to countless species of wildlife and birds that depend on the delicate vegetation and abundance of fish to survive. The islands also play an important role in protecting the mainland from hurricanes.

Barrier islands are a work in progress. With each passing storm the islands change. Some move, like the tiny Sand Island off the Alabama coast. In 2001 it was in Alabama waters, now it's in Mississippi.

People love to frolic on the white beaches of these coastal islands and have moved in droves to live there to escape the cold, harsh northern winters. But there is a price to pay for living in "paradise." Overdevelopment on many of the islands is causing the fragile ecosystem to break down. And there is an economic and human price to pay as well, with the constant threat of devastating hurricanes looming on the horizon each and every summer.

0.4 Pass a swampy area on the left and dunes to the right.

0.5 Pass a bench on the right at a little oasis of shade.

0.6 Come to a Y at a double blaze. There is a great view of Grand Lagoon on the left. A sign here shows the way to the observation tower (to the right). Take the right fork to the southeast.

0.7 Cross the paved park road to the south and follow it around as it swings to the southeast. In less than 0.1 mile, you will come to a new pavilion where nature shows are given. There are great views of Big Lagoon here on the walkway that wraps around the building. When done, head back to the road and turn right (northeast). Continue following the road to the east. A split-rail fence on your right shows the way with orange blazes painted on it.

1.0 Come to a Y with a sign that points to the observation tower (to the right). Take the right fork to the southeast. You will see the orange blaze on your right.

1.1 Turn right off the road and onto the boardwalk that encircles the tower.

Estuary Trail

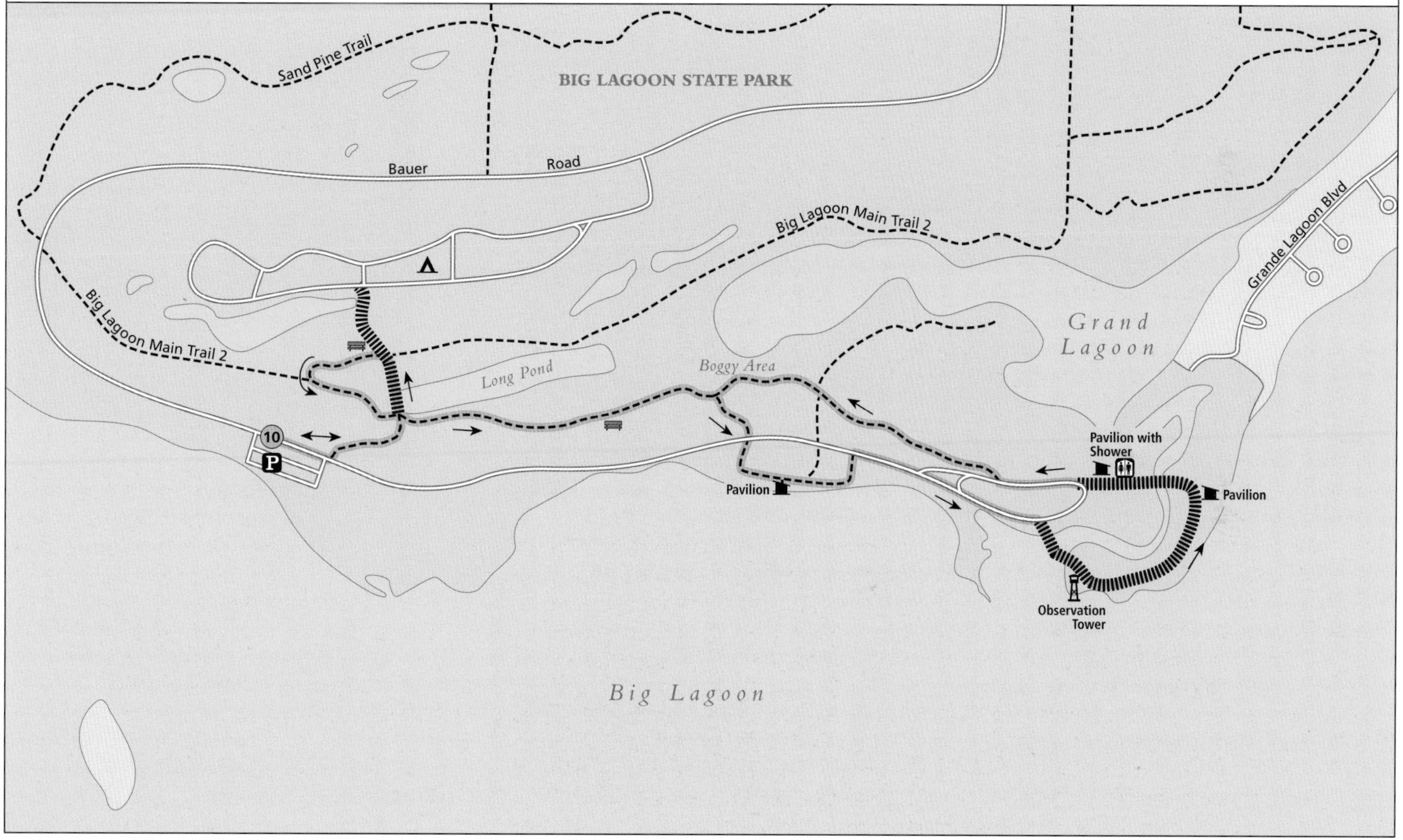

Grande Lagoon Blvd

Grand Lagoon

Pavilion

Pavilion with Shower

Observation Tower

Pavilion

Boggy Area

Big Lagoon Main Trail 2

BIG LAGOON STATE PARK

Sand Pine Trail

Road

Bauer

Long Pond

Big Lagoon

Big Lagoon Main Trail 2

10

P

N

Kilometer
0   0.4

Mile
0   0.4

1.2 Come to a Y with a double orange blaze. The left fork to the south takes you to the observation tower. Take the left fork. After visiting the tower, turn around and head back to the Y at the double orange blaze and turn right (southeast), continuing on the boardwalk.

1.3 After a pavilion, exit the boardwalk for a short beach walk along the Big Lagoon itself.

1.4 Take a short cement sidewalk past another pavilion, and once again you're on the boardwalk.

1.5 Pass a pavilion with a shower and restroom. In 20 yards you're back on the road. Follow it around to your right (west).

1.6 Pass a sign that reads "FVA." Turn off the road to the right (north), and you're back on the trail with orange blazes.

1.8 Come to a Y with a double blaze. Take the left fork to the west.

1.9 Come to a sign pointing to the right (north) that reads "Long Pond West Branch." If you're up to it, take the right fork for a short 0.4-mile out-and-back to the edge of Long Pond for some exceptional views; otherwise, keep going straight to the west, passing a bench on your left. In less than 0.1 mile, cross a boggy area that could be fairly deep in water after a rain.

2.0 Pass the sign at mile 0.6 showing the way to the observation tower. Continue straight to the west.

2.3 Arrive back at the first boardwalk. Take the right fork (north) and follow the bridge and boardwalk across Long Pond, with some really nice views and signs warning you not to swim here due to alligators.

2.4 The boardwalk ends but picks up again in a few feet. A sandy footpath intersects here. Turn left (west) onto the sandy footpath. The trail has white blazes from here on. (The boardwalk continues straight to the north as the Governor's Pavilion Trail.)

2.5 Pass a bench on the right. In less than 0.1 mile, come to a T intersection with another trail (there is a set of double white blazes here). Turn left (southeast) onto this trail. In a few yards pass another trail on your right. Continue straight to the southeast.

2.6 You're back at the boardwalk. Scamper under the boardwalk and use the stairs on the opposite side to climb back up onto it. Turn left (south) and head back to the parking lot.

2.8 Arrive back at the parking lot.

Hike Information

Local Information: City of Pensacola, 222 W. Main St., Pensacola, FL 32502; (850) 435-1603; cityofpensacola.com

Local Events/Attractions: Pensacola Ice Flyers Hockey, Pensacola Civic Center, 201 E. Gregory St., Pensacola; (850) 466-3111; pensacolaiceflyers.com. Hockey Southern-style with the Ice Flyers, a member of the Southern Professional Hockey League and winner of the SPHL President's Cup (league championship) in 2013 and 2014.

Lodging: Big Lagoon State Park Campground, 12301 Gulf Beach Hwy., Pensacola; (850) 492-1595; recreation.gov. Situated in a beautiful pine forest, the campground has 75 improved sites with water, electricity, and picnic tables.

Restaurants: McGuire's Irish Pub, 600 E. Gregory St., Pensacola; (850) 433-6789; mcguiresirishpub.com. An old-time, turn-of-the-century, New York–style saloon with great Irish food, music, and fun—oh, and over a million signed dollar bills on the wall.

Florida Honorable Mentions

There are plenty of great hikes all along the Florida Gulf Coast that didn't make the A list. Although many are shorter in length, they offer fantastic scenery and interesting wildlife. Pay a visit and let us know what you think. Maybe the hike should be upgraded, or maybe you know of a little-known hike that would make a good honorable mention.

A Jay B. Starkey Wilderness Park

In 1937 Jay B. Starkey purchased this property, which is located in New Port Richey, and made it into a profitable cattle ranch and timber operation. In 1975 Mr. Starkey donated several hundred acres of the property to the Southwest Florida Water Management District, which in turn dedicated itself to protecting this landscape for generations to come. Today hikers, equestrians, and cyclists can enjoy over 6.7 miles of paved biking and jogging trails, 10 miles of equestrian trails, and 27 miles of hiking trails. The hiking trails are magnificent as they take you through a wide variety of ecosystems including pine flatwoods, cypress domes, streams, swamps, and freshwater marshes. With 27 miles of trail, you may want to put on your overnight pack and do a little backpacking. Backcountry camping is allowed in the park, in addition to standard primitive camping areas. The park is open from 6:30 a.m. to sunset every day. For more information contact the Jay B. Starkey Wilderness Park at (727) 834-3247 or visit online at swfwmd.state.fl.us/recreation/areas/starkey-park.html.

B Rainbow Springs Nature Trail

Rainbow Springs is a very popular state park—and for good reason. This is the site of a first-magnitude spring—that is, a spring that discharges over 100 cubic feet of water every second! According to the state lands department, all thirty-three first-magnitude springs flow more continuous water each day than the entire population of Florida can drink. With this mega-spring as its centerpiece, visitors can go snorkeling, swimming, canoeing, and tubing in the cold, clear waters. The park has a wonderful 2.5-mile loop trail, the Nature Trail, that meanders through a landscape of meadows and pines, past the beautiful Rainbow River, and the site of a once-burgeoning industry in these parts, phosphate mining. The park is open from 8 a.m. to sunset every day. There is a small day-use fee; children under 6 are free. Additional fees are required for tubing. Contact Rainbow Springs State Park for more information at (352) 465-8555 or online at floridastateparks.org/park/Rainbow-Springs.

C Dr. Julian G. Bruce St. George Island State Park

One of the most beautiful barrier island parks around is St. George Island State Park. Consistently year after year the beaches at this park are ranked in the top five best in the nation. For hikers there are two trails here. The 5-mile out-and-back to Gap Point is a beautiful hike over oak scrub–covered dunes and salt marshes. This is a tough hike through fine beach sand and there is no shade, so be prepared. There is, however, backcountry camping at the far end of the trail where you can pack your gear in and camp for the night. The East Slough Trail is a 1-mile-long trail along the banks of the slough where you are rewarded with a gorgeous view of the water. Park hours are from 8 a.m. to sunset. There is a small day-use fee; children 12 and under are free. Contact St. George Island State Park for more information at (850) 927-2111 or online at floridastateparks.org/park/St-George-Island.

D Topsail Hill Preserve State Park

Between Choctawhatchee Bay and the Gulf of Mexico, wedged in between Panama City Beach and Destin, is a beautiful state preserve, Topsail Hill. The name comes from the famous 25-foot-tall sand dune located in the park that resembles a ship's topsail. Topsail is described as the most intact coastal ecosystem in all of Florida. The main trail through the park is just over 10 miles long and is made up of a series of paths including the Morris Lake and Campbell Lake trails and miles of old logging and jeep roads. The trails loop and wind their way over ancient coastal dunes; through scrub, cypress dome, and old-growth longleaf pine forests; and around freshwater coastal dune lakes and wetlands. There's a bit of history to see on your hike as well. Just south of Morris Lake are remnants of the first missile development program in the United States. Old iron tracks and rebar are all that remain of the testing that went on here during WWII. And take a close look at the pine trees. Cat-face scars will be seen, cut into the longleaf long ago, and are reminders that at one time this area had a bustling turpentine industry. Plus you will be rewarded for your effort with magnificent views of Morris Lake and the blue-green waters of the Gulf of Mexico. The park is open every day from 8 a.m. to sunset. A small admission is charged. For more information contact Topsail Hill Preserve State Park at (850) 267-8330 or visit online at floridastateparks.org/park/Topsail-Hill.

E Naval Live Oaks Preserve

We have hiked several trails along the barrier islands that make up the Gulf Islands National Seashore. Well, add one more to your list—Naval Live Oaks. Located northeast of hike 9, Fort Pickens, in Ocean Breeze, Naval Live Oaks is a sprawling 1,300-acre preserve that was the site of the first national tree farm. In 1828 President John Quincy Adams set aside this area for military purposes, using its significant growth of live oaks to build and repair navy ships. The property has remained in government custody ever since. There are many paths you can follow through the preserve. A great walk for the entire family is the Brackenridge Nature Trail. This 0.5-mile-long boardwalk has informative interpretive signs so you can teach your children about the great outdoors, and impressive views of Santa Rosa Sound at the far end of the walk and at the visitor center. The trailhead is at the visitor center (be sure to view the 12-minute video on the history of the area). On the opposite side of US 98, there are miles of old logging roads you can explore. The main trails here are the Andrew Jackson, Old Borrow Pit, and Beaver Pond. Mix and match your hike to visit the beaver pond or the banks and panoramic view of Pensacola Bay. There is no fee to use the trails at Naval Live Oaks. For more information visit nps.gov/guis/planyourvisit/naval-live-oaks.htm or call (850) 934-9654.

Alabama

labama's Gulf Coast is sometimes referred to as the "Redneck Riviera." You might think that's a slam on the region, but it's actually a term of endearment. It's a place where the average hard-working person or family can come and have fun frolicking in the sun on the beaches, dining on the best seafood around, living life to the fullest but not at the prices of the real Riviera.

For taking up so little real estate on the Gulf of Mexico, the Alabama Gulf Coast sports an incredible natural environment. It all begins miles away from the white beaches north of the city of Mobile where the runoffs from surrounding states flow into Alabama's rivers and converge, creating the second-largest river delta in the country, the Mobile-Tensaw Delta. The delta is second only to the Mississippi Delta.

As with all regions of the Gulf Coast, the American alligator has recovered quite nicely from being on the endangered species list and now has reclaimed the waters of the delta and bayous as its home. The largest population of black bear in the state lives here as well as the once-endangered brown pelican.

This region is also home to the white sand beaches of Gulf Shores and Orange Beach, where the Pine Beach Trail at the Bon Secour National Wildlife Refuge takes hikers directly to the sandy shores. The refuge protects such endangered species as the Alabama beach mouse and the loggerhead sea turtle.

History abounds in this region as well. The Battle of Mobile Bay was fought here during the Civil War. It was in this battle that Union admiral David Farragut reportedly uttered the immortal words, "Damn the torpedoes, full speed ahead!" The battle occurred at Fort Morgan just west of the Bon Secour National Wildlife Refuge. Just north along the Mobile River in Spanish Fort is Historic Blakeley State Park, the site of the Battle of Blakeley, which is recognized as the last major battle of the Civil War.

For the most part you will experience typical Gulf Coast weather here. Being subtropical, late summer heat is accentuated by high humidity that often hits 100 percent, which makes outdoor activity a bit uncomfortable and sometimes dangerous.

The warm air and Mobile's location on the Gulf of Mexico mean that sudden and very heavy rainfall can be expected without warning. The storms are short, but the rain is plentiful. In fact, Mobile has held the National Weather Service title of "wettest city in America" a number of times.

Fall and winter in L.A. (Lower Alabama) is wonderful, to say the least. Most of the time, moderate temperatures, averaging in the low to mid-70s, last well into fall. During this time the humidity is quite low, making hiking a real pleasure. Temperatures in January average around 52°F. Now don't get me wrong, it does get cold here in Dixie. Temperatures have dropped below freezing, even to single digits. In 2014 the area was covered with an inch of ice from the famous Polar Vortex. But those days are short-lived, and literally the next day it will be in the 70s again.

11 Perdido River Trail

The Perdido River Trail is a wonderful day hike along this black-water river that forms the coastal border of Alabama and Florida. This 2.8-mile out-and-back meanders alongside the river, with plenty of views and opportunities to take a dip from one of the many sandbars. The trail passes through beautiful white Atlantic cedar bogs, and there is a good chance you'll see bald eagles, ospreys, and maybe an alligator or two.

Start: Parking area / trailhead alongside river

Distance: 2.8-mile out-and-back

Hiking time: About 2 hours

Difficulty: Easy to moderate over level sandy terrain and through some bogs

Trail surface: Dirt logging roads, sand and dirt footpaths

Best seasons: Year-round

Other trail users: None

Canine compatibility: Dogs permitted

Land status: State wildlife management area

Nearest town: Robertsdale

Fees and permits: None

Schedule: Year-round, sunrise–sunset

Maps: USGS Barrineau Park, FL; maps available online

Trail contact: Alabama Hiking Trail Society, PO Box 231164, Montgomery, AL 36123; hikealabama.org

Special considerations: This trail is located in a state wildlife management area. In the fall and winter, check hunting seasons and times before heading out at outdooralabama.com/hunting and wear hunter orange during these times.

Finding the trailhead: From Robertsdale at I-65 exit 53 (Wilcox Road), head north on CR 64 for 7.1 miles. Turn right onto AL 112 (Old Pensacola Road). Travel 9.4 miles and turn left at Duck Place Road (Barrineau Park Road). Immediately after you turn onto the paved Duck Place Road, turn right onto the dirt River Road. Follow River Road for approximately 1.7 miles, then turn left onto Nims Fork Road. Travel 0.3 mile and turn right onto an unnamed road. Travel approximately 0.5 mile around a curve to the left, then turn right onto another unnamed road. Follow this road approximately 0.4 mile and cross railroad tracks, then take a right at the fork. Travel approximately 0.7 mile and turn left onto yet another unnamed road. Travel 1 mile. The road makes a sharp curve to the right. After the curve, continue another 1.7 miles to a triangle clearing where you can park. The trail begins on the north side of this parking area. GPS: N30 39.477' / W87 24.244'

The Hike

Baldwin County is one of the, if not *the*, fastest-growing counties in Alabama. Hundreds of thousands of people are moving to the area for the beaches and the laid-back way of life. With all of this development you wouldn't think that there would be room, or even a place, to take a hike in a wilderness environment, but there is and this is it—the Perdido River Trail.

The trail is located on the banks of its namesake river that borders Florida and Alabama. The hike described here is a 2.8-mile out-and-back over a nice mix of dirt and sand footpaths and old logging roads that take you through amazing Atlantic

Hiking in the snow? No, just one of the many sandbars along the Perdido River Trail.

white cedar bogs and past beautiful white sandbars. All in all it makes a wonderful outing for families and individuals looking for a day hike in the woods with plenty to do and see along the way, and best of all it's only a stone's throw from the white beaches of the Gulf of Mexico.

The reason that there is a trail here at all is because of the efforts of the Conservation Fund and Nature Conservancy (two national land conservation organizations) and the Alabama Forever Wild program. The land was originally owned by International Paper (IP), but in 2006 the company decided to sell. Fearing that this unique environment and important watershed would be divvied up into subdivisions, the Conservation Fund and Nature Conservancy moved quickly to make IP an offer, which the company accepted. Forever Wild then purchased the property from the other organizations.

In addition to protecting the area and its natural beauty, the state began working to open it up for public recreation. The result is an amazing area for birding, wildlife

ALABAMA'S NEW LONG TRAIL—THE ALABAMA TRAIL

In the not-too-distant future, a new long trail will be available for hikers to set out on—the Alabama Trail. The trail is the brainchild of the Alabama Hiking Trail Society (AHTS), a non-profit organization whose mission is to build and maintain hiking trails across the state, including this new long trail.

The goal is to have a linear footpath that will stretch from Fort Morgan on Alabama's Gulf Coast to the city of Florence in northwest Alabama and then head across the state to Huntsville and the Tennessee state line, a trek of over 500 miles. When completed the path will highlight all of the natural beauty the state has to offer—white beaches along the Gulf, maritime forests and wetlands, black-water rivers, deep canyons, towering waterfalls, and the last mountains in the Appalachian chain.

It's an ambitious project, to say the least, and one that is well under way along Alabama's Gulf Coast, where local volunteers have been granted easements and right-of-ways and built over 50 miles of their 120 miles of trail, including the first backpacking trail on the state's coast, the Perdido River Trail (hike 11).

Other trails featured in this guide that are being included in the Alabama Trail are the Blue Trail, Graham Creek Preserve (hike 12); the Pine Beach Trail (hike 13); and the Jeff Friend / Centennial Trail, Bon Secour National Wildlife Refuge (hike 14).

Learn more about the project and how you can become involved in making it a reality by visiting AHTS online at hikealabama.org.

viewing, swimming, canoeing, hiking, hunting, fishing, horseback riding . . . well, you get the idea.

There are actually two recreational trails here. The first is a new 20-mile paddling trail. The other is the first backpacking trail on Alabama's Gulf Coast, the Perdido River Trail. Eventually this trail will be part of a new long trail, the Alabama Trail, that will eventually stretch from the Gulf to Tennessee. The complete Perdido River Trail along the river is about 15 miles in length, with camping allowed along the many sandbars it passes and in brand-new trail shelters (see "Trail contact" for information on where to learn more).

I will throw a shameful plug in here and tip my hat to a group that I am proud to be part of, the Gulf Coast Chapter of the Alabama Hiking Trail Society. It is our volunteers that are getting out there and building this remarkable trail year-round, including during some incredibly hot weather.

While the entire trail is complete and ready to backpack, the section I am describing here is a subset that will take you down the first few miles of the trail, a nice 2.8-mile out-and-back that ends at a gigantic white sandbar, the perfect place to spend some time catching rays, picnicking, and swimming in the deep, cool water. (Remember, there are no lifeguards. Swimming is at your own risk, and children need to be under adult supervision.)

A picturesque view of the black-water river awaits you at the trailhead. A black-water river is tinted a dark tea color from the tannin of the trees that line its banks. From here you will get your first glimpse of the many white sandbars that line the river. Directly across the river is Florida. Keep your eyes to the sky here. I have seen numerous bald eagles soaring overhead just after parking the car.

The trailhead is located on the southernmost end of the longer trail in a dirt and gravel cul-de-sac that is also the parking area. The area has enough room for maybe ten cars, but there is plenty of extra parking along the old logging road that leads to the trailhead. This area is also used by paddlers as a takeout for the 20-mile-long Perdido River Canoe Trail, so it could get crowded from spring to fall.

The trail is blazed yellow, and where the path makes a sharp turn, it uses what is affectionately known as the "dit-dot" method of blazing—two dollar-bill-size blazes, one on top of the other. The top blaze indicates the direction of the turn: If it's offset to the left, the trail turns left; to the right, the trail turns right.

The first part of the hike is along an old logging road that runs parallel to the river on your right (east). Every now and then you will get a glimpse of the river until mile 0.7, when you will come to a short and very obvious 30-foot side trail to a nice bluff giving you excellent views of the river and maybe a paddler or two sailing past. From here the path ducks into the woods and takes you through some magnificent stands of Atlantic white cedar in picturesque bogs. This is a good place to see some wildlife, including white-tailed deer, quail, armadillo, and coyote.

Keep in mind that you are hiking through some substantial bogs here. If you plan on hiking in the summer, be sure to slather on plenty of insect repellent. The trail finally arrives at the large sandbar. Believe me, you won't miss it! Bring along a lunch and something to swim in, and enjoy the water and beach. This is a favorite spot for locals in the summer, so it could get crowded on hot days. You will notice that the blazes continue to the north. That is the remaining 2.6 miles of the completed trail that takes you through a pine savannah. Unless you plan to continue on a longer trip, this is your turnaround to head back to the trailhead.

Here are a couple of things to keep in mind. First, the river is in a low-lying area, so flash flooding is possible. Keep your eyes and ears open for severe weather, and leave if the weather is threatening. And remember that the property is shared with hunters in the fall and winter. Please refer to the "Special considerations" section and contact the Alabama Department of Conservation and Natural Resources for dates.

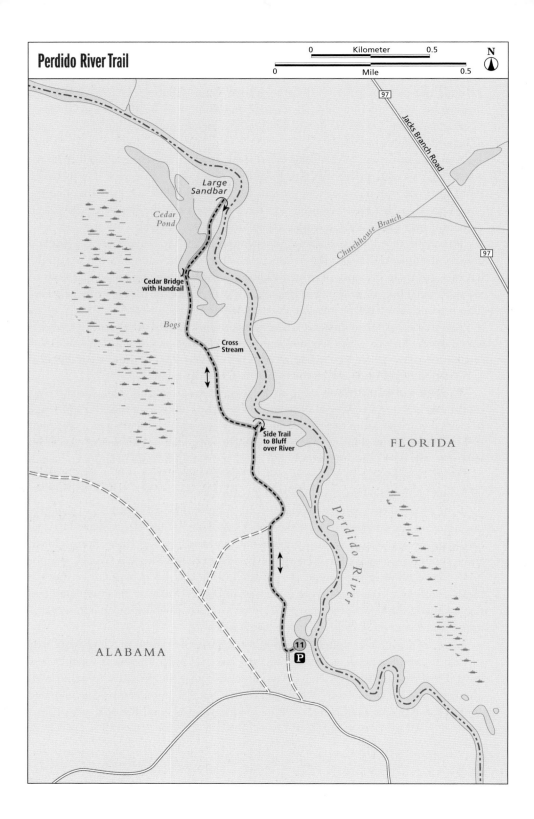

Perdido River Trail

0 — Kilometer — 0.5
0 — Mile — 0.5

N

Large
Sandbar

Cedar
Pond

Cedar Bridge
with Handrail

Bogs

Cross
Stream

Side Trail
to Bluff
over River

FLORIDA

ALABAMA

Churchhouse Branch

Jacks Branch Road

97

97

Perdido River

11

P

Miles and Directions

0.0 Start from the parking area / trailhead. Head to the southwest on the dirt road that you drove in on. In less than 200 feet, turn right (northwest) onto a dirt road.

0.4 Come to a Y in the road. Take the right fork (northeast).

0.7 A short, 30-foot side trail to the right (east) leads to a bluff some 20 feet above the river, with excellent views. Continue northwest on the dirt road. In less than 0.1 mile, the trail makes its way off the dirt road and into the woods on a dirt footpath. You will cross several boggy areas through this section. After a few days of rain, this could be thick in mud or even rather deep puddles.

0.9 Cross a narrow, 1- to 2-foot-wide stream (it's easy to hop across). The trail narrows to 2 feet wide, with thick foliage on either side.

1.0 Cross over another boggy area. One part has a narrow, 3-foot-wide stream that you will cross on a cedar log footbridge.

1.2 Cross another stream, this time over a cedar log bridge with a handrail. After crossing the bridge, you will be walking through stands of tall Atlantic white cedars. You will also start getting views of the river once again to your right (east).

1.3 Pass a nice, deep cedar pond on the left (west). The pond is seasonal, depending on rainfall. The trail bed turns sandy here and follows the top of a 20-foot bluff along the river.

1.4 Come to a large sandbar. This is your turnaround, but you will want to linger. It also makes for an excellent campsite if you want to spend the night.

2.8 Arrive back at the trailhead.

Hike Information

Local Information: Central Baldwin Chamber of Commerce, 23150 AL 59, Robertsdale, AL 36567; (251) 947-4809; centralbaldwin.com

Local Events/Attractions: Flavors of the South Food and Wine Showcase, 19477 Fairground Rd., Robertsdale; (251) 947-2626; robertsdale.org. Held annually the last week of July, this event showcases the finest food and wine from Alabama's Gulf Coast.

Restaurants: Mama Lou's Restaurant, 22288 Pine St., Robertsdale; (251) 947-1988; mamalousbuffet.com

Organizations: Alabama Forever Wild, Alabama Department of Conservation and Natural Resources, 64 N. Union St., Montgomery, AL 36130; (334) 242-3484; alabamaforeverwild.com

12 Blue Trail

The city of Foley, Alabama, has preserved a 484-acre tract of land, Graham Creek Nature Preserve, a property that is brimming with an amazing array of wildlife and native plants. The Blue Trail is an easy-walking 3.2-mile loop through the preserve, on which you may run across bobcats, coyotes, gopher tortoises, and hundreds of migratory birds, not to mention swaying pine savannah grasses, flowering magnolias, and acres of beautiful white-topped pitcher plants.

Start: Trailhead across from parking area
Distance: 3.2-mile figure eight
Hiking time: About 2 hours
Difficulty: Easy over firm level terrain
Trail surface: Dirt, sand, grass
Best seasons: Early Mar to mid-May, mid-Sept to mid-Nov
Other trail users: Cyclists, disc golfers
Canine compatibility: Leashed dogs permitted

Land status: City nature preserve
Nearest town: Foley
Fees and permits: None
Schedule: Year-round, dawn to dusk
Maps: USGS Gulf Shores, AL; trail map available in kiosk at parking area
Trail contact: City of Foley, 407 E. Laurel Ave., PO Box 1750, Foley, AL 36536; (251) 952-4041; visitfoley.org

Finding the trailhead: From the intersection of US 98 and AL 59 in Foley, take AL 59 south 3.5 miles and turn left onto CR 12. Travel 1 mile and turn right onto Wolf Bay Drive. Drive 1 mile on Wolf Bay Drive. The road will make a sharp left curve just before the park entrance. Turn right into the preserve (a large Graham Creek Nature Preserve sign marks the turn). Follow the dirt road 0.2 mile. The parking area is to the left at a kiosk. The trailhead is across the road from the parking area and is marked with a round orange disk with an arrow on it attached to a 4-by-4-inch post. GPS: N30 20.734' / W87 37.471'

The Hike

Graham Creek Nature Preserve is a 484-acre tract of land that is a testament to the City of Foley, local utility company Riviera Utilities, and the hard work of city environmental manager Leslie Gahagan to protect this environmentally significant property. Without such protection the land would have been engulfed by the growth of one of the fastest-growing counties in the state.

The preserve is named for the creek that flows through the property and feeds Wolf Bay, a brackish body of water that borders Florida and Alabama and one that creates a unique and diverse environment where wildlife abounds. It's not unusual to see bald eagles, ospreys, Florida manatees, red-cockaded woodpeckers, gopher tortoises, coyotes, and American alligators.

The preserve sports two hiking trails: the main Blue Trail, which is described here, and a smaller 2-mile subset of the Blue Trail called the Red Trail. Both trails are

Water lilies on a pond at Graham Creek Nature Preserve

marked with round metal medallions mounted on 4-by-4-inch posts. The Blue Trail uses blue medallions; the red trail uses red medallions. Major mile markers such as 1.0, 2.0, and 2.5 miles are indicated along the path as well.

Parking is located about 0.2 mile south of the preserve's main entrance next to an information kiosk that describes the park's habitat and also has brochures to help guide you through your journey. Just remember to practice Leave No Trace and pack the brochures out with you.

The trailhead is located across the road from the parking lot and is marked with a round orange medallion. The orange marker indicates the path of the preserve's 7.5-mile-long bike path. Follow the orange marker about 100 feet, where you'll come to the first marker of the Blue Trail. Just a note, don't let the brochure at the kiosk throw you. As of this writing, the trail is labeled on the map in the brochure as being marked in green but it's actually blue.

As for the trail itself, it is a nice, easy walk over flat dirt roads. One striking feature of this hike is the large fields that you will skirt along the route. The first, coming almost immediately after beginning the hike, is part of the preserve's nine-hole disc golf course. Watch for flying Frisbees!

At 0.3 mile you will cross Graham Creek itself as it cuts through the path. The stream isn't deep—that is, unless you hike the trail after one of south Alabama's infamous heavy afternoon downpours. Unless the stream is dry, the rocks can be slippery. All around you are towering longleaf pines, and depending on the season you are hiking the trail, you will see over 700 plant species including lilies, arums, sunflowers, and several different species of rare orchids such as the rosebud orchid.

If you decide you want to shorten the trip, you can do so at mile 0.9 by taking the Red Trail back to the trailhead, but don't shortchange yourself. There is plenty more to see. At mile 1.7, just as the trail crosses a boggy area, you will get your first glimpse of white-topped pitcher plants. These are rare carnivorous plants much like a Venus flytrap that grow in the bogs surrounding pine savannahs. But wait, there's more! At the 2-mile mark you will make a turn to the north and be surrounded by hundreds of these beautiful cupped plants. Remember, the peak blooming season for these plants is March through early May.

Besides hiking, Graham Creek Nature Preserve provides plenty of additional recreational activities like biking and disc golf, as mentioned earlier. There is also a wonderful canoe launch on the creek just a few yards south of the parking area that provides access to the creek and bay so you can further explore.

A large picnic pavilion is also available, along with nice, clean restrooms near the preserve's entrance. The preserve hosts many tours and special events throughout the year. Visit their website at visitfoley.org for a listing.

Miles and Directions

0.0 Start from the trailhead across from the parking lot and head west. The trail runs along the south side of a large field that is also a disc golf course.

0.1 The trail bends to the left (south). It is now marked with color-coded medallions for all three trails: blue for this 3-mile trail, red for the 2-mile walking trail, and orange for the 7.5-mile bike trail.

0.3 Cross Graham Creek. The crossing isn't deep under normal conditions but can be after a good afternoon thunderstorm. Be careful of slippery rocks.

0.4 A spur of the Orange Bike Trail enters from the right (west).

0.5 The Orange Bike Trail leaves the walking trails to the left (east).

0.6 The Orange Bike Trail rejoins the walking trails as they all head to the west.

0.7 Reach a major four-way intersection where all three trails loop around each other. Turn left here and head south.

0.9 The Red Trail exits to right (west) at the northeast corner of a large field; continue straight ahead (south). The Orange Bike Trail continues to follow the path you're on.

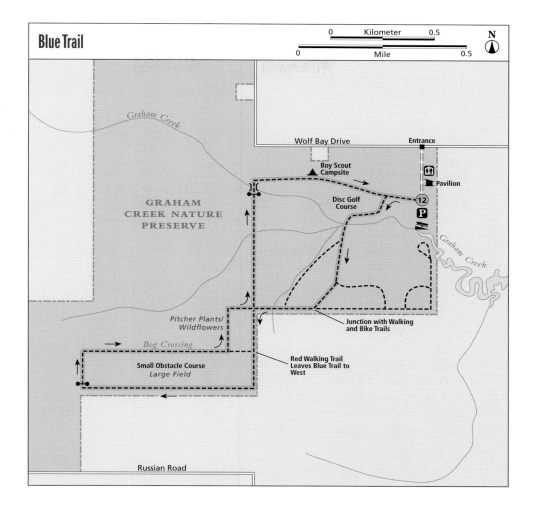

GRAHAM CREEK NATURE PRESERVE

Graham Creek

Wolf Bay Drive

Entrance

Boy Scout Campsite

Disc Golf Course

Pavilion

Graham Creek

Pitcher Plants/ Wildflowers

Junction with Walking and Bike Trails

Bog Crossing

Red Walking Trail Leaves Blue Trail to West

Small Obstacle Course
Large Field

Russian Road

1.0 Turn right (west). Travel along the south side of the large field. This part of the trail runs along the southernmost property line.

1.2 Pass a small obstacle course with a climbing wall and tubes on the right (north).

1.5 Come to a closed gate on the left. The path goes straight to a dead end. Turn right here and head north.

1.6 Turn right (east). You are now traveling on the north side of the field.

1.7. Come to a boggy area where a small creek crosses the trail. Keep your eyes peeled for the first signs of white-topped pitcher plants.

2.0 Turn left (north) and rejoin the Red Trail. The Orange Bike Trail continues straight. Hundreds of pitcher plants and different varieties of wildflowers will be seen in this pine savannah in the spring.

2.3 Return to the intersection with the Red Trail at mile 0.9 and turn left (north). The Orange Bike Trail rejoins here.

2.6 Pass through an open gate and cross a short bridge over Graham Creek.

2.7 The trail bends to the right (east).

2.8 You are now walking on the north side of the first field where you started the hike. The disc golf course will be on your right (south).

3.2 Arrive back at the trailhead.

Hike Information

Local Information: South Baldwin Chamber of Commerce, 112 W. Laurel Ave., PO Box 1117, Foley, AL 36536; (877) 461-3712; southbaldwinchamber.com

Local Events/Attractions: Alabama Festival of Flavor, US 98 and Alston Street, Foley; (877) 461-3712; southbaldwinchamber.com/major-events/alabama-festival-of-flavor-overview. You'll find a little bit of this and a little bit of that, but all of it Alabama. This 6-block party is held the middle of October and features football tailgating food, music, wine and beer tastings, unique Alabama craftsmen and artisans, and much more.

Restaurants: Fish River Grill #2, 608 S. McKenzie St., Foley; (251) 952-3474; fishrivergrill.com. Literally piles of the best seafood from Alabama's Gulf Coast.

13 Pine Beach Trail

The Pine Beach Trail at the Bon Secour National Wildlife Refuge is one of south Alabama's most popular hiking destinations, and with good reason. This 3.4-mile out-and-back is a transitional coastal hike beginning in a beautiful maritime wetland with Spanish moss–draped oak trees and deep rows of saw palmetto and wild rosemary, and ending at the pristine and secluded white-sand beaches of the Gulf of Mexico. Many species of animals call this area home, including the American alligator, bald eagle, osprey, and Alabama beach mouse. This is also a prime nesting area for loggerhead sea turtles.

Start: Pine Beach trailhead off AL 180
Distance: 3.4-mile out-and-back
Hiking time: About 2.5 hours
Difficulty: Moderate because of extended powdery sand dune walking
Trail surface: Dirt and gravel road, fine deep sand
Best seasons: Sept to May
Other trail users: None
Canine compatibility: Dogs prohibited

Land status: National wildlife refuge
Nearest town: Gulf Shores
Fees and permits: None
Schedule: Year-round, dawn to dusk
Maps: USGS Pine Beach, AL; brochures with map available at trailhead kiosk
Trail contact: US Fish and Wildlife Service, AL 180, Gulf Shores, AL 36542; (251) 540-7720; fws.gov/bonsecour

Finding the trailhead: From the intersection of AL 59 and AL 180, take AL 180 west 9 miles. Trailhead parking will be on the left and is well-marked with a sign. GPS: N30 14.872'/W87 49.761'

The Hike

A long finger of land hugs the Alabama Gulf Coast between Mobile Bay and the Gulf of Mexico. In the middle of this finger of land, which is known as the Fort Morgan peninsula, there is an area over 7,000 acres in size called the Bon Secour National Wildlife Refuge where you will find this remarkable hike.

The Bon Secour National Wildlife Refuge was established by Congress on June 9, 1980, and is located in one of the last undisturbed areas of coastal barrier remaining in the state. The refuge is aptly named. Bon secour is a French term that means "safe harbor" and that is just what this refuge is, a safe harbor for a wide range of wildlife. Within the confines of the refuge, you will see hundreds of species of waterfowl and migratory birds such as ospreys, great blue herons, brown pelicans, cattle egrets, and peregrines. You will be treated to your everyday variety of wildlife like squirrel, rabbit, and raccoon, but you'll also find armadillo, American alligator, and bobcat.

Speaking of wildlife, the refuge plays host to a few endangered species including the Alabama beach mouse, which lives in the dunes; the piping plover, a shorebird that nests on beaches; and the loggerhead sea turtle, which nests on its beaches. Bon Secour has a unique program where the public can help the sea turtle by monitoring their nesting grounds during nesting season (May through September). Contact the refuge at (866) SEA-TURTLE (732-8878) to learn more.

There is only one way you can experience all of the wildlife and beautiful landscapes of Bon Secour, and that is by hitting one of the refuge's four hiking trails, one of which is the Pine Beach Trail. This 3.4-mile out-and-back trail takes you through all that the refuge has to offer, beginning in a maritime forest with wetlands and ending at the pristine white beaches of the Gulf of Mexico.

Starting at the trailhead you will see huge Spanish moss–laden live oak trees, then meander along the wide dirt footpath through a maritime forest of magnolia, red

Hikers make it over the final dune ridge before the Gulf of Mexico on the Pine Beach Trail.

cedar, wild olive trees, and saw palmettos. The trail is not blazed but is easy to follow over an old dirt and gravel roadbed.

As you stroll along the path, you will pass blueberry and huckleberry bushes, but don't pick the fruit. These plants are federally protected because they are an important food source for the wildlife that lives here. Be sure to pick up the "Pine Beach Trail Guide" brochure at the kiosk before you head out to help you identify the many trees you'll see.

Just over halfway through the hike, you'll pass the junction with the Centennial Trail. Soon after you will arrive at an impressive elevated wildlife-viewing platform that is a perfect place to stop and have a snack or lunch and take in the view of the freshwater Gator Lake and saltwater Little Lagoon, which are only separated by a thin strip of land. The path follows the wide sand and gravel road between Little Lagoon and Gator Lake, and once you pass them the landscape begins to change and soon you will be walking among the white sand dunes of the Alabama Gulf Coast. Sea oats wave in the breeze as you make your way to the Gulf. The trail through here is plainly marked with metal hiker signs mounted on T-posts. Remember to stay on the trail! The dunes are sensitive habitats for plants and wildlife and as such are federally protected. Some areas are actually roped off, a "subtle" reminder of the rules.

Along this section of the trail, you will pass the foundations of two houses. These were beach houses that unfortunately met their match, Hurricane Frederick, in 1979. Hurricanes are a key player along the Alabama Gulf Coast. In 2004 Hurricane Ivan made a direct hit here, with winds over 130 miles per hour, a 16-foot storm surge, and a total of $3.9 million in damages. The US Fish and Wildlife Service did a remarkable job with cleanup and actually recycled over 30 percent of the debris that washed up onshore.

At last the trail heads over the final large frontal dune and you are treated to an amazing expansive view of the Gulf of Mexico. This is one of the most secluded areas of Gulf beach you will find in Alabama, with not a soul to be seen for miles.

Miles and Directions

0.0   Start at the Pine Beach Trail trailhead located at the south end of the parking area.

0.3   Pass a beautiful wetland to the right (west). The water is dotted with water lily.

0.5   Pass a sign on the left describing how the US Fish and Wildlife Service perform prescribed burns to enhance the habitat for wildlife. Behind the sign you will see the results of the burns.

0.7   Come to a very spacious and clean portable toilet. The facility has a solar-powered fan for ventilation. In about 100 feet you will come to the intersection of the Jeff Friend / Centennial Trail to the left (east). Continue straight (south).

0.8   Arrive at the wildlife-viewing platform. When you're ready, continue straight south on the trail, crossing a single-lane wooden bridge over a small bayou. The trail now travels between the two bodies of water and gradually becomes a sand path.

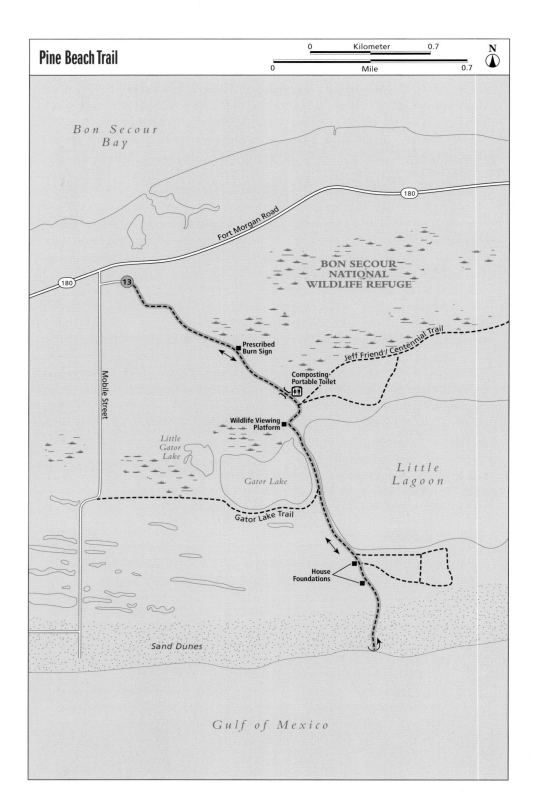

Pine Beach Trail

Bon Secour
Bay

Fort Morgan Road

180

180

Mobile Street

13

BON SECOUR
NATIONAL
WILDLIFE REFUGE

Prescribed
Burn Sign

Jeff Friend / Centennial Trail

Composting
Portable Toilet

Wildlife Viewing
Platform

Little
Gator
Lake

Gator Lake

Little
Lagoon

Gator Lake Trail

House
Foundations

Sand Dunes

Gulf of Mexico

Kilometer

0   0.7

0   0.7

Mile

N

1.2 The Gator Lake Trail enters from the right (west) and is marked with a sign. The sign also indicates the direction to the beach and back to the trailhead. Continue straight (south).

1.3 Come to a Y in the trail. Take the right fork (south). A sign here points the direction. The left fork is private property. You now begin walking on beautiful, fine white sand dunes. The walking becomes tougher from here to the Gulf in the deep sand. The trail is now marked with 4-by-5-inch hiker signs mounted on 4-by-4-inch posts. *FYI:* Make sure you stay on the path! The dunes are federally protected habitats.

1.4 Pass the foundation of a house to the right (west) destroyed by Hurricane Frederick.

1.5 Come to another Y in the trail. Take the right fork to the south. The left fork is closed to hikers. In a few yards you will come to another house foundation.

1.6 Climb over sand dunes to get your first glimpse of the Gulf of Mexico. The trail is lined with ropes to keep hikers off the dunes.

1.7 Arrive at the Gulf of Mexico. Feel free to walk the beach, explore, collect some shells, and enjoy the serenity that the Pine Beach Trail offers. When you're ready, turn around and retrace your steps to the trailhead.

3.4 Arrive back at the trailhead.

Hike Information

Local Information: Gulf Shores and Orange Beach Tourism, 3150 Gulf Shores Pkwy., Gulf Shores, AL 36542; (800) 745-7263; gulfshores.com

Local Events/Attractions: Interstate Mullet Toss, Flora-Bama Lounge, 17401 Perdido Key Dr., Pensacola; (251) 980-5118; florabama.com. This annual event is held the last weekend of April and, as the name implies, is an interstate event where contestants vie for prizes as they toss mullet (dead, of course) across the state line. Proceeds benefit various charities.

Lodging: Gulf State Park, 22050 Campground Rd., Gulf Shores; (251) 948-7275; camping reservations (800) 252-7275. The campground has 496 sites available.

Restaurants: Original Oyster House, 701 AL 59, Gulf Shores; (251) 948-2445; theoysterhouse.com

Hike Tours: Ranger-led tours are available throughout the year. Contact refuge headquarters at (251) 540-7720 for a current schedule.

Organizations: Friends of Bon Secour, 12295 AL 180, Gulf Shores, AL 36542; fws.gov/bonsecour/friends.htm

14 Jeff Friend / Centennial Trail

This is a beautiful hike of exploration that takes you through the transitional maritime forests and wetlands of Alabama's Gulf Coast. It includes the Centennial Trail, which gives you a chance to visit beautiful wetlands with wildflowers and waterfowl. For those of you with very young children, the 1-mile-long Jeff Friend Trail loop is a wonderful option where you can show them the wonders of nature as it takes you to the banks of Little Lagoon.

Start: Jeff Friend trailhead parking lot
Distance: 5.0-mile lollipop
Hiking time: about 2.5 to 3 hours
Difficulty: moderate due to length and some soft sand walking
Trail surface: Gravel, dirt, sand, boardwalk
Best seasons: Late Sept to mid-May
Other trail users: None
Canine compatibility: Dogs prohibited
Land status: National wildlife refuge

Nearest town: Gulf Shores
Fees and permits: None
Schedule: Year-round; electronic gate at parking lot open 6 a.m.–8 p.m. Apr–Oct, 7 a.m.–6 p.m. Nov–Mar
Maps: USGS Pine Beach, AL; brochures with trail map available at trailhead kiosk
Trail contact: US Fish and Wildlife Service, AL 180, Gulf Shores, AL 36542; (251) 540-7720; fws.gov/bonsecour

Finding the trailhead: From the intersection of AL 59 and AL 180, take AL 180 west 5.6 miles. Trailhead parking will be on the left and is well-marked with a sign. GPS: N30 14.668'/W87 47.235'

The Hike

From maritime wetlands and forests to dune ecosystems, Bon Secour is a real gem on the Alabama Gulf Coast. The refuge has four trails in all to explore the landscapes and wildlife, including the Pine Beach and Gator Lake Trails. The other two, the Jeff Friend and Centennial Trails, interconnect and allow you to explore the transitional area between the maritime forest and the dunes of the Gulf.

The combination of these two trails makes for a nice 5-mile lollipop hike. The hike starts at the Jeff Friend Trail trailhead just off AL 180. The Jeff Friend Trail is a 1-mile ADA-accessible loop that leads you to a beautiful wetland via a boardwalk and a wide gravel path that is held in place by a plastic underlayment that allows for drainage. The trail circles around the banks of the saltwater Little Lagoon. (***Option:*** By itself this trail makes a great hike to take your children on. It's a short, easy walk with enough interesting features to keep them occupied and entertained. It will take about 1 hour, including time to explore.)

A summer sun glitters over Little Lagoon along the Jeff Friend Trail.

At the intersection with the Jeff Friend Trail at 0.3 mile, continue west on the Centennial Trail. The width of the trail varies from a nice, enclosed 4-foot-wide dirt path to 10-foot-plus-wide sand trail. Several times on this trek you will cross some beautiful wetlands over wooden boardwalks, the largest being at mile 2.1. Here the wetland comes to life from spring to summer with blooming water lilies, wildflowers, and waterfowl. Be sure to have your camera ready. Keep in mind that the boardwalk is just above the surface of the wetland, so after one of south Alabama's notorious wet summers, it may actually be underwater. In that case you may have to turn around or use a small strip of higher ground to the south that parallels the boardwalk to walk around the water, but that's not a guarantee.

Wildlife is abundant along the trail, and signs along the path tell the stories of armadillos, coach whip snakes, pine woods tree frogs, gopher tortoises, and many more animals. One of the interesting sights as you walk this trail is evidence of the power of hurricanes. As you near the boardwalk at mile 2.1, you will see trees simply snapped off like broken matchsticks.

Now remember, and it goes without saying, you are walking through a wetland here, and in the hot summer months mosquitoes are everywhere. Be sure to douse down with insect spray before heading out.

The Centennial Trail ends at the intersection with the Pine Beach Trail. If you have to heed the call of Nature, a few yards to your right is a very nice composting toilet. A short 0.3-mile walk to the south on the Pine Beach Trail takes you to an elevated viewing platform overlooking Gator Lake and Little Lagoon, a great place to stop for a rest, have lunch, and watch for birds and wildlife, especially in the early morning hours.

The Pine Beach intersection is the turnaround for this trip, where you retrace your steps back to the Jeff Friend Trail. An option if you want an even longer hike would be to turn to the south on the Pine Beach Trail and walk the 1 mile to the Gulf of Mexico (that increases the length of this trip to 7 miles).

Arriving back at the Jeff Friend Trail, take the right fork to the south to take the boardwalk stroll along the banks of Little Lagoon.

The trails at Bon Secour are not heavily marked but are easy enough to follow, and where needed, small metallic brown hiker signs with arrows point the way. Several times along the trail you will pass dirt access roads coming in from different areas. Heed the signs and don't go exploring down them. These are closed to the public.

Miles and Directions

0.0 Start from the east side of the parking lot. Head east 70 feet to the trailhead (the kiosk is very obvious from the parking lot). A sign here reads "Loop Trail 1 Mile, No Pets." Head to the right (west). The trail is a wide gravel path with thick rows of saw palmetto and oaks laden with Spanish moss lining the way.

0.2 Pass an informative sign explaining maritime wetlands on the left and a bench on the right.

0.3 Come to a Y in the trail. The left fork (south) will be used for our return trip; continue on the right fork and head west on the Centennial Trail. A sign here points the way and identifies the trail. The trail from here on out alternates from dirt to sand base and back again. (***Option:*** For the 1-mile loop hike, turn left and continue on the Jeff Friend Trail to return to the trailhead.)

0.4 Cross a series of three boardwalks over wetlands, each separated by a 30- to 40-foot dirt path. Bamboo grows alongside the walkways.

0.6 The boardwalks end. Continue to the west. Some of the trail in this area is low-lying and can be muddy, if not covered with water, after a heavy rain.

0.7 Cross a short, 30-foot boardwalk.

0.8 Cross another boardwalk, about 100 feet long. At the end is a bench.

1.1 A dirt road enters from the right (north). There is an "Area Closed" sign here telling you not to take the road, and a Centennial Trail sign with an arrow points the direction (west). In about 0.5 mile pass another bench. The canopy thins out here, a disadvantage on hot summer days.

1.4 Pass another bench.

1.5 A dirt road enters from the right (north). An "Area Closed" sign indicates the road is closed to the public. Follow the arrow on the Centennial Trail sign and continue straight (west). All around you is evidence of damage from hurricanes of the not-too-distant past.

1.6 Cross a 30-foot boardwalk.

1.8 Pass another bench on the right (north). Also to the north you will see the western end of a large wetland.

2.1 Cross the largest boardwalk of the trip over a beautiful wetland. Halfway across is a nice bench and a wide platform for you to view the plants and wildlife. ***FYI:*** After a heavy rain the walkway could be underwater. If that's the case, you may be able to walk around the crossing on the uphill side of the wetland.

2.2 Come to the end of the boardwalk. The canopy again provides good shade. Look for deer moss along the trail. The trail from here to the intersection with the Pine Beach Trail is mostly a dirt path. Little Lagoon can be seen through the trees to the southeast.

2.3 Come to the intersection of the Centennial Trail and the Pine Beach Trail. Turn around here and retrace your steps to the Jeff Friend Trail intersection. ***FYI:*** About 250 feet to the right (north) on the Pine Beach Trail is a nice composting toilet. If you turn left onto the Pine Beach Trail and travel about 0.3 mile, you will come to a large elevated wildlife-viewing platform.

4.4 Arrive back at the Y intersection of the Centennial Trail and Jeff Friend Trail. Take the right fork to the south. Once again the trail is gravel.

4.6 Come to a bench on the right and a short boardwalk over a small slough next to a very pretty wetland on your left. In 200 feet you will come to a long boardwalk that takes you past beautiful views of Little Lagoon.

4.7 Still on the boardwalk, come to a small deck on your right with a bench.

4.8 The boardwalk ends and the trail is once again gravel.

5.0 Arrive back at the trailhead.

Jeff Friend / Centennial Trail

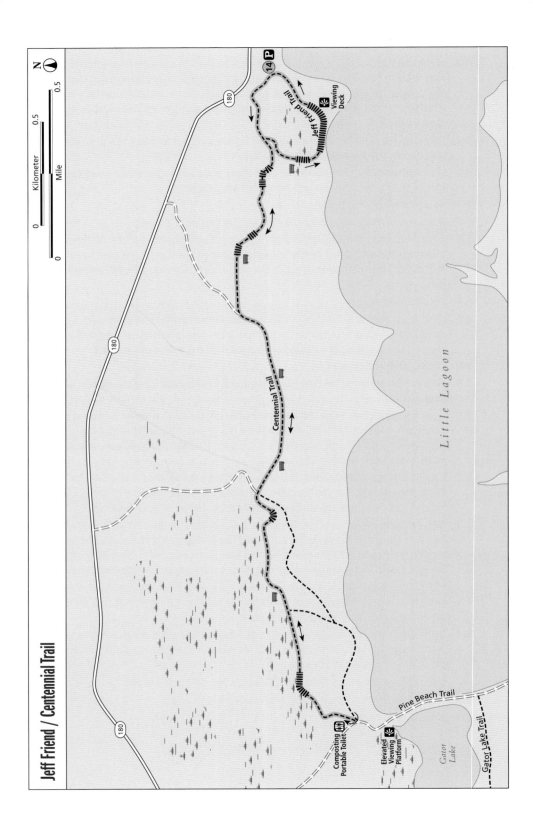

Centennial Trail

Jeff Friend Trail

Viewing Deck

Little Lagoon

Composting Portable Toilet

Elevated Viewing Platform

Gator Lake

Pine Beach Trail

Gator Lake Trail

180

14

P

N

Kilometer

Mile

0   0.5

0   0.5

Hike Information

Local Information: Gulf Shores and Orange Beach Tourism, 3150 Gulf Shores Pkwy., Gulf Shores, AL 36542; (800) 745-7263; gulfshores.com

Local Events/Attractions: John L. Borom Alabama Coastal BirdFest; (251) 625-0814; alabama coastalbirdfest.com. Held annually the first weekend of October at various locations throughout Baldwin County, the event features guest speakers on birding and plenty of opportunity to bird-watch with experts by boat and on foot all across Alabama's Gulf Coast.

Lodging: Gulf State Park, 22050 Campground Rd., Gulf Shores; (251) 948-7275; camping reservations (800) 252-7275. The campground has 496 sites available.

Restaurants: Lucy Buffett's Lulu, 200 East 25th Avenue, Gulf Shores; (251) 967-5858; lulu buffett.com

Hike Tours: Ranger-led tours are available throughout the year. Contact refuge headquarters at (251) 540-7720 for a current schedule.

Organizations: Friends of Bon Secour, 12295 AL 180, Gulf Shores, AL 36542; fws.gov/bonsecour/friends.htm

15 Historic Blakeley State Park

It's almost like taking a trip back in time to the mid-1800s as you hike through Historic Blakeley State Park. The setting is like a postcard of the archetypal South: long, flowing Spanish moss hanging from the trees, shady walkways along the riverbank, and let us not forget Civil War history. While General Lee was surrendering to Grant in Virginia, the last major battle of the war was being waged here. Today the park is a Civil War National Historic Site and a great hike along the banks of the second-largest river delta in the country.

Start: Parking lot along Mobile Bay
Distance: 4.1-mile multi-loop
Hiking time: About 2.5 hours
Difficulty: Moderate due to length, easy if you break the hike down into one of the shorter sections
Trail surface: Dirt path, gravel road, boardwalk
Best seasons: Sept to May
Other trail users: Cyclists, motorists (on road sections), equestrians
Canine compatibility: Leashed dogs permitted

Land status: State park
Nearest town: Spanish Fort
Fees and permits: Admission fee (children under 6 free)
Schedule: Year-round, 9 a.m.–dusk
Maps: USGS Bridgehead, AL; brochure with map available at office
Trail contact: Historic Blakeley State Park, 34745 AL 225, Spanish Fort, AL 36527; (251) 626-0798; blakeleypark.com

Finding the trailhead: From the intersection of US 98 and AL 225 in Spanish Fort, take AL 225 north 5 miles. The park entrance is on the left. Once you pay the attendant, travel 2 miles, continuing straight on Franklin Street to its end at the boat ramp. This is the trailhead for this hike. GPS: N30 44.851' / W87 55.400'

The Hike

History abounds along the trails at Historic Blakeley State Park. The land where the park is situated has changed hands many times, beginning with the Paleo Indians who lived here some 4,000 years ago. Since that time the land would fall under the rule of several countries during its history, including Spain in the late 1500s and France in the early 1700s, followed by Britain and then the United States in 1813. Soon after becoming a US territory, Josiah Blakeley stepped into the picture and bought this property and established the town of Blakeley.

The town was chartered in 1814 and became a bustling port city that rose to rival neighboring Mobile, but by 1828 a series of yellow fever epidemics coupled with the greed of land speculators forced the city of 4,000 into a spiral of decay. By the mid-1800s it was abandoned, eventually to be reclaimed by nature. Today all that remains of the old port town are the 400-year-old live oaks that once lined the city streets

A look at the Union redoubt used during the Battle of Blakeley

and a recently unearthed foundation, the original brick and wood base of the town's courthouse that you will pass by on this hike.

But history wasn't done with Blakeley quite yet. On April 8, 1865, 55,000 Union and Confederate soldiers converged in the fields surrounding the old town. The Union army intended to seize Fort Blakeley and then cross Mobile Bay to capture the city of Mobile. The fighting was fierce—216 killed, 955 wounded, and 3,054 captured (3,050 of those Confederates). It was a decisive Union victory, but what made the battle significant had little to do with the casualties. On the second day of this two-day campaign, Confederate general Robert E. Lee surrendered to Union general Ulysses S. Grant at Appomattox Courthouse in central Virginia, thus making the battle at Blakeley the last major battle of the Civil War.

Speed ahead more than a hundred years to 1974, when the Alabama Historic Commission placed the site on the National Register of Historic Places and the effort to preserve the battle site began. Trails were built, breastworks were located, and in 1993 Congress designated the site a Class A Civil War Site. Three years later it was added to the National Civil War Trail list. Be sure to pick up a brochure at the entrance gate that describes the battle through numbered signs along the trail.

Within the 3,800 acres of Historic Blakeley State Park are a total of 15 miles of nature and historic trails. The trails cross one another so that you can form shorter or longer loops to suit your schedule or what you want to see.

▶ Shortly before the Civil War, the State of Louisiana issued a note of currency worth $10 called a dix—French for "ten"—and eventually the South became known as "Dixie." Montgomery, Alabama, was the first capital of the Confederacy, and until recently the official motto of Alabama was "The Heart of Dixie."

Not only is Blakeley steeped with history, but it is filled with natural beauty as well. This hike will take you past the Wehle Nature Center, which is used for conferences and special presentations (visit the park's website for schedules). There is also a display behind the building of some of the wildlife that calls the Mobile-Tensaw River Delta home.

The trail will also take you down a boardwalk along the banks of the second-largest river delta in the country and one of the largest intact wetland systems left in America, with over 300,000 acres of swampland, river bottom, and marshes. The delta plays host to 300 species of birds, 70 percent of all of Alabama's reptiles, and 40 different species of mammals. It is one of the largest drainage basins in the world, with runoffs from four states feeding into it and into the Gulf of Mexico. Blakeley is at the very southern end of the delta but has exceptional views of some marshland as well as views across the river of the city of Mobile.

The hike begins at the park's boat ramp at the very end of the main road into the park. There is room for about fifteen cars here and a nice portable toilet. Your trip begins along the Jacque Pate Nature Trail. Along this section you will be walking through river bottomland. Many of the trees in this area have signs indicating what you will see. Some species include live oak, saw palmetto, and yellow poplar.

The Cockleshell Mound Trail then takes you past the Wehle Nature Center and to a dirt road that leads you to the battlefield where some of the best-preserved breastworks and redoubts from the Civil War can be seen. You will also head over to the Union side to see the "Zig Zag," an approach trench that took the Union soldiers right up to the Confederates doorstep at the redoubts.

The path returns the way you came, taking a turn on the nature trail farther down Franklin Street to the site of the old courthouse, the Mary G. Grice pavilion, and then the walk along Mobile Bay on the boardwalk.

Miles and Directions

0.0 Start at the parking lot along Mobile Bay. In a few yards turn left onto the Jacque Pate Nature Trail, a narrow dirt and sand path through thick forest. Many tree species are identified with signage. The trail is not blazed but easy enough to follow. In 100 feet come to the Cockleshell Mound Trail boardwalk and walk across to the other side of a wetland.

0.2 On the other side, make a left turn to the north onto an unnamed trail. In 20 feet cross another boardwalk. As of this writing, the boardwalk was in disrepair with loose boards and tipped to an angle; be cautious crossing.

0.3 Climb down a steep set of stairs. The treads are far apart, so be very careful climbing down. Many people walk next to the stairs, which is causing an erosion issue.

0.4 Come to the intersection with Green Street Extension, a wide dirt and gravel road. Turn left (east) onto the road. From here on to the battlefield, the trail is open with little shade.

0.5 Pass the Wehle Nature Center.

0.6 Green Street Extension dead-ends at Battlefield Road. Turn left (north) onto the road and head to the battlefield.

0.8 Cross Baptizing Branch, with a wetland on the right.

1.0 Pass Marker #3. Turn right (south) on a dirt road and head to the redoubt.

1.1 Arrive at Redoubt #2. Walk around on the right side.

1.3 At Marker #16, turn right (southeast) and head across the grassy battlefield. In less than 0.1 mile, arrive at another dirt road. Turn right (south) onto the dirt road.

1.4 Pass Marker #15. In few yards pass a dirt road on the right and Marker #5, then in a few feet Marker #6. Union trenches can be seen along this stretch.

1.5 Arrive back at Battlefield Road at Marker #14 and turn right (east) onto it.

1.6 Pass Marker #7 on the left (this will be the return route for the loop end of this section). Continue straight (east) on the dirt road and in a few feet pass Marker #9. One hundred feet later, cross the Union breastworks.

1.7 Arrive at the Union redoubt. Walk to the far end and turn left (west). Follow the clear-cut in the thick grass to the left (southwest), following the "Zig Zag" on the left.

1.9 Come to Marker #8. Turn right and head back to the main park road. In 200 feet return to Battlefield Road. Turn right (west) onto the road and head back to Green Street Extension at mile 0.4.

2.5 Turn right onto Green Street Extension and head back the way you came.

3.2 At the intersection with the Cockleshell Mound Trail, continue straight on Green Street Extension until you come to a cul-de-sac in the dirt road. A sign with a blue arrow about 10 feet off the ground is hung on a tree indicating the route to take. Follow the arrow onto a sandy footpath to the right (southwest). Once again the trail travels through a thick forest with a good canopy.

3.4 Return to the Cockleshell Mound Boardwalk and cross it to the northwest. In less than 0.1 mile, come to the end of the boardwalk at the Jacque Pate Nature Trail. A sign here reads "Parking Area 0.1 Mile" (arrow pointing to right) / "Trail Fork 0.2 Mile" (arrow pointing to left). If you take the right turn to the north, you will return to the parking lot. Instead, turn left (south) onto the nature trail. The vegetation is very thick here.

3.6 Come to a Y at a large live oak tree (the tree is indicated by an informational sign). Take right fork (west) onto a short spur trail. In less than 0.1 mile, you will be back at Franklin Street. If you want to return to your vehicle, turn right (north); otherwise, turn left onto the road and head south.

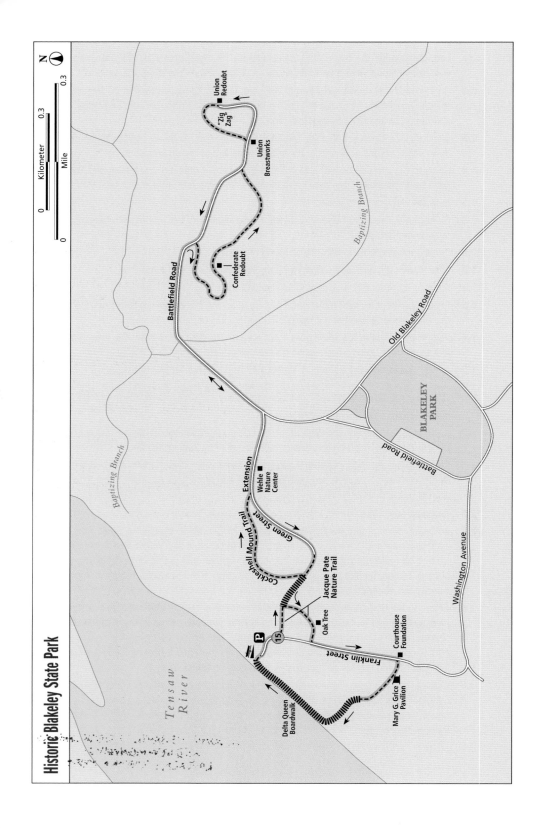

Historic Blakeley State Park

3.7 Pass the foundation of the old courthouse. Turn right (west) here, cross the road through a wood fence, and head toward the Mary G. Grice pavilion. In a few yards arrive at the pavilion. There are picnic tables and grills here. Behind and to the right of the pavilion is a sign describing big-leaf magnolia trees and a large cement barbecue grill. The Nature Trail begins here, with descriptive signs for Florida anise, live oak, saw palmetto, yellow poplar, American beech, and pignut hickory. In less than 0.1 mile, arrive at the delta boardwalk. Follow it to the north.

4.0 Come to the end of the boardwalk (the Delta Queen tour boat is docked here). Turn right onto the dirt road.

4.1 Arrive back at the trailhead.

Options: There are several intersections along the way, so you can make the hike as long or as short as you like. The hike described here can easily be divided into three separate routes. The first is the loop from the trailhead to the courthouse foundation, then back to the trailhead on the boardwalk along the delta. The second would be a nature loop from the trailhead to the Wehle Nature Center and back. Finally, you can do a simple battlefield walk from the Wehle Nature Center and loop around the battlefield for a 2-mile hike.

Hike Information

Local Information: Eastern Shore Chamber of Commerce, 29750 Larry Cawyer Dr., Daphne, AL 36526; (251) 621-8222; eschamber.com

Local Events/Attractions: Annual Battle of Blakeley Reenactment, 34745 AL 225, Spanish Fort; (251) 626-6798; blakeleypark.com. The event occurs around the weekend of the actual battle date of April 9.

Blakeley Bluegrass Festival, 34745 AL 225, Spanish Fort; (251) 626-6798; blakeleypark.com. Held annually in mid-October.

Lodging: Blakeley Historic State Park Campgrounds, 34745 AL 225, Spanish Fort; (251) 626-0798; blakeleypark.com. Two separate campgrounds, one for RV use the other for tent and pop-ups only.

Restaurants: Blue Gill, 3775 Battleship Pkwy., Spanish Fort; (251) 625-1998; bluegillrestaurant .com. Original Oyster House, 3733A Battleship Pkwy., Spanish Fort; (251) 626-2188; theoyster house.com.

16 Village Point Park Preserve

Over 300 years of history, including the massive Jackson Oak where Andrew Jackson reportedly rallied his troops before the Battle of New Orleans and the D'Olive Cemetery established in the late 1700s; fascinating wildlife such as American alligators; and beautiful native plants make the Village Point Park Preserve hike a great trek for your entire family. The trail winds along the banks of Mobile Bay, where para-surfers glide across the waves and fishermen try their hand at landing the big one or filling their nets with crab.

Start: Village Point Park Preserve trailhead at Bayfront Park
Distance: 1.8-mile lollipop
Hiking time: About 1.5 hours
Difficulty: Easy over level dirt footpaths, some beach walk
Trail surface: Gravel and dirt roads, boardwalks
Best seasons: Late Feb to mid-May, mid-Sept to early Nov
Other trail users: Cyclists

Canine compatibility: Leashed dogs permitted
Land status: City nature preserve
Nearest town: Daphne
Fees and permits: None
Schedule: Year-round, sunrise to sunset
Maps: USGS Bridgehead, AL; brochures with map available online (see "Trail contact")
Trail contact: City of Daphne Parks and Recreation Department, 2605 US 98, PO Box 400, Daphne, AL 36526; (251) 621-3703; daphneal.com/residents/parks-recreation

Finding the trailhead: From the intersection of I-10 and US 98 in Daphne, take US 98 south 1.7 miles. Turn right onto Main Street (a Publix shopping center is on the right at the turn). In 200 feet turn right onto Bay Front Drive. Travel 0.4 mile to the parking area. The trailhead is well-marked on the west side of the parking lot next to Mobile Bay. GPS: N33 37.793' / W87 55.117'

The Hike

It's rare that you get so much history and natural beauty in a single trail within the heart of a city, but that's what you'll find on the trails of Village Point Park Preserve in Daphne.

The park is located on the eastern shore of Mobile Bay in the city of Daphne. The town is situated on the southern end of the second-largest river delta in the country, the Mobile-Tensaw Delta, a fertile land teeming with wildlife, fish, and reptiles, making it a perfect location for civilization to take root. Native Americans, including Choctaws, Tensaw, Creeks, and Seminoles, called this land home thousands of years ago.

This area, however, has suffered from an identity crisis. Following the early residents, the area was settled by Spain in 1557. The Spaniards named the land La Aleda, or "the village." Next, the French moved in to claim the territory in the early 1700s, only to lose it to the British after the French and Indian War of 1763. Finally, the United States took control following the defeat of the British in the War of 1812.

A paddler relaxes just offshore of the Village Point Park Preserve trail.

The park itself was created in 2004 by the City of Daphne to protect its history and fragile environment. The hike described here was named a National Recreational Trail in 2011 and will take you back in time to explore a little of that history as it makes its way over a boardwalk around the mighty Jackson Oak, a giant, sprawling, Spanish moss–laden oak tree where some historians believe General Andrew Jackson made an address to his troops before the famous Battle of New Orleans.

The trail also takes you to D'Olive Cemetery. In the early 1800s Village Point was the site of the D'Olive Plantation, the home of the oldest family in Daphne and Baldwin County. The cemetery is all that remains of the plantation. The tombstones reveal the family's French ancestry, with many of them engraved in French. You will learn more about the D'Olive family and Jackson Oak at audio kiosks located at each site.

Besides history, Village Point Park Preserve is a favorite location for nature lovers. Just after leaving the trailhead, the path takes you over a beautiful wetland with floating lilies, a wonderful view of Mobile Bay to the west, and a good chance for you to see American alligators in their natural habitat. I can't stress it enough, alligators are naturally afraid of humans, but feeding them changes the rules. Do not feed the alligators!

From there the trail takes a short side trip to Mobile Bay itself. A small boardwalk takes you over a slough to a nice sand island where legend has it that pirate Jean Lafitte would hide among the bluffs. This is a perfect location to take in a gorgeous sunset over the bay.

Most of the trail from here on out uses wide gravel and dirt service roads. You won't find much motorized traffic here, only the occasional city truck doing trail maintenance. The tall pines and magnolias along this section provide a nice, shady canopy. Depending on the time of year you hike the trail, you will see a wide variety of wildflowers and trees, many of which are identified with signage.

The walk around Jackson Oak is over a composite boardwalk and deck, allowing you good access to the tree but keeping you far enough away. Several ancient live oaks in south Alabama have been killed intentionally by vandals, and the City of Daphne wants to keep this one safe.

The only exception to the service road and boardwalks the trail uses comes at the west end of the trail's loop. Here the path takes you into the woods on a more traditional, 2-foot-wide dirt footpath on the D'Olive Plantation Nature Trail. Along this section many of the trees are identified with signs, including six state champion trees.

Miles and Directions

0.0 Start from the Village Point Park Preserve trailhead located about 250 feet west of the parking lot on Mobile Bay. The trailhead is well-marked. The hike begins on a boardwalk over a wetland.

0.2 Come to the end of the boardwalk. The trail becomes a wide dirt and gravel road and heads off in two directions, to the left (east) and straight ahead. For now, continue straight ahead to the south.

0.3 The trail turns to the right (west), crosses a bridge over a slough, and comes out on a small sand island. There is a fishing pier at the end of the bridge. When you're ready, turn around and retrace your steps to the end of the first boardwalk at mile 0.2.

0.5 Return to the south end of the boardwalk and turn right (east).

0.6 Come to a T intersection with another dirt road. Turn left here and head east. A right turn dead-ends at a locked fence and gate.

0.8 Pass a side trail with a bridge over Yancey Creek to your right (south). This is an access trail to the Harbor Place condominiums and is private property. Don't go there. Continue straight (east). In about 400 feet come to a fork in the trail. This is the southwest end of the trail's east loop. Take the right fork. In just a few feet, turn right (south) onto the D'Olive Plantation Nature Trail. There is a small sign indicating the trail entrance, but it can be hard to see when the area is overgrown. The trail is a narrow, 2-foot-wide dirt footpath through a thick forest with a good, shady canopy.

1.0 Come to a boardwalk that encircles the massive Jackson Oak. The boardwalk is made of a composite material to alleviate problems with rotting. There is an audio kiosk here that tells the history of the oak tree, along with picnic tables off to the side. After the board-

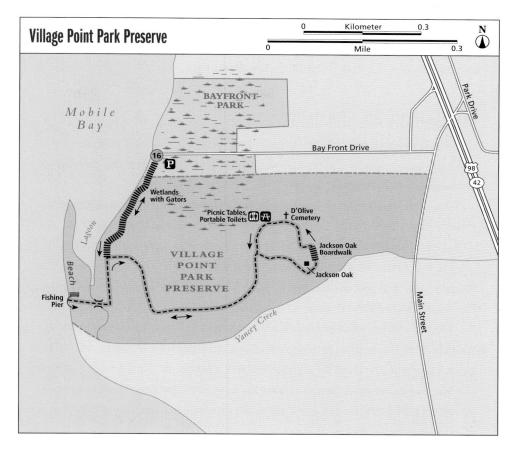

Village Point Park Preserve

Mobile Bay

BAYFRONT PARK

Bay Front Drive

Park Drive

98
42

Wetlands with Gators

Picnic Tables, Portable Toilets

D'Olive Cemetery

Jackson Oak Boardwalk

Jackson Oak

VILLAGE POINT PARK PRESERVE

Lagoon

Beach

Fishing Pier

Yancey Creek

Main Street

walk, continue on the dirt footpath to the north and in 200 feet cross a dirt service road. A sign points the way to D'Olive Cemetery.

1.1 Arrive at D'Olive Cemetery. Another audio kiosk is located here that tells the history of the D'Olive family and their plantation. After exploring the cemetery, continue west on the trail. In just a few hundred feet, there are portable toilets and picnic tables. Shortly after that arrive at the south end of the loop.

1.6 Return to the boardwalk. Turn right (north).

1.8 Arrive back at the trailhead.

Hike Information

Local Information: Eastern Shore Chamber of Commerce, 29750 Larry Cawyer Dr., Daphne, AL 36526; (251) 621-8222; eschamber.com

Local Events/Attractions: Jubilee Festival, Main Street, Daphne; (251) 621-8222; eschamber .com/area_jubilee.php. Held September of each year, the Jubilee Festival is a celebration of living on the Alabama Gulf Coast with plenty of entertainment, arts and crafts, and food.

5 Rivers Delta Safaris, Bartram Landing, 30841 Five Rivers Blvd., Spanish Fort; (251) 259-8531; 5rds.com. The Mobile-Tensaw Delta is the second-largest river delta in the country, and

5 Rivers Delta Safaris can take you right into the bayous with American alligators, black bears, and more with ecotours, canoe and kayak trips, and camping trips.

Restaurants: Market by the Bay Takeout Restaurant, 29145 US 98, Daphne; (251) 621-9994; marketbythebay.com. Serves up great local seafood at affordable prices.

THE BIRTH OF THE SUBMARINE

In late 1861 two engineers from New Orleans, James McClintock and Baxter Watson, began working on an invention that, at the time, was only part of science fiction. They were designing the world's first submarine.

They began with a design for a three-man vessel that would stealthily glide beneath the waves. It wasn't until wealthy lawyer and merchant Horace Lawson Hunley joined the men by financing their invention that the sub leapt from the drawing board and into the water.

The first submarine was completed in February 1862 and successfully tested in New Orleans's Lake Pontchartrain, but by then Union forces were heading toward the Crescent City. The men burned the sub, picked up their designs, and headed to Mobile, Alabama.

Within months of arriving in Alabama, the team built a second much larger vessel, the *American Diver*. The inventors opted against using a steam motor for propulsion and instead used a hand crank that turned the propeller. Evidence indicates that the sub might have been near Fort Morgan during the Battle of Mobile Bay but couldn't get enough speed up to be of any value. A second attack was planned, but as the submarine was being towed to the fort, a storm raced through and sank the ship.

Just before the *American Diver* sank, a third submarine, the CSS *Hunley*, was under construction. Tests in Mobile Bay proved successful, and when word of the fall of Vicksburg and Gettysburg arrived in the Port City, the *Hunley* was loaded onto a flatcar and transported to Charleston, South Carolina, where it would join the war.

On a cold February night in 1864, the *Hunley*, armed with a torpedo or mine on a boom that protruded from her bow, rammed the Union warship *Housatonic*. The mine exploded and the ship eventually sank. The *Hunley* surfaced briefly to signal that their mission was accomplished, but after that the crew and sub were never heard from again.

Travel ahead to the year 2000, when the wreck of the *Hunley* was discovered off the Carolina coast. In 2001 the sub was raised, its crew moved to their final resting place, and the task of solving the mystery of how the submarine sank began.

The sub is currently on display at the Warren Lasch Conservation Center in North Charleston, South Carolina. Learn more at hunley.org.

17 Muddy Creek Interpretive Trail

The Muddy Creek Interpretive Trail is a perfect example of how a major industry can take the lead and preserve the environment while providing recreational opportunity for the public. This beautiful family-friendly hike features many boardwalks that lead you through and educate you about the amazing wetlands and longleaf pine ecosystems found on Alabama's Gulf Coast.

Start: Parking lot on Industrial Road
Distance: 2.2-mile lollipop
Hiking time: About 1.5 hours
Difficulty: Easy over flat, level dirt paths and boardwalk
Trail surface: Dirt and clay footpaths, boardwalks
Best seasons: Late Feb to mid-May
Other trail users: None

Canine compatibility: Leashed dogs permitted
Land status: City nature preserve
Nearest town: Theodore
Fees and permits: None
Schedule: Year-round, dawn to dusk
Maps: USGS Theodore, AL
Trail contact: Alabama State Port Authority, 250 N. Water St., Mobile, AL 36602; (251) 441-7001; asdd.com

Finding the trailhead: From the intersection of US 90 and Bellingrath Gardens Road in Theodore, take Bellingrath Gardens Road south 2.2 miles. Turn left onto Industrial Road and travel 1 mile. The paved parking lot is on the left. GPS: N30 31.029' / W88 09.158'

The Hike

I have hiked all of the trails you can hike on the Alabama Gulf Coast, which only makes sense since I live there. Yes, I have hiked all of the trails in L.A. (Lower Alabama), or so I thought. One day an e-mail pops up on my computer. It was an invitation to hike the Muddy Creek Interpretive Trail in the town of Theodore. Curious, I shot the author an e-mail and asked where Muddy Creek was and what it was like. They answered that they didn't know. They had only heard a vague mention of it themselves from a friend and thought they would check it out. And so did I, and I'm glad I did.

You wouldn't think that there would be much to the hike when you consider the trail's location. You are in the bustling town of Theodore on the west side of one of the state's biggest counties, Mobile. As you drive to the trailhead, you turn down a road called Industrial Road and drive through an area known for its chemical plants, not hiking trails. But son of a gun, there it was, and what a great little hike it was.

The Muddy Creek Interpretive Trail is a 2.2-mile lollipop through wetland areas on the western bank of Mobile Bay. The property itself is owned by the Alabama State Port Authority, the same folks who handle shipping in and out of the busy port city. The trail project began in 1998, when it was decided that the best use

Parts of the Muddy Creek Interpretive Trail are a soft bed of green moss.

of the property was to preserve and enhance the wetland as part of a wetland mitigation measure. Five long, hard years later, the trail was completed.

Some of the goals of the Muddy Creek project included the removal and control of invasive exotic plant species, restoration of native wetland and upland plant ecosystems, installation of nesting boxes, replanting of 66 acres of upland agricultural fields with native longleaf pines, and the development of an interpretive trail and boardwalk system.

▶ **Mobile, Alabama, is the home of five Major League Baseball Hall of Fame players, placing the city third on the list for growing the most, behind only New York and Los Angeles. They are Satchel Paige, "Hammerin'" Hank Aaron, Willie McCovey, Billy Williams, and "The Wizard" Ozzie Smith.**

The first goal, the removal of invasive plants, proved challenging. The process was all done by hand—everything from pulling bushes to hand-cutting trees to treating stumps with herbicide then replanting native species. By the time the project was completed, it had become the largest invasive plant removal ever in the state. The resulting interpretive trail is a fascinating educational experience and nice walk in the woods, one that is suitable for families with children of all ages, over wide, packed dirt paths and long boardwalks. If you have younger children, you may want to cut the trip short due to the length.

The path is well-marked with metal directional signs, and at key turns in the trail, a large map of the route shows you where you are. Throughout the trek there are informational signs that identify the many species of native trees you will pass, such as tupelo gum, sweet bay, red maple, wax myrtle, and bald cypress. Signs also describe the wetland ecosystem and the Muddy Creek project itself.

The hike begins along a 0.2-mile paved section of trail, but after that it is a wide, hard-packed dirt and clay path. Several long boardwalks are encountered on the trip over beautiful wetlands and streams, including the trail's namesake. Remember, water in streams and wetlands can be seasonal in Alabama. The best time to visit is late February to mid-May, when the spring rains are plentiful along the Gulf and the creek is wide and flowing, and the wildflowers and trees are blooming. The boardwalks are wide, with tall handrails and an occasional viewing platform or bench.

One of the more interesting boardwalks, at the northern end of the loop, takes you through a beaver pond management area. As the sign will tell you, beavers were once considered nuisances but it was found that the careful management of beaver ponds results in a healthier wetland system.

As you head back, you will be treated to a few sections of trail where the footing is thick green moss. The cushion of the moss is quite the transition from the hard-packed dirt, and on sunny days the moss has a beautiful green glow to it.

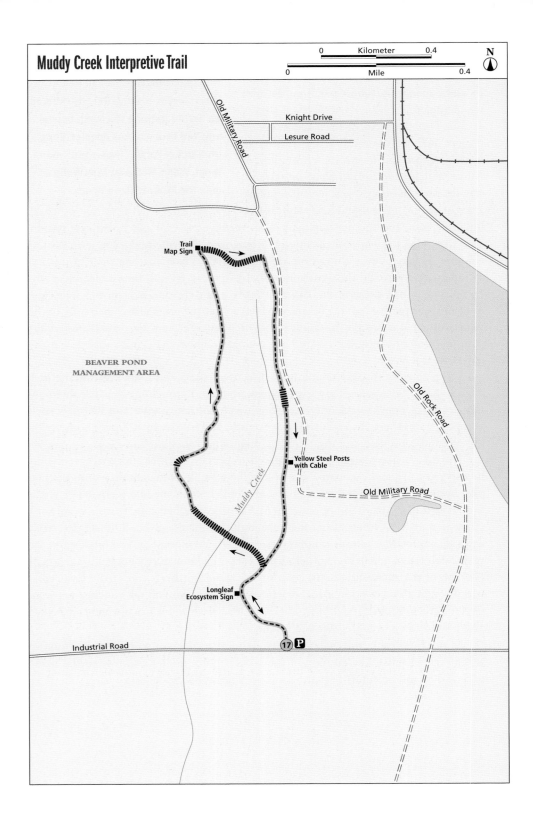

Muddy Creek Interpretive Trail

0   Kilometer   0.4

0   Mile   0.4

N

Old Military Road

Knight Drive

Lesure Road

Trail
Map Sign

BEAVER POND
MANAGEMENT AREA

Muddy Creek

Old Rock Road

Yellow Steel Posts
with Cable

Old Military Road

Longleaf
Ecosystem Sign

Industrial Road

17 P

Miles and Directions

0.0 Start at the parking lot trailhead on Industrial Road. A Muddy Creek Interpretive Trail sign is here that shows the route of the trail. Head north on a paved path a few yards and come to a Y. The right fork is a dirt road. Turn left (west) and continue following the paved path. You will soon see the first of many signs describing the habitat you will be walking through.

0.2 The paved path comes to a T intersection with another paved road. Cross the road to the north and enter the woods on a narrow footpath. Through this section you will be surrounded by longleaf pines.

0.3 Come to a Y in the trail. A map here shows you where you are. The right fork is the route you will be returning on. Take the left fork (northwest). A long boardwalk begins in about 30 feet. The boardwalks are very nice, with high railings. Through here you'll see tupelo gum, sweet bay, elderberry, red maple, and bald cypress trees.

0.4 The boardwalk crosses Muddy Creek. *FYI:* The streams and wetlands are seasonal and may be dry at certain times of the year.

0.5 The boardwalk ends at another trail map sign and turns to the right (north).

0.6 Cross a short, 30-foot boardwalk.

0.7 The trail gets very dense with longleaf pines and wax myrtles.

1.1 Pass another trail map sign and in a few yards cross another boardwalk. This is the north end of the loop.

1.2 Pass a series of signs with information on beavers and their importance to the wetland.

1.3 The boardwalk ends at another trail map sign and the trail turns to the right (south).

1.6 Pass another trail map sign and cross another short boardwalk.

1.7 For a few hundred feet the trail bed is soft, green moss. Along this section you'll see a steel cable with yellow metal posts through the trees to your left (east). This is a barrier for a dirt road that parallels the trail.

1.9 Return to the Y at the southern end of the loop. Take the left fork to the south and retrace your steps to the trailhead.

2.2 Arrive back at the trailhead.

Hike Information

Local Information: Mobile Bay Visitors and Convention Bureau, PO Box 204, Mobile, AL 36601; (800) 566-2453; mobile.org

Local Events/Attractions: Bellingrath Gardens and Homes, 12401 Bellingrath Gardens Rd., Theodore; (800) 247-8420; bellingrath.org. An array of color, fragrances, and scenic views are in store for you year-round at this world-renowned garden. Don't miss the Magic Christmas in Lights display from Thanksgiving to New Year's Day.

Restaurants: Time to Eat, 7351 Theodore Dawes Rd., Theodore; (251) 654-0228; timetoeatmobile .com. Offers mountains of some of the best Southern down-home cooking for dine-in or takeout.

18 Audubon Bird Sanctuary

While you can easily hike the Audubon Bird Sanctuary loop on Dauphin Island in an hour, you will want to linger to catch the morning sun glinting off the shimmering waters of Galliard Lake as wading birds look for breakfast, bathe in the soothing sounds of a choir of songbirds, and frolic in the crashing waves of the Gulf of Mexico.

Start: Parking lot off Bienville Boulevard
Distance: 1.7-mile loop
Hiking time: About 1 hour
Difficulty: Easy over level dirt footpaths and boardwalks
Trail surface: Dirt, sand, boardwalks
Best seasons: Mid-Sept to May
Other trail users: None
Canine compatibility: Leashed dogs permitted
Land status: City nature preserve

Nearest town: Dauphin Island
Fees and permits: None
Schedule: Year-round, sunrise to sunset
Maps: USGS Little Dauphin Island, AL, and Fort Morgan, AL; trail map and birding brochure available online
Trail contact: Dauphin Island Park and Beach Board, 109 Bienville Blvd., Dauphin Island, AL 36528; (251) 861-3607; dauphinisland.org/audubon-bird-sanctuary

Finding the trailhead: From Dauphin Island at the intersection of AL 193 and Bienville Boulevard, take Bienville Boulevard east 1.6 miles. Turn right at a small "Bird Sanctuary" sign onto a narrow, one-lane, unnamed gravel road. Follow the road less than 0.1 mile to the parking lot. The trail begins at the kiosk on the south side of the parking lot. GPS: N30 15.021'/W88 05.240'

The Hike

You know you're in for a treat when you hear that the Audubon Bird Sanctuary, located on Alabama's Dauphin Island, is world-renowned as being in the top four places for bird viewing. In fact, the National Audubon Society says that the sanctuary is "globally important for migration."

The Audubon Bird Sanctuary loop takes you deep into one of the last and most secluded areas on the burgeoning island. Although the trail is only 1.7 miles in length and can easily be walked in an hour, you will find yourself wanting to linger to soak in all that nature has to offer here.

If you're into birding, before you head out be sure to pick up a copy of the trail guide and checklist at the trailhead kiosk in the parking lot. The list names about a hundred common birds known to live in or migrate to the sanctuary. Migration season generally runs from mid-September through October and mid-March through May, but during the winter months you will be treated to a wide variety of waterfowl, wading birds, and wintering woodland birds such as the yellow-crowned night heron, great egret, and belted kingfisher. You may see one of several species of birds of prey soaring high in the sky, like red-shouldered and red-tailed hawks and bald eagles.

A beautiful spot to sit and reflect along the trail at the Audubon Bird Sanctuary

The loop uses four different trails that wind through a diverse habitat. The hike begins on the Lake Loop Trail on a long boardwalk and dirt footpath with detailed interpretive signage describing the environment and wildlife around you. The trail has two very short spurs that lead to beautiful views of Galliard Lake.

The Dune Edge Trail takes you from the forest of yaupon, wax myrtle, longleaf and slash pines, southern magnolia, and saw palmetto to the Gulf of Mexico. Take the time to stop and listen to the chorus of songbirds that will serenade you here, including rufous-sided towhee, cardinal, and mockingbird.

The trail travels between Oleander Pond and Swamp and the Gulf of Mexico, just behind the island's primary dunes. Distorted sand live oaks line the path, providing a rugged landscape and little shade. Off in the distance the Sand Island Lighthouse, which was built in 1873, can be seen. The trail is lined with wildflowers like meadow-eyed beauties, blue flag (which are actually violet), beach heather, and sandhill rosemary.

A boardwalk leads you to a beach observation deck with a bench where you can sit and take in the expansive view of the Gulf from high atop the primary dune. A nesting box is located here, and you may see an osprey nesting. The boardwalk then leads directly to the Gulf, where you can walk in the sand and swim, but remember, there are no lifeguards here so swimming is at your own risk. And your dog will love you for taking him to the only dog-friendly beach on Alabama's Gulf Coast.

Up to this point the trails have been either wide dirt and hard-packed sand footpaths or boardwalk and ADA-accessible. After the beach boardwalk the trail becomes narrow, 2 to 3 feet wide, and thick with sand as it makes its way to the west side of the swamp on the Swamp Overlook Trail and an impressive observation platform overlooking the water feature. Here you will see many varieties of wintering birds congregating. From here the loop joins the Campground Trail and returns to the trailhead and parking lot.

In addition to this hike through the bird sanctuary, be sure to visit historic Fort Gaines located only 1 mile to the east of the sanctuary. The fort, along with Fort Morgan on the opposite side of the bay, was one of the last defenses protecting the city of Mobile from Union troops during the Civil War. Together both forts played an important role in what has become known as the Battle of Mobile Bay, the biggest naval engagement of the war.

A fun way to get to the sanctuary is by taking the Mobile Bay Ferry that sails between Fort Morgan and Fort Gaines. There is a fee and the ferry shuts down for the winter and when tropical storms or hurricanes are approaching. For information call (251) 861-3000.

Miles and Directions

0.0   Start from the south side of the parking lot to the right of the information kiosk, which contains a large map and copies of the trail guide / bird checklist. This is the Lake Loop Trail, with a thick canopy of longleaf and slash pines and southern magnolias. This trail has excellent interpretive signage along the route. In a few yards you will be walking on a 4-foot-wide boardwalk.

0.1   The Lake Loop Trail continues straight (south). Turn right onto the Dune Edge Trail. The boardwalk ends in a few feet and the trail becomes a 6-foot-wide dirt path.

0.2   The Upper Woodlands Trail begins to your right (west); continue straight (south) on the Dune Edge Trail.

0.3   A short, 50-foot side trail takes you to the banks of Galliard Lake. There is a bench for viewing the many birds that live here and the wildflowers. When ready, turn around and then turn left (southwest) onto the Dune Edge Trail.

0.4   Pass a bench. In less than 0.1 mile, come to another short side trail to the lake on your left (east). The opposite end of the Upper Woodlands Trail comes in from the right (west). Continue south on the Dune Edge Trail.

0.5   Come to a Y. To the left (east) the Dune Edge Trail continues. You'll come back to that in a moment. Right now continue straight to the south (a sign here points the way to the Gulf of Mexico). The trail is now a boardwalk as it heads over a dune. In less than 0.1 mile, a short boardwalk heads off the main walkway to the left (east) to an observation deck with great views of the Gulf; check out the osprey nest high above. Continue south on the main boardwalk.

Audubon Bird Sanctuary

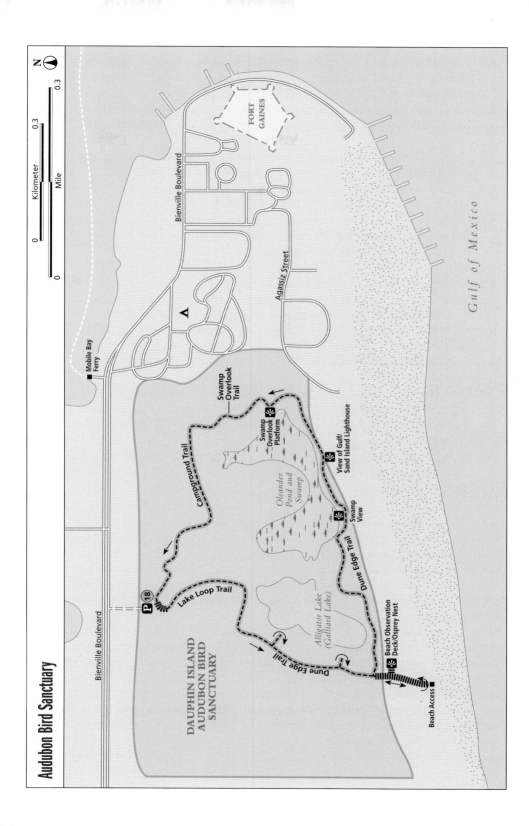

N

Kilometer
0   0.3

Mile
0   0.3

Mobile Bay Ferry

Bienville Boulevard

Bienville Boulevard

Agassiz Street

FORT GAINES

DAUPHIN ISLAND AUDUBON BIRD SANCTUARY

Campground Trail

Swamp Overlook Trail

Swamp Overlook Platform

View of Gulf/ Sand Island Lighthouse

Oleander Pond and Swamp

Swamp View

Dune Edge Trail

Lake Loop Trail

Alligator Lake (Galliard Lake)

Dune Edge Trail

Beach Observation Deck/Osprey Nest

Beach Access

Gulf of Mexico

P 18

0.6 Arrive at the Gulf and a nice little beach for swimming, or if you have your dog, let him play. (Remember, there are no lifeguards here. Swim at your own risk.) When ready, turn around and head back to the Y.

0.7 Back at the Y, turn right (east) and continue on the Dune Edge Trail. The trail narrows to 2 to 3 feet wide and is no longer ADA-accessible from this point on. There is a nice, thick canopy here.

0.8 A short trail leads up a dune to your right (south) with a Gulf view. In less than 0.1 mile, the Lake Loop Trail joins with the Dune Edge Trail. Continue straight (east).

0.9 The Lake Loop Trail exits to the left (north). There is a kiosk with a map here. Continue straight (east) on the Dune Edge Trail. The canopy thins and the trail is sandy.

1.0 The path is narrow as it passes between Oleander Pond and Swamp on the left (north) and the Gulf of Mexico to the right (south). Along this stretch you will have excellent views of the swamp and its wildlife, and to your right views of the Gulf and the Sand Island Lighthouse in the distance.

1.1 Best view of the Sand Island Lighthouse to the right (south).

1.2 Come to a Y. The right fork leads to the campground. Take the left fork and head north on a boardwalk on the Swamp Overlook Trail. In less than 0.1 mile, come to the swamp overlook platform. When done viewing, turn around and continue northeast on the Swamp Overlook Trail.

1.3 The Campground Trail comes in from the right (east). Continue straight on the Swamp Overlook Trail.

1.4 Come to an intersection. The campground is to the right (east), the banding area ahead (north); turn left (west) onto the Campground Trail. The path is an old, wide, dirt service road. Evidence of past hurricanes can be seen, with splintered and defoliated pines along the trail.

1.5 Come to a sign indicating the lake is straight ahead to the west. Turn right (north) here and onto the access trail back to the parking lot.

1.7 Arrive back at the trailhead.

Hike Information

Local Information: Town of Dauphin Island, 1011 Bienville Blvd., Dauphin Island, AL 36528; (251) 861-5525; townofdauphinisland.org

Local Events/Attractions: Alabama Deep Sea Fishing Rodeo, PO Box 16606, Dauphin Island; (251) 471-0025; adsfr.com. The Alabama Deep Sea Fishing Rodeo is touted as the largest such event in the world. Began in 1920 by the Mobile Jaycees, the event attracts over 3,000 anglers and 75,000 spectators.

Dauphin Island Sea Lab, 101 Bienville Blvd., Dauphin Island; (251) 861-7500; disl.org. Home of the Marine Environmental Resources Consortium, the Sea Lab is an educational facility for colleges and universities to study the Gulf of Mexico but also has plenty for the public to do, including the Estuarium and Public Aquarium.

Lodging: Dauphin Island Campground, 109 Bienville Blvd., Dauphin Island; (251) 861-2742; dauphinisland.org/campground. A beautiful campground located between the Audubon Bird Sanctuary, historic Fort Gaines, and the Mobile Bay Ferry. The campground has 151 sites for RVs and tents, an off-leash dog park, bicycle rentals, and many more amenities.

Restaurants: Barnacle Bill's, 698 Le Moyne Dr., Dauphin Island; (251) 861-8300; barnaclebills.net

Alabama Honorable Mentions

There are plenty of great hikes all along the Alabama Gulf Coast that didn't make the A list. Although many are shorter in length, they offer fantastic scenery and interesting wildlife. Pay a visit and let us know what you think. Maybe the hike should be upgraded, or maybe you know of another little-known hike that would make a good honorable mention.

F Hugh Branyon Backcountry Trail

I don't usually include paved multiuse trails in my hiking guides, but I have to make an exception for the Hugh Branyon Backcountry Trail in Orange Beach. This trail system has six trails totaling 11 miles and was named a National Recreational Trail just a few years ago. The trails are unique in that they take you through six different ecosystems. Located in the city of Orange Beach and the northern side of Gulf State Park, the trail allows hikers, joggers, and cyclists to experience a beautiful butterfly garden, freshwater marshes, hardwood swamps, and maybe bobcats, white-tailed deer, or an American alligator. For more information about the Hugh Branyon Backcountry Trail, the location of the trailheads, guided tours, and a trail app for your phone, visit backcountrytrail.com or contact the City of Orange Beach at (251) 981-1180.

G Gator Lake Trail

The fourth trail at the Bon Secour National Wildlife Refuge in Gulf Shores is a beautiful, and easy, out-and-back hike that allows hikers of all ages to experience the wonders of the refuge. The trail is 1.5 miles long and takes you over rolling sand dunes past the trail's namesake, the freshwater Gator Lake, a beautiful water feature that reflects the deep blue Southern skies. The path is dotted with beautiful black-eyed Susans, wild rosemary, blazing star, and, of course, wildlife including dozens of species of migratory birds, monarch butterflies, and maybe an alligator or two. For more information, including guided tour schedules, contact the US Fish and Wildlife Service office at Bon Secour at (251) 540-7720 or online at fws.gov/bonsecour.

H Splinter Hill Bog

On the back roads of Baldwin County, Alabama, there is a little park that the Nature Conservancy describes as having the most "visually impressive pitcher plants in the world." It's called Splinter Hill Bog, a 627-acre tract located at the headwaters of the Perdido River that borders Alabama and Florida. The tract is in a pine seepage bog where in early spring you will find yourself surrounded by literally thousands of the beautiful white-tubed carnivorous plants. And there's plenty of wildlife to view as well. Hunting is allowed on this state-owned property, so please visit Alabama's Forever Wild program online at alabamaforeverwild.com/ or call (334) 242-3484 for details.

Mississippi

I t's called the "Magnolia State," and believe me, you will see plenty of the sweet-smelling Southern landmark throughout the hikes we feature in Mississippi.

Mississippi and Alabama have the smallest Gulf footprints of the five states that ring the coast, but that doesn't mean that there isn't some great hiking opportunities here. Like Alabama, Mississippi's Gulf Coast is a large drainage basin with hundreds of rivers funneling waters from other states down into the Gulf of Mexico; the largest of these drainage areas culminates in the largest river delta in the country, the Mississippi.

The Mississippi Gulf Coast landscape is characterized by maritime forests of oak and those southern magnolias with their white fragrant blossoms; tidal flats, salt marshes, and salt pannes where migratory birds flock to share the fertile grounds with the year-round residents; and beautiful wide, lazy black-water rivers that course through the state to their ultimate destination in the Gulf. The grasses of pine savannah wave in the breeze in longleaf pine forests, while white-topped pitcher plants stand stoically awaiting their next meal.

With so many water features and the extended warm weather of the South, it's safe to say that you need to bring insect repellent to ward off those mosquitoes and ticks.

Just like the Alabama Gulf Coast, you can't beat hiking here in the fall and winter. Temperatures are moderate, averaging in the low to mid-70s well into fall. In January the average high is around 52°F, with lows around 40°F. Yes, there are days when the temps drop below freezing or even into single digits, but those times are short-lived and last only a day or maybe two at the most.

19 Escatawpa Trail

Here's something a little different: a trail at a state welcome center and a fine one at that. The Escatawpa Trail is an easy 1.4-mile loop located at the Mississippi Welcome Center on I-10 West at the Alabama state line. It's a surprising little trail with an abundance of beautiful wildflowers and two panoramic views of the Escatawpa River from viewing platforms high above the river on a bluff.

Start: Trailhead on west side of I-10 (westbound) Mississippi Welcome Center
Distance: 1.4-mile loop
Hiking time: About 1 hour
Difficulty: Easy over level dirt paths and boardwalk
Trail surface: Dirt, gravel, boardwalk
Best seasons: Sept to May
Other trail users: None

Canine compatibility: Leashed dogs permitted
Land status: National wildlife refuge
Nearest town: Moss Point
Fees and permits: None
Schedule: Year-round, sunrise–sunset
Maps: USGS Kreole, MS
Trail contact: Grand Bay National Wildlife Refuge, 7200 Crane Lane, Gautier, MS 39553; (228) 497-6322; fws.gov/refuge/grand_bay

Finding the trailhead: From the intersection of CR 11 and I-10 in Grand Bay, Alabama, take I-10 west 6 miles. Turn into the Mississippi Welcome Center and follow the signs for car parking. Continue straight past the welcome center. At the east end of the parking lot, come to a Y. Take the right fork, and in less than 0.1 mile, turn left into the parking lot. The trailhead is at the western side of the parking area. GPS: N30 27.717' / W88 26.242'

The Hike

So, you're traveling down I-10 westbound from Alabama to Mississippi. You're tired from a long drive; your legs are numb from hours of nonstop travel. You need a break. You pull into the Mississippi Welcome Center just past the Alabama state line and get out of the car to stretch your legs. Instead of just walking up to the vending machine or restroom, how about taking a little hike? No joke, there is a beautiful little 1.4-mile loop trail located right at the welcome center, the Escatawpa Trail.

The land and trail are managed by the Grand Bay National Wildlife Refuge, part of the US Fish and Wildlife Service. Combined with the land in the area that is managed by the Grand Bay National Estuarine Research Reserve, and which the Grand Bay refuge overlaps, over 18,000 acres of virtually undisturbed coastal habitat including maritime forests, tidal flats, salt marshes, and salt pannes are protected. A panne is a watery depression within a salt and brackish marsh that has a much higher salt content than the surrounding marsh. The refuge is said to have the most extensive and best examples of salt panne on the Gulf Coast. The refuge is also home to the largest remaining expanse of pine savannah on the Gulf Coast.

A wonderful view from high atop the banks of the black-water Escatawpa River.

The Escatawpa River is an 80-mile-long, black-water river that flows along the Alabama-Mississippi state line from Washington County, Alabama, to Robertson Lake in Moss Point, Mississippi. The river is a deep, dark brown or reddish color because of the tannin from the trees that line its banks, including bald cypress, black gum, and Atlantic white cedar.

In the 1980s the National Park Service (NPS) evaluated the river so that it could be placed on the National Wild and Scenic River list and protected from development and pollution. For whatever reason the river never made the list, even though the NPS described it as being "the finest undeveloped black water stream in the nation."

The footing of the Escatawpa River Trail is generally a combination of hard-packed dirt or gravel and boardwalks. The boardwalks will be found on the aptly named Boardwalk Trail through a marsh and at the half-mile mark at an overlook that gives you a remarkable view of the river. The path is wide, about 5 feet throughout.

Tall longleaf pines line the path, which is accentuated with beautiful wildflowers such as the yellow savannah honeycomb, the white with red center swamp rose mallow, and the narrow-leaf water primrose with its flat, smooth yellow leaves. Bright green saw palmetto makes an appearance on the hike, and as the trail meanders through the marsh, look for pitcher plants.

The trail is part of the Escatawpa River Observatory Birding Trail and is a prime location to spy Mississippi kites, chuck-will's-widows, brown-headed nuthatches, pileated and red-headed woodpeckers, or yellow prothonotary warblers.

If you hike the trail first thing in the morning and you pass any hikers coming your way, tell them thank-you. A lot of golden orb spider webs cross the trail in the morning, and if a hiker is heading your way, he or she has cleared the path for you. The web is a thick green material that is strong enough to catch birds in it.

As you walk, keep an eye on where you step. The refuge plays host to four species of venomous snakes: copperhead, cottonmouth, rattlesnake, and coral snake.

Of course, having the trailhead at the welcome center means there is traffic noise from I-10, but only a short distance in, you are immersed in quiet solitude. So, park the car, skip the vending machine, and take a walk to the Escatawpa River.

▶ **Mississippi facts to amaze your friends: Root beer was invented in 1898 by Adolf Barq Sr. in Biloxi, and the world's largest shrimp is on display at the Old Spanish Fort Museum in Pascagoula.**

Miles and Directions

0.0 Start from the trailhead at a steel gate clearly marked "Escatawpa Trail," on the west side of the Mississippi Welcome Center on I-10 West. There are informational kiosks here. In less than 0.1 mile, cross a 150-foot boardwalk and almost immediately after come to a Y and a sign that reads "Boardwalk Loop" (points left) / "To Overlook" (points right). Take the right (west) fork.

0.1 Pass a steel bench on the right.

0.3 Cross a 180-foot-long boardwalk over a wetland.

0.5 Cross another boardwalk and bridge over a runoff to the river. In less than 0.1 mile, come to a sign at a T intersection that reads "Outer Loop" and "Overlook" with an arrow pointing to the right (northwest). Turn right and head to the overlook.

0.6 Arrive at the Escatawpa River overlook. When done viewing, retrace your steps to the intersection and turn right (southwest) back onto the main trail. The trail is mostly grass through this section, more of an old service road.

0.8 Pass a bench on the right. A sign here points to the left and back the way you came. A service road heads straight to the south. Turn left (southeast) to continue on the trail.

1.0 Pass a bench on the right.

1.1 Come to an intersection at a boardwalk. A sign points the way to the parking lot (right) and the boardwalk loop (left). Turn left onto the boardwalk loop, crossing a wetland. Look for pitcher plants.

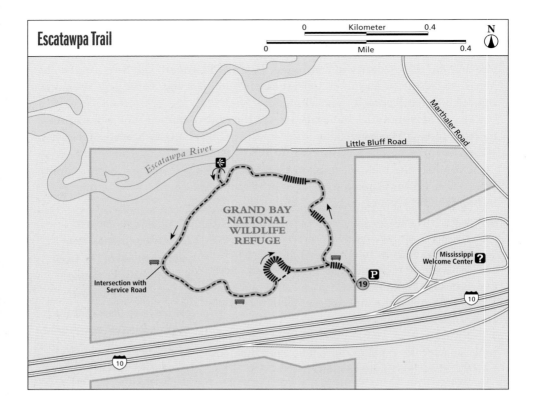

1.2 Rejoin the trail you left at mile 1.1. Turn left (east) to head back to the parking lot. In a few yards the boardwalk ends and the trail is gravel again.

1.3 Arrive back at the Y at mile 0.1. Turn right (east).

1.4 Arrive back at the trailhead.

Hike Information

Local Information: Mississippi Gulf Coast Regional Convention and Visitors Bureau, 2350 Beach Blvd., Ste. A, Biloxi, MS 39531; (888) 467-4853; gulfcoast.org

Local Events/Attractions: Jackson County Fair, Jackson County Fairgrounds, 2902 Shortcut Rd., Pascagoula; (228) 762-6043; co.jackson.ms.us/departments/fair.php. A good old-fashioned American fair with thrill rides, food (on a stick, of course), music, and more.

Restaurants: Tay's BBQ, 6522 MS 63, Moss Point; (228) 474-7050

20 Fontainebleau Walking Trail

Experience the transitional Gulf habitat of Mississippi along the Fontainebleau Loop at the Mississippi Sandhill Crane National Wildlife Refuge. While short in length, the loop opens up this world of bayhead swamps, pine savannahs, and pine forests to those who venture out. Orchids, pitcher plants, and pine savannah grasses greet you around every turn as you make your way around a salt marsh and to the banks of Davis Bayou.

Start: Trailhead on north side of parking lot
Distance: 1.1-mile loop
Hiking time: About 1 hour
Difficulty: Easy over level dirt footpaths and boardwalk
Trail surface: Dirt footpath, boardwalk
Best seasons: Late Sept to mid-May
Other trail users: None
Canine compatibility: Leashed dogs permitted

Land status: National wildlife refuge
Nearest town: Ocean Springs
Fees and permits: None
Schedule: Year-round, 8 a.m.–sunset
Maps: USGS Ocean Springs, MS
Trail contact: Mississippi Sandhill Crane National Wildlife Refuge, 7200 Crane Lane, Gautier, MS 39553; (228) 497-6322; fws.gov/mississippisandhillcrane

Finding the trailhead: From the intersection of US 90 and Hanshaw Road in Ocean Springs, take Hanshaw Road south 0.7 mile. Turn left into the parking area. The trailhead is on the north side of the parking lot. GPS: N30 23.879' / W88 45.432'

The Hike

The Mississippi Sandhill Crane National Wildlife Refuge is the second of two refuges in coastal Mississippi, the other being Grand Bay. Located in Ocean Springs just north of Ocean Springs Middle School, the refuge is an oasis in the middle of the town, preserving a rich transitional habitat from bayhead swamps to pine savannahs and forests along the banks of Davis Bayou.

The refuge is named for the fact that cranes reside here, but you may ask, "Where are they?" The fact is that the Mississippi sandhill crane is among the rarest species of birds in the world. Only a hundred cranes currently live in the refuge so you may or may not see one up close, but you may see or hear one flying overhead. Even though the current population seems small, consider this: In 1970, when the crane was found to be an endangered species, there were only thirty here. It's a slow and steady recovery as the pine savannah—the crane's natural habitat—is being restored by the US Fish and Wildlife Service (USFWS).

And that's the type of habitat you would have found on this land a hundred years ago, but as the wetlands were drained to make room for subdivisions, businesses, and farming, the savannah began to rapidly disappear. This gave Mother Nature the

Wildflowers grace this trail at the Mississippi Sandhill Crane National Wildlife Refuge.

opportunity to take control and change the grassland into a forest, almost completely wiping out such plants as the white-top sedge, black needlerush, and several species of pitcher plants. The USFWS has been working diligently to bring the land back to its natural state, and you will see some of the results along this hike.

The hike is a short, 1.1-mile loop that's easily walkable in an hour, but you may find yourself lingering at the overlooks on Davis Bayou. *Bayou* is a variation of a Native American word that means "river," but a bayou is not a river. The flow changes direction with the change in tide. This allows fresh and brackish water to intermingle, creating an amazing habitat for fish, birds, and wildlife.

The trail will take you through a series of habitats beginning with a southern mixed hardwood forest. From there it meanders down into a wet pine savannah where coastal savannah grasses wave in the breeze among a scattering of longleaf pine and where you will find birds like the brown-headed nuthatch. Eventually you will arrive at the banks of Davis Bayou and not one but two overlooks to view the marsh and bayou itself.

There is an informational kiosk at the trailhead with brochures, including a trail map. Along the trail you will find several interpretive signs that point out significant points of interest about the area you're walking through.

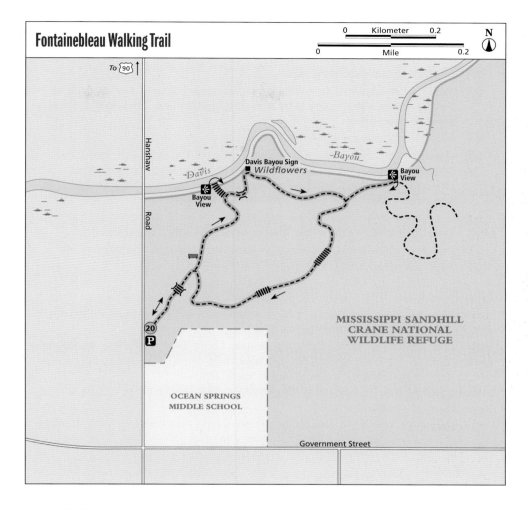

Fontainebleau Walking Trail

To 90

Hanshaw Road

Davis Bayou Sign
Wildflowers
Davis
-Bayou-
Bayou View
Bayou View

MISSISSIPPI SANDHILL
CRANE NATIONAL
WILDLIFE REFUGE

20
P

OCEAN SPRINGS
MIDDLE SCHOOL

Government Street

N

0   Kilometer   0.2
0   Mile   0.2

The footing is a gravel bed with plastic underlayment all the way to the first over-look at mile 0.2, making this section ADA-accessible. After that the footing becomes dirt and sand and a bit hilly, making the use of a wheelchair here impossible. Saw palmettos, ferns, orchids, and the violet-blue spike of pickerelweed as well as several species of carnivorous plants, including pitcher plants and butterworts, will be seen.

Miles and Directions

0.0 Start from the trailhead kiosk on the north side of the parking lot. In less than 0.1 mile, cross a 50-foot composite bridge over a boggy area that turns into boardwalk.

0.1 Pass a trail on the right—this is your return after the loop. Arrive at a sign about the pine flatwoods and a bench. The vines make a tunnel.

0.2 Arrive at a sign about the ridge. A 50-foot boardwalk leads to a bayou overlook. When done viewing, turn around and return to the sign and the trail.

0.3 Cross a 30-foot bridge over a slough. There are lots of palmettos here and a view of the bayou to the left. In less than 0.1 mile, come to a sign about Davis Bayou and lots of wildflowers.

0.4 Come to a sign about fire in the woods.

0.5 Arrive at a T intersection. To the right is the loop back to the parking lot. Turn left and head east. In less than 0.1 mile, come to the edge of the bayou for views. Turn around and head back to the intersection.

0.6 Back at the T intersection, go left (south-southwest).

0.7 Cross a 30-foot boardwalk over wetland with a sign about "Life on the Edge," followed by low-lying areas that could be boggy and wet after rain. It's very open here through the pines trees. In less than 0.1 mile, pass a view to the left of open pine forest and a Gulf prairie sign.

0.8 Cross another 30-foot boardwalk over wetland with a "Where Are the Cranes" sign, followed by a low-lying area with water. A brown sign with an arrow points to the right.

1.0 Arrive at a T intersection with a trail sign pointing to the left. Turn left onto the gravel trail.

1.1 Arrive back at the trailhead.

Hike Information

Local Information: Mississippi Gulf Coast Regional Convention and Visitors Bureau, 2350 Beach Blvd., Ste. A, Biloxi, MS 39531; (888) 467-4853; gulfcoast.org

Local Events/Attractions: Jackson County Fair, Jackson County Fairgrounds, 2902 Shortcut Rd., Pascagoula; (228) 762-6043; co.jackson.ms.us/departments/fair.php. A good old-fashioned American fair with thrill rides, food (on a stick, of course), music, and more.

Restaurants: Doughboys Pizza and Poboys, 6512 Washington Ave., Ocean Springs; (228) 875-7828; facebook.com/doughboysonline?fref=ts

21 Davis Bayou Trail

While this nearly 2-mile hike is partially a walk down Davis Bayou's Park Road, there are some great views of the bayou marsh, a numbered nature trail through a saltwater marsh lined with pine and sweet southern magnolia, and a bit of CCC history. The hike is easy enough for any member of your family, and the Nature's Way Loop at the end can be split out as a separate, shorter 0.5-mile hike.

Start: East end of parking lot near visitor center
Distance: 1.9-mile lollipop with out and back
Hiking time: About 1 hour
Difficulty: Easy over gravel sidewalk, dirt footpath
Trail surface: Gravel, dirt
Best seasons: Year-round
Other trail users: None
Canine compatibility: Leashed dogs permitted

Land status: National park
Nearest town: Ocean Springs
Fees and permits: None
Schedule: Year-round, 8 a.m.–sunset
Maps: USGS Ocean Springs, MS; brochures with map available at visitor center
Trail contact: Gulf Islands National Seashore, 3500 Park Rd., Ocean Springs, MS 39564; (228) 875-9057, ext. 100; nps.gov/guis

Finding the trailhead: From the intersection of US 90 and Park Road in Ocean Springs, take Park Road south 2.1 miles. Come to a Y. Take the right fork, and in less than 0.1 mile, turn right into the parking lot. The trailhead is on the east side of the parking lot. GPS: N30 23.495'/W88 47.359'

The Hike

Just when you thought you've seen it all when it comes to hiking at Gulf Islands National Seashore, you can add one more stop to your list—the salt marshes and bayous of the Davis Bayou area.

This recreation area is located literally in the heart of the bustling little coastal town of Ocean Springs. Cross one of the town's main thoroughfares, Government Street, where the road is wall-to-wall shopping centers, and poof, you're suddenly in a land that seems far removed from the crowds.

Davis Bayou is a great little getaway, especially for families. The park is quiet and peaceful. Early morning hiking is a joy here, especially when a light fog has rolled in off the bayou. It's very serene and the best time to view some of the wildlife that calls the area home, including white-tailed deer, river otters, raccoons, and maybe a nutria, that large rodent-like creature that roams the Southern backwaters. Keep a close eye out for squirrel tree frogs or cricket frogs and, of course, alligators. Your best chance to see one is just as you cross Stark Bayou on this hike. Carefully cross Park Road to the east to a little observation area, and you're almost guaranteed to see one of the "resident" gators on display.

A side trail leads you to the ruins of an old CCC recreation and dining hall from the 1930s.

A trip to Davis Bayou wouldn't be complete without visiting the exceptional William M. Colmer Visitor Center. The center has exhibits, an orientation film about the park, a book and gift store, and very knowledgeable and friendly staff and volunteers. The visitor center is open daily from 8:30 a.m. to 4:30 p.m., closed for Thanksgiving, Christmas, and New Year's Day.

I call this the Davis Bayou Trail though it actually uses two trails, the CCC Overlook Trail and Nature's Way Loop, plus a bit of a "road walk" to take a good close-up look at the salt marsh and bayou. The bulk of the trail uses a narrow shoulder along the side of Park Road. The shoulder is a gravel footpath, about 2 feet wide, so be watchful of cars. Even though you're doing a little road walk, there is still a wonderful view of the salt marsh 0.2 mile into the hike from a composite and wood walkway that crosses the bayou.

At 0.3 mile you leave the road for a 0.5-mile walk down the CCC Overlook Trail. The trail is a wide, 5- to 6-foot dirt path, and the ground is littered with a soft blanket of leaves and pine needles. As you walk, you will see a short, 6-inch cement wall on each side of the trail. The wall continues until you arrive at a large cement semicircle. This is all that remains of a Civilian Conservation Corps (CCC) recreation and dining hall. During the Great Depression between 1933 and 1941, men aged 18

EXPLORING GULF ISLANDS NATIONAL SEASHORE

The Gulf Coast is truly blessed to have some of the finest barrier islands anywhere in the country. Beautiful bright white beaches, emerald green oceans, waving sea oats, wetlands that are alive with every kind of animal and bird imaginable—they truly are an American treasure.

The islands that make up the seashore stretch some 160 miles from Cat Island in Mississippi to Okaloosa, Florida. In 1971 Congress passed legislation to create the Gulf Islands National Seashore and protect this fragile environment and the historically significant structures that were built here hundreds of years ago.

Barrier islands are not only important habitat for many species of wildlife, but they are also important breaks for the mainland. The islands are situated between the Gulf of Mexico and the mainland, separated by bays and sounds. This "wall" of sand protects the mainland from violent hurricanes by slowing them down, even if just a little; otherwise, the effects would be more devastating than they already are.

Besides the wetlands and refuges described in this book, the islands hold an amazing historical record. Several forts built before the Civil War are located here, including Fort Pickens (hike 9), Forts Gaines and Morgan in Alabama, and Fort Massachusetts in Mississippi. Although not officially part of the National Park system, Fort Morgan is still located within this barrier island chain and is where the historic Battle of Mobile Bay occurred during the Civil War. During the battle Admiral Farragut allegedly uttered those immortal words, "Damn the torpedoes, full speed ahead!" Fort Massachusetts is located on Ship Island and can only be reached by a special ferry out of Biloxi. Learn more about the ferry and reserve a seat online at msshipisland.com.

Naval Live Oaks in Gulf Breeze, Florida, was developed by the US government in 1828 as a live oak farm with the sole purpose of supplying the navy with wood for its ships. And then there are the historic lighthouses that dot the northern Gulf coast, beautiful structures that have, for the most part, weathered time, elements, and wars, like St. Marks (hike 5) and Ship Island.

But the main attraction of Gulf Islands National Seashore is the wildlife. Exotic birds like white and brown pelicans, seven different species of plovers, and a long list of bitterns and herons are only a few of the 300-plus species that live on the islands. And many endangered species of animals find protection here, like the loggerhead and leatherback sea turtles who find the beaches prime nesting areas, manatees, and the Perdido Key beach mouse.

The barrier islands are breathtaking, the history remarkable, and the wildlife amazing. With all that the Gulf Islands National Seashore has going for it, you would think someone would have written a book about it. Oh, wait, they have. Check out Robert Falls's excellent book, *Exploring Gulf Islands National Seashore*, published by FalconGuides. And also visit the park's website for more information at nps.gov/guis.

to 23 (later 17 to 28) were given the opportunity to do some good, honest work for pay while providing a remarkable infrastructure for the nation.

Much of the CCC's work was building the many state parks that dot the country, and the area you are standing on was part of one of those projects. From 1938 to 1941 these men built picnic areas, cabins, and trails here for what would become Magnolia State Park, an appropriate name for a park in the "Magnolia State." They also planted over a million trees to help stop erosion and provided training for another 200 men joining the Corps. In 1971 the park was merged into the newly established Gulf Islands National Seashore.

From here you return to Park Road to continue on your trek. At mile 0.8 the trail turns off Park Road and onto Robert McGhee Road. As you hit the 1-mile mark, the gravel shoulder expands into a pull-off parking area big enough for probably six cars. This is the beginning of the Nature's Way Loop and is clearly marked with a sign and a box that holds brochures. These brochures help guide you along this section of the trail with numbered descriptions of the plants and views you will see. The numbers correspond to the numbers on green-painted, 4-by-4-inch cement posts along the trail.

Once you turn off the road and onto the trail, you will cross a short footbridge over a runoff ditch. The footpath is dirt with a good covering of leaves and pine needles. Loblolly pine and palmetto fill the landscape to each side. Almost immediately after turning onto Nature's Way Loop, you will have an excellent view of the marsh to your right and then climb a hill over a set of stairs made by 12-by-12-inch posts. There are a number of these stairs going up the short sides of ravines scattered about the loop.

At mile 1.4 you have the option of turning left at a T intersection to finish the loop at the gravel parking area or turning right to begin the trip back (there is a sign here pointing the way to the visitor center). For this trip I turned right and headed back to the road, where you make another right turn to the south and retrace your steps back to the parking lot. (Skip the CCC Overlook Trail on the way back, unless you want to revisit.) **Option:** If you finish out the loop at the gravel parking area, turn left to the west and walk less than 0.1 mile to view Stark Bayou from a bridge.

Miles and Directions

0.0   Start from the east side of the parking lot. A sign telling about the Davis Bayou trails is here. This is a narrow dirt footpath covered in leaves and pine needles. Loblolly pine and palmetto line the path. In less than 0.1 mile, come out to Park Road. Turn left (north) onto the gravel shoulder. The shoulder is very narrow so use caution.

0.2   The gravel shoulder is now a composite and wood walkway over a bayou. There are excellent views of the marsh here. On the other side the gravel path resumes.

0.3   Turn left (west) onto the CCC Overlook Trail. Cross a ditch at the turn over a short footbridge. A sign here clearly marks the turn. The path is a wide dirt path through here.

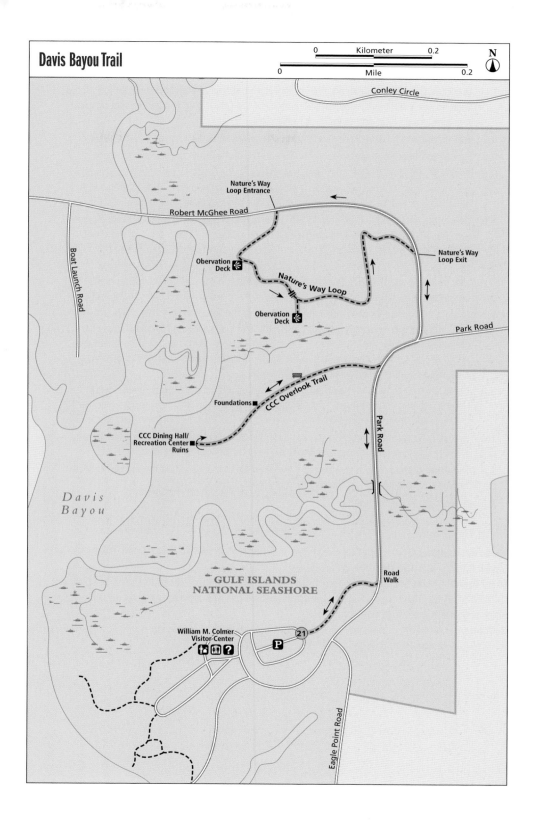

0.4 Pass a bench on the right.

0.5 See the first of a small (6-inch-tall) cement wall or foundation on each side of the trail. In less than 0.1 mile, come to a Y. The left fork is an old animal trail. Take the right fork to the west. In just a few yards, arrive at the remains of the CCC dining hall and recreation building. Turn around here and head back to the road.

0.7 Back at the road, turn left (northeast) onto the gravel shoulder.

0.8 Turn left off Park Road onto Robert McGhee Road. Continue on the gravel shoulder.

0.9 Pass a side trail on the left. This will be where the Nature's Way Loop returns (a sign here points the way to the visitor center). Continue straight as the road swings to the west. In a few yards you will pass a road marked "Authorized Vehicles Only" on the right.

1.0 Come to a gravel pull-off area where about six cars can park. Turn left here (south) onto the Nature's Way Loop. The first few yards are over a boardwalk with views of the bayou and marsh to your right. In less than 0.1 mile, come to a Y. Take the right fork to the south.

1.1 Come to a Y. Take the right fork to the southwest and come to an observation deck that overlooks the marsh. Turn around and head back to the main trail and turn right (southeast).

1.2 Cross a 20-foot boardwalk, then climb 15 steps to the top of a hill on the other side. In less than 0.1 mile, come to another Y. The right fork is a "social trail" that will rejoin the main trail later. Take the left fork to the northeast. In a few yards cross a short boardwalk and come to a Y. Take the right fork to the south and soon come to another marsh overlook. Return to the main trail and turn right (east).

1.4 Come to a bench at a T intersection. A sign here points to the right and reads "Visitor Center." You can either turn left and continue the loop a short distance, coming back to the 1-mile mark, or turn right to begin the trip back. For this description, turn right (east).

1.4 Returning to the road, turn right (south) onto the gravel footpath and begin retracing your steps to the trailhead. Do not take the CCC Overlook Trail on the return trip.

1.8 The gravel path ends at a sign pointing the direction to the visitor center and picnic area. Turn right here onto the dirt footpath.

1.9 Arrive back at the trailhead.

Hike Information

Local Information: Mississippi Gulf Coast Regional Convention and Visitors Bureau, PO Box 8298, Ocean Springs, MS 39535-8298; gulfcoast.org

Local Events/Attractions: Busted Wrench Garage, Museum, and Gift Shop, 2311 9th St., Gulfport; (228) 864-9082; bustedwrench.com. A must for classic car, motorcycle, and boat enthusiasts, all under a 6,000-square-foot exhibit hall roof.

Restaurants: Anthony's Steaks and Seafood, 1217 Washington Ave., Ocean Springs; (228) 872-4564. Great seafood and their famous Baked Cat Island Oysters.

22 Pirate's Alley Nature Trail

I know the kids will want to spend most of the day in Buccaneer State Park's wave pool, but I'm pretty sure they will also love this short and easy romp along the Pirate's Alley Nature Trail. The trail is lined with moss-covered oak trees and leads to a panoramic view of a marsh. And hey, it doesn't hurt to tell them that pirate Jean Lafitte once called this area home as he smuggled treasure along the Mississippi Gulf Coast.

Start: Parking lot just north of entrance station / honor box
Distance: 1-mile loop
Hiking time: About 1 hour
Difficulty: Easy over a level dirt/sand footpath and boardwalk
Trail surface: Dirt/sand footpath, boardwalk
Best seasons: Late fall to early spring
Other trail users: Cyclists
Canine compatibility: Leashed dogs permitted

Land status: State park
Nearest town: Waveland
Fees and permits: Day-use fee
Schedule: Year-round, 8 a.m.–sunset
Maps: USGS Waveland, MS; maps available at entrance station
Trail contact: Buccaneer State Park, 1150 South Beach Blvd., Waveland, MS 39576; (228) 467-3822; mdwfp.com/parks -destinations/ms-state-parks/buccaneer.aspx

Finding the trailhead: From the intersection of US 90 and Lower Bay Road, take Lower Bay Road south 2.4 miles. Make a sharp left turn onto Clermont Road and head south 1.3 miles (Clermont Road will turn into Loor Avenue for 0.3 mile). Turn left onto South Beach Boulevard. Travel 0.6 mile and turn left onto State Park Road. In less than 0.1 mile, arrive at the pay station. If no one is at the station, pay your fee at the honor box. Continue straight 400 feet. The parking lot is on the right, and the trailhead is across the street to the west. GPS: N30 15.771' / W89 24.315'

The Hike

When people talk about Hurricane Katrina, they immediately think about the massive flooding that occurred in New Orleans and the images of people stranded on their roofs. That was the big story everyone focused on. But there was another story, one that those of us along the Gulf Coast will never forget—the story of the tiny town of Waveland.

The town is tucked away in the extreme southwestern corner of Mississippi, directly on the Louisiana state line. On the night of August 29, 2005, Hurricane Katrina smashed into the southeast Louisiana coast. Waveland was in the crosshairs.

The town took a direct hit from the category 3 storm. Winds gusted to 160 mph when the eye wall hit and brought a 25-foot storm surge with it. Fifty people died and just about every home and business within a half mile of the beach was washed away. NBC led the news the next day with the headline, "Mississippi Town Nearly Wiped off Map." That included Buccaneer State Park.

A splendid view of a bayou from the Pirate's Alley observation deck

That was then and this is now. The town has been rebuilt and revitalized, and Buccaneer State Park is bigger and better than ever. This is a park for kids of all ages. For the young ones there is a huge playground with a rock wall. For those who love disc golf, the par 3, 18-hole course here doesn't get any better, with a backdrop of the beautiful Gulf of Mexico. There is also a recreation center with video games, foosball, and Ping-Pong, and an activity pool.

The biggest draw for kids is the completely redesigned wave pool. This 4.5-acre pool can generate eight different wave patterns for body surfing, plus there's a kiddie pool and splash pad.

A great little hiking trail is also located in the park, the Pirate's Alley Nature Trail. The trail is short enough for the youngest in your family and is a good way to get them away from the wave pool and on a little adventure.

The trail was named in honor of the pirates who used to ply the Gulf waters and one in particular, Jean Lafitte. People didn't call him a pirate, though. He would

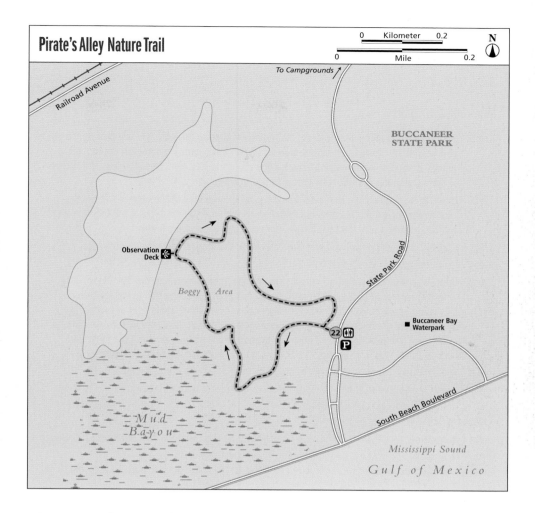

Pirate's Alley Nature Trail

just as soon shoot you if you called him that. To Lafitte, he was a "privateer." In 1805 he operated a warehouse in New Orleans where his "trade" was dealing in selling smuggled goods and slaves. Legend has it that he built a house in Waveland.

The path starts as a hard-packed dirt trail as it winds its way from the parking lot near the park's entrance. This is a nice 1-mile hike through an oak, magnolia, and longleaf pine forest. Brown and white pelicans, egrets, great blue herons, and ospreys soar around you. You'll see and hear many red-headed and pileated woodpeckers, and rabbits, raccoons, and squirrels scurry about. The highlight of the trip is the observation deck that stretches out into a big, wide bayou and wetland.

The hike described here is the inner loop of the larger 1.8-mile loop. Full disclosure, and a word of warning to you all, during my visit the yellow flies were ferocious! Me and my Lab Archer had to cut the trip to just the inner loop. The best time to hike this trail is from late fall to early spring.

The state estimates that over 17,000 trees were destroyed by Katrina, but the landscape is making a remarkable recovery. The canopy is a bit thin, but there is still enough shade to make this stroll in the woods well worth the trip. Oh, and the wave pool, too.

Miles and Directions

0.0 Start from the parking lot and cross the main park road to the west. You will pick up the trail here at the kiosk. The trail is a good 5 feet wide and grassy for most of the trip. You will see plenty of dead trees from the hurricanes of the past ten years. In a few yards come to the intersection with the return loop. Turn left (west).

0.1 Come to an intersection. The cross-trail is the outer loop that, at the time of this writing, was overgrown and impassible, but hopefully by the time you read this, it will be open and you can lengthen your trip by 0.8 mile. Continue straight to the south.

0.3 Come to another intersection with the outer loop. Continue straight to the north.

0.4 Cross boggy area over a few 2-by-2-inch boards.

0.5 Come to a bench, a blackberry patch, and another intersection with the outer loop. Turn onto the outer loop to the right (north). In 50 feet come to a side trail to the left (west). This is a nice, short walk to a wooden observation deck with the highlight of the trip, a beautiful view of the bayou and marsh. When you're done at the overlook, turn around and head back to this intersection. Make a left (north) and continue on the outer loop. This section is low-lying and tends to be boggy with considerable water after a good rain.

0.6 The outer loop continues straight to the north. Turn right (east) onto the inner loop.

1.0 Arrive back at the trailhead. Cross the road to the east to return to your car.

Hike Information

Local Information: Mississippi Gulf Coast Regional Convention and Visitors Bureau, 2350 Beach Blvd., Ste. A, Biloxi, MS 39531; (888) 467-4853; gulfcoast.org

Local Events/Attractions: Infinity Science Center, NASA's Stennis Space Center, 1 Discovery Circle, Stennis Space Center; (228) 533-9025; visitinfinity.com. A fascinating hands-on science center for young and old alike that explores deep space and Earth itself. The admission fee includes a bus tour of Stennis Space Center, where NASA's Saturn V moon rocket and the new Space Launch System engines are tested. Open Mon–Sat, 9 a.m.–4 p.m. Admission is charged; children 3 and under free.

Lodging: Buccaneer State Park Campground, 1150 South Beach Blvd., Waveland; (228) 467-3822; mdwfp.com/parks-destinations/ms-state-parks/buccaneer.aspx. Improved campsites with water and electricity (including beach sites overlooking the Gulf) and primitive sites are available.

Restaurants: Da Kitchen, Too, 714 US 90, Waveland; (228) 467-7242. Great Southern cooking, like crawfish pie, gumbo, and crab cakes.

IN ADDITION
5 'N' 10—FIVE HURRICANES OF THE PAST DECADE FOR THE RECORD BOOKS

It is well known that the Gulf Coast receives its share of hurricanes. In the past ten years the coast has seen some of the costliest and deadliest storms on record come ashore. The worst string came between 2004 and 2008 when five named storms came in and upended everyone's way of life.

It all began on September 16, 2004, when Hurricane Ivan blasted in from the Gulf, making landfall on the Alabama-Florida state line and directly hitting Gulf Shores, Orange Beach, and Pensacola. The storm raced in as a category 3 with sustained winds of 120 mph and a 14-foot storm surge. Ivan ended up killing thirty-three people and totaling $19.8 billion in damages, placing the storm fifth on the list of the costliest in American history.

On September 13, 2008, Hurricane Ike came ashore near Galveston, Texas. Although only a category 2 with winds of 110 mph, the toll was immense mostly due to the sheer size of the storm, over 400 miles wide. In the end 112 people died and damages totaled $27.8 million, making it the third costliest.

Then there was 2005. In an unlikely scenario the Gulf Coast was battered not once, not twice, but three times. The string began on July 10 when Hurricane Dennis paid a call to the coast. The storm was packing winds of 145 mph but at the last minute dropped to 120 as it made landfall on Santa Rosa Island near Pensacola, just a few miles from where Ivan landed a year earlier.

It was August 29, 2005, that the big one hit—Hurricane Katrina. The storm destroyed cities and towns from New Orleans to Alabama, sweeping away entire towns like Waveland, Mississippi. New Orleans was the most famous victim of Katrina. The storm surge was big enough to breech fifty-three levees, causing 80 percent of the city to be underwater. The death toll from the storm including deaths far inland was 1,836, with 1,500 of those in New Orleans. Damages were $105.8 billion, putting Katrina number one on the list.

The last storm to visit the storm-weary Gulf Coast hit the beach on September 24, Hurricane Rita. Rita came in as a category 3 storm, making landfall on the Louisiana-Texas border at Sabine Pass with winds topping 120 mph, a 20-foot storm surge, and 25 inches of rain. The storm caused $11.8 billion in damages, putting it number nine on the costliest list.

Evidence from these storms can still be seen today, especially on the trails in southwest Louisiana. Many of the beautiful and popular boardwalks into the marshes were destroyed, such as the Alligator Marsh Trail at Fontainebleau State Park. Hopefully in the very near future they will be back and better than ever for all to enjoy.

Mississippi Honorable Mentions

The Mississippi Gulf Coast has several more hiking trails for you that didn't make the A list. Some are shorter in length but still offer fantastic scenery and interesting wildlife. While you're on the coast, check them out and let us know what you think. Maybe the hike should be upgraded, or maybe you know of a little-known hike that would make a good honorable mention.

I Indian Point Coastal Preserve

The Indian Point Coastal Preserve is located in the city of Gautier. This 800-acre conservation park is owned by the state and managed by the Mississippi Department of Marine Resources. There are four trails that link together so you can mix and match your hike route. Trails like the Wiregrass, Needlerush, Bayhead, and Burning Dirt wind through the pine forest and savannah to some pretty marsh views along the banks of Mary Walker Bayou. Find out more about the trails at Indian Point by calling (228) 374-5000.

J Ship Island

Part of the Gulf Islands National Seashore, Ship Island is a barrier island off the coast of Mississippi that has camping, swimming, beach fun, and hiking. The island has a 2-mile-long loop trail that is entirely beach walk around the island. It's a beautiful stroll on the beach with the blue waters of the Gulf encircling you, but remember there's no shade at all so be prepared by wearing sunscreen and head protection, and drink plenty of fluids. And once you're done walking, take a tour of historic Fort Massachusetts. You can't drive to the island. The only way there is by an officially sanctioned National Park Service ferry. For more information about the park, contact the National Park Service at (228) 875-9057 or visit online at nps.gov/guis. For ferry information, visit msshipisland.com or call (866) 466-7386.

K Oak Grove Birding Trail

The Oak Grove Birding Trail is part of the Grand Bay National Estuarine Research Reserve (GBNERR) and the Mississippi Coastal Birding Trail. This 1-mile out-and-back is a birder's paradise, with warblers, scarlet tanagers, and a wide variety of songbirds filling the air with, well, song. The path leads you through a mixed hardwood maritime forest that slopes down to the Bayou Heron Marsh and an observation deck. Bring your binoculars and enjoy the show. Visit GBNERR online at grandbayneer.org or call (228) 475-7047.

Louisiana

The fourth state on our tour of the Gulf Coast is Louisiana. Nicknamed the "Pelican State" because of the population of brown pelicans that call these coastal waters home, the state serves as a transitional environment from the swamps and black-water rivers of the north-central Gulf of Mexico to the salt marshes, tidal flats, and barrier islands of the western Gulf coast.

Along the state's eastern coast you will find the swamps and bayous. Beautiful cypress and tupelo swamps with their pea green algae-covered waters and cypress knees jutting out create an eerie scene that makes you think a dangerous animal like an American alligator or cottonmouth snake is lurking, waiting for you. Well, they are lurking but not for you. These trails are the safe way to visit these backwaters, where the trees are draped heavily with Spanish moss.

A precautionary word about alligators, and it can't be said enough: Gators are naturally afraid of humans but feeding them or harassing them in any way changes the rules. They may seem slow-moving on land, but don't let that fool you. They can be pretty fast for a short distance. Keep your children close by at all times and your dog on a leash. In many cases it's not recommended to bring your dog on a hike because of gators. I've listed the warnings where they apply in this section's hikes. Heed them and the advice of park rangers.

On the west side of the state, we begin to see expansive salt marshes where a vibrant community lives. Thousands of species of birds either live here on a permanent basis or part-time as they migrate in and out of the region. The panoramic views are amazing, and the wildlife like those alligators, river otters, roseate spoonbills, and great blue herons are spectacular.

And speaking of spectacular, let's talk about mosquitoes. Locals joke about them as being the "Louisiana Air Force." Case in point: Hiking the Sabine Wetland Walkway (hike 31), it was interesting to sit in my car and watch would-be hikers get out of their vehicle, and start the hike, disappearing around the bend for a moment then reappearing running as fast as they can, swatting swarms of the bug. The lesson—put on that bug spray!

The entire Louisiana Gulf Coast has seen its share of hardship over the last few years, what with hurricanes like Katrina and the BP Oil Spill (see the "In Addition" sidebars on both of these subjects). But these people are resilient and so is nature, and the area is coming back strong.

The weather is the same as on the Alabama and Mississippi coasts, with moderate temperatures averaging in the low to mid-70s well into fall. In January the average high is around 52°F, with lows around 40°F. Below-freezing temperatures do occur here but are short-lived.

23 Fiddler's Loop

Drive out deep into the Gulf of Mexico and explore the Fiddler's Loop Trail at Grand Isle State Park. This moderate loop follows the banks of an inlet of the Gulf of Mexico. Along the route you'll be treated to expansive views of the inlet, an abundance of wildflowers and birds, and the trail's namesake, fiddler crabs. And don't forget to catch a bird's-eye view of the Gulf and Grand Isle itself from the six-story observation tower.

Start: Parking lot at the visitor center and observation tower
Distance: 2.1-mile loop
Hiking time: About 1.5 hours
Difficulty: Easy to moderate when trail is flooded
Trail surface: Dirt, gravel, boardwalk
Best seasons: Year-round
Other trail users: Cyclists
Canine compatibility: Leashed dogs permitted
Land status: State park
Nearest town: Grand Isle

Fees and permits: Park admission fee (children under 3 free); toll on the LA 1 Bridge
Schedule: Year-round; 6 a.m.–9 p.m. Sun–Thurs; 6 a.m.–10 p.m. Fri, Sat, and days preceding holidays
Maps: USGS Barataria Pass, LA; maps available at entrance station
Trail contact: Grand Isle State Park, Admiral Craik Dr., Grand Isle, LA 70358; (888) 787-2559; crt.state.la.us/louisiana-state-parks/parks/grand-isle-state-park

Finding the trailhead: From the intersection of US 90 and LA 1, take exit 215A and follow the ramp around 0.3 mile. Turn right onto LA 1 South. Travel 3 miles and turn left onto Bayou Crossing Road. After crossing the bridge over Bayou Lafourche, turn right onto LA 308 South. In 14.5 miles LA 308 crosses the bayou again and becomes LA 657 / W. 15th Street. In 0.5 mile turn left onto LA 3235. Travel 15.6 miles and LA 3235 becomes LA 1. Travel 8 miles and make a right turn to continue on LA 1. In just a few hundred feet, pay the small toll and continue on LA 1 South another 8.3 miles to where the road makes a sharp turn to the left (east). Continue an additional 15.3 miles on LA 1 South. Make a left onto Admiral Craik Drive. Turn right into Grand Isle State Park and in 100 feet arrive at the entrance station. After paying your fee, head straight 100 feet and turn left at the intersection. Head north on the state park road 0.3 mile. The observation tower, visitor center, and parking are on the right. Start the hike here. GPS: N29 15.654' / W89 57.130'

The Hike

It is a long, beautiful drive south of New Orleans down LA 1 to Grand Isle, Louisiana, and this great hike on the Fiddler's Loop Trail. The drive down takes you through quaint little towns with tall shrimp boats lining every bayou and expansive views of the intricate marshlands and rivers as you cross the 19-mile-long LA 1 Bridge. Remember, there is a small toll to cross the bridge.

A long boardwalk crossing on the eastern end of the Fiddler's Loop Trail

Being so far south and so far out into the Gulf with virtually only one highway as a lifeline to the mainland, you may wonder who would live here, but let me tell you, Grand Isle is one hoppin' little beach town. People flock here for the beaches, which they swim in most months of the year, and, of course, the fishing. Grand Isle is recognized as one of the top ten fishing spots in the world. A 0.2-mile-long lighted fishing pier juts out into the Gulf, and each July a world-famous tarpon rodeo is held here. Some of the best Gulf seafood is harvested from the waters around the island, and the people, well, they are super-friendly and hospitable.

Grand Isle State Park sits on the northern tip of this barrier island, which serves as a natural breakwater that protects the miles of canals and bayous north of here that lead to the Mississippi River. Bayou Fifi forms the west coast; Barataria Pass is on the north and east; the Gulf of Mexico is to the south.

The trail begins at the parking lot next to the six-story-tall observation tower and visitor center. You can climb to the top now or wait until you return to your vehicle, but it's not to be missed. There is a spectacular view of the Gulf and the pass, and to the north you can see Isle Grande Terre, another location where legend has it privateer Jean Lafitte tended to his "business." The visitor center here has a few nice exhibits depicting how man and the elements have shaped this community.

From the parking lot, circle around to the west and southwest and come to a gravel road to the northwest. This is where the trail actually begins. A long fishing pier into the lagoon is at the end of this path, but we're going to turn left (southwest) and pick up a narrow dirt (and often slippery mud) trail. You are now on the loop that will eventually come back to this spot from the opposite direction.

The hike along the east side of the lagoon offers beautiful views of the water feature, with deep Southern skies reflecting off its surface. This is where you will find many fishermen wetting their line or casting their net for blue crab. You will have to jump one 4-foot-wide slough along the west end of the trail, but the jump isn't that bad. From here the trail crosses the park road on the south side of the entrance station, circles around to the north, then crosses the road again, this time just north of the entrance station. This can be the only confusing part of the hike. The trail on the other side can be hard to pick up. As you cross the road, look for a series of yellow posts on the opposite side. Pick up the trail right next to the posts.

Birders and wildflower lovers will love this section of the trail. The path is narrow here, with thick brush on either side. To your left behind the shrubs is Admiral Craik Drive. The lagoon is to your right. On this side of the loop, you will see American golden plover, upland sandpiper, sometimes long-billed curlew, and frigate bird, to name only a few. And from spring through late summer, wildflowers brighten the hike. Not just a few but thousands are lined up row upon row, most notably on the north side of the lagoon.

Finally the path reaches the north end of the lagoon and crosses the inlet over a long wooden boardwalk. It is an amazing view of the lagoon, with the observation tower in the distance on one side and the pass with recreational boats plying its waters to the left.

While this is a great hike, there are a couple of words of caution to pass along. First, the trail circles a lagoon that connects directly to the pass and Gulf, which means that the trail, being so close to the edge, can flood during high tide, making completing the loop difficult or impossible. During my visit the tide had occurred hours before but the path after the long bridge on the north side of the trail was still calf deep in water.

And don't forget, this is a barrier island and is virtually void of trees for shade, so if you're hiking this trail in any kind of heat, you had better prepare with something to protect your head, sunscreen, and plenty to drink.

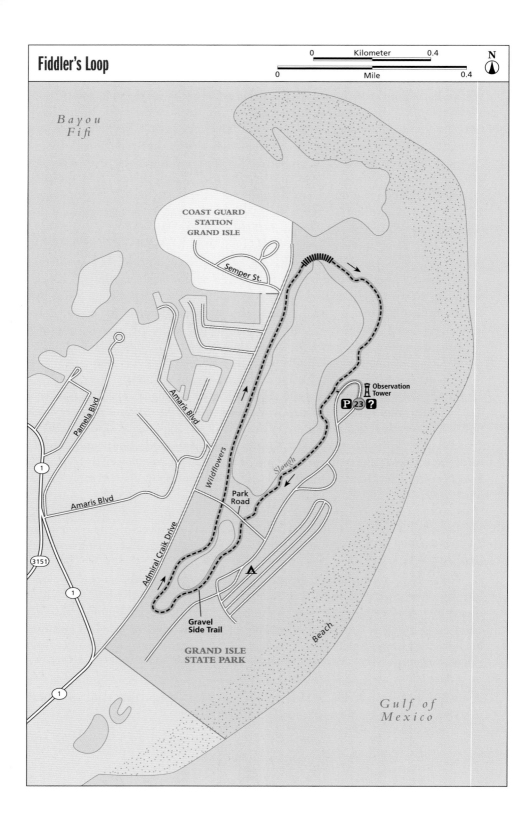

Fiddler's Loop

Kilometer
0   0.4

Mile
0   0.4

N

Bayou Fifi

COAST GUARD
STATION
GRAND ISLE

Semper St.

Observation
Tower

P 23 ?

Pamela Blvd

Amaris Blvd

Wildflowers

Amaris Blvd

Park
Road

Slough

Admiral Craik Drive

Gravel
Side Trail

GRAND ISLE
STATE PARK

Beach

*Gulf of
Mexico*

1

3151

1

1

Miles and Directions

0.0 Start from the visitor center / observation tower. Head away from the parking lot following the road to the north.

0.1 Turn right (west) onto a gravel road. There is a fishing pier on the end. In 50 feet turn left (southwest) onto a narrow 2-foot-wide dirt path with some gravel. This section of the trail is often mucky and slick from tide and rain. Look for fiddler crabs.

0.4 Hop a 4- to 5-foot-wide slough. Small minnows can be seen swimming here.

0.5 Cross the park's entrance road to the south. The entrance station is to your right. Pick up the trail on the other side.

0.6 Pass a gravel side trail back to the park road on your left (south).

0.7 The trail bends to the northeast and becomes deeper sand/dirt for a bit. You will be paralleling Admiral Craik Drive that is outside the park; the road will be on your left (west) and the lagoon to your right. You will lose sight of the water for a bit through here. Wildflowers literally line the path.

0.9 The lagoon is seen again on your right (east).

1.0 Cross the park entrance road to the north (the entrance station is on your right). On the other side you will walk past five yellow-painted creosote poles with chains between them on your left. This stretch is a favorite spot for fishermen.

1.5 Come to an area that is very boggy and wet after a good rain or high tide, then begin crossing a long boardwalk with beautiful views of the lagoon and the Gulf of Mexico.

1.6 Come to the end of the boardwalk, and when they say the trail may flood after high tide, they aren't kidding. You could be ankle to knee deep here.

2.0 Arrive back at the gravel road at mile 0.1. Turn left and in 50 feet turn left again onto the park road. Follow the road back around to the visitor center.

2.1 Arrive back at the visitor center.

Hike Information

Local Information: Town of Grand Isle, PO Box 200, Grand Isle, LA 70358; (985) 787-3196; townofgrandisle.com

Local Events/Attractions: Butterfly Dome, 2757 LA 1, Grand Isle; (985) 787-2229. Take a guided or self-guided tour of the world of butterflies in this unique dome. The dome is funded through donations. Call in advance for the tour.

Lodging: Grand Isle State Park Campground, Admiral Craik Drive, Grand Isle; (888) 787-2559; crt.state.la.us/louisiana-state-parks/parks/grand-isle-state-park. The park has 49 improved sites with power and water and 10 beach campsites.

Restaurants: Bridge Side Marina Deli, 1618 LA 1, Grand Isle; (225) 787-2419

IN ADDITION
THE GREAT SPILL—DEEPWATER HORIZON 2010

Whenever I travel to sing the praises of the Gulf of Mexico and its many recreational activities, I am inevitably asked about the Deepwater Horizon Oil Spill, or as it is known around the world, the BP Oil Spill, and how the Gulf Coast is recuperating from it.

In 2010 the British Petroleum (BP) oil rig Deepwater Horizon exploded, killing eleven rig workers and pouring an estimated 4.9 million barrels of oil into the Gulf. Beaches and marshland were affected in some form or another from as far east as Pensacola, Florida, to Louisiana. The effects ranged from tiny tar balls washing up on beaches to large mats of oil inundating wetlands.

To make matters worse, in an effort to clean the oil from the surface, dispersants were dropped from planes, the idea being that it would break up the oil cloud. Scientists are now looking to see what effect those chemicals had on the Gulf waters and its inhabitants and if the chemicals simply caused the oil to sink to the bottom.

While the cleanup has been steadily progressing and much of the waters of the Gulf are returning to some semblance of normal, some areas are still feeling the effects. For example, in August of 2014 some Louisiana inshore shrimping grounds remained closed.

Overall, though, the Gulf is looking pretty good considering what it went through, and Mother Nature and the resilient residents of the coast are finally getting back on their feet.

24 Barataria Preserve Trail

Moss-draped oaks, placid green waters of a cypress-tupelo swamp, and lots of wildlife make the Barataria Preserve Trail a must-visit when in the New Orleans area. Three separate trails, mostly boardwalk, make up the path through this national park preserve. Amazing wildflowers line many of the paths; crawfish mounds dot the landscape; ruby-throated hummingbirds dart about; and don't be surprised if you come up on a white-tailed deer walking the boardwalk.

Start: Visitor center parking lot
Distance: 4.6-mile out-and-back with several shorter options
Hiking time: About 2.5 to 3 hours
Difficulty: Easy to moderate depending on length of trip you choose
Trail surface: Boardwalks (ADA-accessible except the Marsh Overlook Trail), dirt paths
Best seasons: Year-round
Other trail users: None
Canine compatibility: Dogs not permitted

Land status: National park preserve
Nearest town: Marrero
Fees and permits: None
Schedule: Year-round except federal holidays and Mardi Gras Day, 9 a.m.–sunset
Maps: USGS Bertrandville, LA; maps available at visitor center
Trail contact: Jean Lafitte National Historic Park and Preserve, 419 Decatur St., New Orleans, LA 70130-1035; (504) 689-3690; nps.gov/jela/barataria-preserve.htm

Finding the trailhead: From the intersection of US 90 Business Route and LA 45 in Marrero, take LA 45 south 2.9 miles. Turn left onto LA 3134 South. Travel 5.4 miles and turn right onto LA 45 North. Continue 1 mile. The preserve entrance and visitor center will be on the left. GPS: N29 47.034' / W90 06.906'

The Hike

I don't think there is a better place to experience Louisiana's wetlands than at the Barataria Preserve, part of the Jean Lafitte National Historic Park and Preserve. Operated by the National Park Service, this 23,000-acre tract has a little bit of everything when it comes to ecosystems—marshes, bayous, swamps, and hardwood forests.

Located only minutes from New Orleans, this preserve provides a resting place for migrating birds commuting on the Mississippi Flyway heading to either Texas or Canada. Other birds that call the preserve home include white ibis, mallard duck, bank swallow, tufted titmouse, and pileated woodpecker. And that's only a few of the over 200 species of birds that live here or migrate in.

Keep your eyes peeled as you walk the trails here. You may spot a bobcat, nine-ringed armadillo, marsh rabbit, nutria, or minx. And yes, there are alligators here, too.

Native Americans called this land home over 1,000 years ago, as is evidenced by an ancient "midden," or refuse pile, you will pass on the trail. "Privateer" Jean Lafitte

The perfect exhibit of what a cedar and tupelo swamp should look like is on display on the Visitor Center Trail portion of this hike.

and his band of "Baratarians" plied these waters partaking in a little illegal enterprise of supplying slaves and luxury items to the wealthy plantation owners of the region.

Most of the trails at Barataria are boardwalk and therefore ADA-accessible, the exception being the Marsh Overlook Trail along Bayou Coquille. While there is a boardwalk there, it is older and travel would be rough, to say the least. There are also some formidable stairs at the far end of the trail that lead to the overlook that wheelchairs wouldn't be able to navigate. For the most part the path is a composite boardwalk, but like I said, the exception is the Marsh Overlook Trail and dirt footing on the Bayou Coquille Trail.

The hike begins at the visitor center. There is a nice restroom here to the right with, get this, two filtered water fountains: a standard fountain and one where you can fill up larger water bottles. To the left is the visitor center itself, with exhibits and plenty of information. To get to the trail, walk between the two buildings and you'll see the boardwalk.

This first section of trail is called the Visitor Center Trail, for obvious reasons, and is one of the most popular. Even on weekdays the path is lined with people. Often you may catch up with a tour being led by a ranger. The path travels through an absolutely amazing cypress swamp as it makes its way to the banks of the marsh and the Lower Kenta Canal. The green waters and cypress knees are everything you would expect to see in a swamp.

When you arrive at the far end of the boardwalk, turn around and retrace your steps to the intersection with the Palmetto Trail. This path is less traveled, probably because of its length, but one that shouldn't be missed. Hundreds of palmetto fans line the trail. Being less traveled, don't be surprised if you round a bend and there are white-tailed deer walking down the boardwalk, nibbling at the brush on the sides.

MARDI GRAS MADNESS

From Texas to Florida the two weeks prior to Lent is a mad time—it's Mardi Gras! While just about every town on the Gulf Coast celebrates with their own parades and balls, no celebrations can compare with the ones held in the cities that started it all here in the United States, Mobile and New Orleans.

Mardi Gras, or "Fat Tuesday," began as a celebration by Catholics on the day before Ash Wednesday. Call it their last hurrah before the forty days of Lent begins. The history of Mardi Gras in the United States can be traced back to seventeenth-century France and the House of the Bourbons. The holiday was called Boef Gras, or "Fatted Calf." As France began to establish herself in the north Gulf Coast region of the New World, the party came with them, and in 1703 the settlement of Fort Louis de la Mobile, present-day Mobile, held the first recognized Mardi Gras celebration. The following year the first mystic society, Masque de la Mobile, was formed, which later became what we call "krewes" today. They are the ones who are responsible for putting on the grand parades.

The celebration quickly spread to New Orleans, and by the early 1740s instead of parades, Louisiana's governor established elegant society balls. These are still held in cities all along the Gulf Coast, with plenty of food, dancing, drinking, and the coronation of the society's king and queen.

In the city of Mobile, you can expect an average of twenty-four parades a year, while in New Orleans the average is thirty-four. And, of course, that doesn't include the dozens that occur in the surrounding towns.

You can tell you're in the Deep South from this scene ripped from a postcard.

At the end of the Palmetto Trail, you will come to a parking lot. If you were only to hike the Bayou Coquille and Marsh Overlook Trails, this is where you would begin. If you're doing the full hike, cross the parking lot to the north and pick up the Bayou Coquille Trail on the opposite side.

This trail is wall-to-wall information. The path has many informative signs describing the marsh ecosystem and the plants, wildlife, and history of the area. The footing is a combination of dirt and wooden bridges and boardwalks and travels atop a natural levee formed by centuries of floods that have left sediment deposited here. Allow plenty of time to take in all of the information. This is also a very popular trail and can be crowded.

Finally you will arrive at the end of the Bayou Coquille Trail and begin walking the Marsh Overlook Trail. The boardwalk is made of wood and is older through here; it's only a few inches above the marsh waters but the scenery is wonderful, with the swampy marsh and its wildflowers like clasping coneflower (which resembles black-eyed Susan), southern coast violet, and yellow iris, and the green waters of the cypress swamp right next to you. The trail ends at an elevated wooden observation deck where you will get a panoramic view of the marsh.

The total length of the hike is 4.6 miles if you walk from end to end and back again. For most hikers that would be a breeze, but for families with smaller children, it would be impossible. Instead, consider doing one of the shorter hikes. A favorite for small children and their parents is simply doing the 0.5-mile out-and-back Visitor Center Trail. Another favorite option, and something a little longer, would be doing the Bayou Coquille and Marsh Overlook Trails, a total of 1.8 miles of out-and-back hiking but with plenty to see, including the marsh overlook.

And if you still want to explore this preserve, directly across LA 3134 from the visitor center is another almost 6 miles of trails. A map is available at the visitor center. See "Louisiana Honorable Mentions" for more information.

Miles and Directions

0.0 Start from the visitor center on the aptly named Visitor Center Trail. The trail is a boardwalk between the visitor center and restrooms and heads to the west. It is a wide, wooden ADA-accessible boardwalk through a beautiful swamp.

0.2 Come to the intersection with the Palmetto Trail to your right (north). Right now continue straight on the Visitor Center Trail.

0.3 Come to the end of the Visitor Center Trail. After viewing the marsh, turn around and retrace your steps to the Palmetto Trail intersection.

0.4 Arrive back at the intersection with the Palmetto Trail and turn left (north) onto the trail. The boardwalk is now a composite boardwalk.

0.7 Pass glades of purple flowers and soon walls of palmetto, hence the name of the trail.

1.2 Come to the end of the Palmetto Trail at the preserve's second parking lot. Walk straight across the parking lot to the northwest, crossing a small wooden bridge in the middle of the lot. You will then pick up the Bayou Coquille Trail on the northwest side of the parking lot. The entrance is clearly marked with an information kiosk.

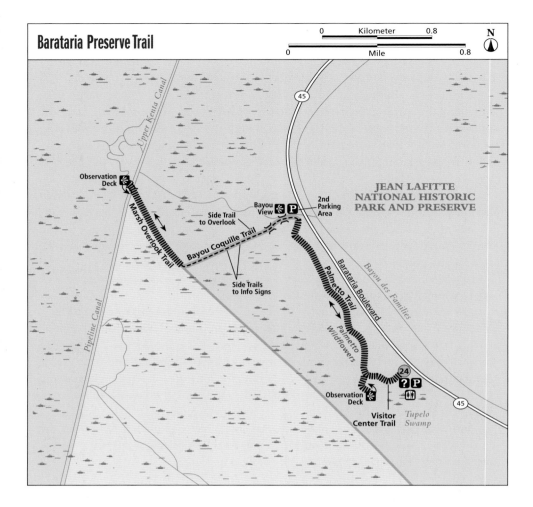

Barataria Preserve Trail

JEAN LAFITTE
NATIONAL HISTORIC
PARK AND PRESERVE

1.3 Come to the Bayou Coquille trailhead. From here to the trail's end, the path is a mix of composite or wooden boardwalks and dirt footpaths. You will be walking directly beside a beautiful green swamp and the bayou itself. In less than 0.1 mile, come to an information sign about the Bayou Coquille Trail. A service road intersects from the left (south). Continue straight to the southwest.

1.4 Cross a 200-foot bridge with benches and nice views of the bayou. In less than 0.1 mile, cross a 75-foot boardwalk.

1.5 Cross a short boardwalk.

1.6 Come to a short, 100-foot side trail on the right (northwest) to a nice overlook and information about the "flooded forest." When done turn around, head back to the main trail, then turn right (southwest). In less than 0.1 mile, cross a boardwalk, then come to a short side trail on the left (south) that leads to an overlook and the impressive cypress tree named "The Monarch of the Swamp." Back at the main trail, turn left (southwest) and cross another boardwalk. In the fall the hardwoods turn to autumn color and the leaves drop and cover the path.

1.7 Another side trail takes you to an information sign about the "Spell of the Swamp" to the north. In less than 0.1 mile, cross a 100-foot boardwalk with benches.

1.8 Cross another boardwalk and a few yards later another boardwalk.

1.9 Cross a long boardwalk with benches, trash cans, and recycle bins. In less than 0.1 mile, come to the end of the composite boardwalk and the wooden boardwalk of the Marsh Overlook Trail begins. Turn to the right (northwest) onto the Marsh Overlook Trail.

2.0 Come to an intersection with a short side trail off to your right (north) with nice views of the surrounding marsh and bayou.

2.3 Come to a T intersection. You will see the boardwalk and a suspension bridge to your left (northwest). For now, turn right (southeast) and in a few feet come to an observation deck with an information sign about "Sinkers" and a Kodak moment—a view of the suspension bridge crossing the bayou with beautiful bayou plants surrounding it. When done viewing, go back to the main trail, turn right (northwest), and cross the bridge.

2.4 Just after the bridge, pass a set of stairs on the left (south) that leads to the banks of the bayou; with beautiful clover-like plants floating in the water and the bridge in the background, it is worth a visit. Continue straight a few yards from the bridge and come to the end of the boardwalk on an observation deck with benches and an expansive view of the marsh. This is the end of the Marsh Overlook Trail. Turn around and retrace your steps back to the trailhead.

4.6 Arrive back at the trailhead.

Hike Information

Local Information: Jefferson Convention and Visitors Bureau, 1221 Elmwood Blvd., Ste. 411, New Orleans, LA 70123; (877) 572-7474; experiencejefferson.com

Local Events/Attractions: Westwego Farmers and Fisheries Market, 484 Sala Ave. and Fourth St., Westwego; (504) 341-3424. A beautiful open market with the freshest seafood, produce, and unique arts and crafts.

Restaurants: Raising Cane's Chicken Fingers, 4817 Lapalco Blvd., Marrero; (504) 328-9550. A local fast-food chain that began on the campus of LSU with amazing chicken fingers and sides.

Other Resources: An audio tour is available, provided by the US Fish and Wildlife Service. Phone (504) 799-0802 then press the number indicated on the sign at the stop you are at.

25 Bayou Segnette Nature Trail

The Bayou Segnette Nature Trail is an easy walking path with several options that allow you to take even the smallest child out for adventure in the woods. The trail winds through a forest of cypress trees with gnarled roots. At the far end the trail comes out to a restroom and picnic area where the kids can reenergize, or frolic on the playground equipment.

Start: Wildcat Walk trailhead on Drake Avenue
Distance: 1.5-mile double loop
Hiking time: About 1 hour
Difficulty: Easy over level dirt paths
Trail surface: Dirt, short road walk
Best seasons: Year-round
Other trail users: None
Canine compatibility: Leashed dogs permitted
Land status: State park
Nearest town: Westwego
Fees and permits: Admission fee (as of publication, seniors 62 and over and children under 3 free)

Schedule: Year-round; 7 a.m.–9 p.m. Sun–Thurs; 7 a.m.–10 p.m. Fri, Sat, and the day preceding holidays
Maps: USGS New Orleans West, LA; maps available at entrance station
Trail contact: Bayou Segnette State Park, 7777 Westbank Expwy., Westwego, LA 70094; (888) 677-2296; crt .state.la.us/louisiana-state-parks/parks/ bayou-segnette-state-park

Finding the trailhead: From the intersection of US 90 Business Route / Westbank Expressway and Drake Avenue in Westwego, take Drake Avenue south 0.4 mile. Turn right into the park. In 0.1 mile arrive at the pay station. After paying your fee, continue straight 0.2 mile. The trailhead is on your right. GPS: N29 53.921' / W90 09.499'

The Hike

OK, this one isn't for you hard-core hikers. This is for the kids, and I'm pretty sure they will love it. Bayou Segnette State Park is located only minutes from the heart of New Orleans but offers a unique wilderness-like environment to explore along the marsh and swampland.

Besides the hiking trail I'll talk about in just a minute, the park has plenty of amenities to make your visit pleasant, including picnic areas, playgrounds, nice clean restrooms, and a wave pool. Did I mention that kids will love this place?

The park is located in the middle of a network of some of New Orleans's famous canals and bayous. If you love to fish, this is a great spot to wet your line. Try your hand at reeling in bass, catfish, perch, or bream, and the saltwater intrusion of the marsh area gives you a chance to snag a redfish.

A bayou crossing at the intersection of the West-We-Go and Raccoon Right-A-Way Trails

As for the wilderness-like environment, there is a wide variety of plants and animals that beckon to be discovered by both young and old along the park's nature trail. Coypu, or nutria, live here. These are very large rodent-like animals that can weigh between 8 and 11 pounds when fully grown. They were introduced to the United States by fur traders but have since become quite a nuisance, as they ferociously eat, and destroy, riverside vegetation. They live in burrows along riverbanks and are often mistaken for muskrat.

Some of the happier animals you may see on your visit include opossum, raccoon, and armadillo. Red-tailed hawks, kites, and northern cardinals will be seen here as well, along with an occasional bald eagle.

The Bayou Segnette Nature Trail is made up of three separate trails: the Wildcat Walk (0.2 mile one-way); West-We-Go Trail (0.5 mile one-way), which is named for the town where the park resides, Westwego; and the Raccoon Right-A-Way (0.2 mile one-way). There is also a 0.2-mile section of road walk. The trails are not blazed but are easy-to-follow wide dirt footpaths. The paths are well-marked where one trail ends and another begins.

Our hike begins just off Drake Avenue near the banks of Whisky Bayou. There is a small parking lot here with enough room for three, maybe four, cars. This is the trailhead for the Wildcat Walk, a dense hardwood forest where birds love to hang out since it is away from the crowded playground area.

At the opposite end of the trail, you will cross the park road and pick up the West-We-Go Trail. This path leads you through an old cypress swamp; the gnarled roots of the trees can be quite creepy in the dark, dense forest in the early morning or late evening. Along a short stretch of this trail, you will be walking near US 90 and will hear cars passing by, but it's not too disturbing.

▷ **Beignets were first brought to the United States by the Acadians that settled in Louisiana around 1755. At the time, these pastries were little fried fritters that were sometimes filled with fruit. Today, these Cajun doughnuts are square pieces of fried dough with a good dose of powdered sugar and are the best!**

When you come to the end of West-We-Go, you will cross the park road once again, using the crosswalk, and make your way across one of the canals over a wooden walkway next to the road. There are nice views of the canal here and a good chance to spy egrets or herons catching crawfish for a snack.

After crossing the canal you will cross the road again, using the crosswalk, and arrive at the Raccoon Right-A-Way Trail. This path is just a nice walk in the woods, with many rabbits scurrying about. At the end you will once again arrive at the park road, and directly across the street are the playground, picnic area, and restrooms. To get back to your car, turn left here and follow the road, crossing over the canal again, until you reach the north end of the Wildcat Walk, which you will take back to the trailhead.

There are several options for hiking this trail with small children. You can park at the picnic area and simply do the Raccoon Right-A-Way loop or the West-We-Go loop, or just do a short out-and-back of the Wildcat Walk. Either way, get the kids out and have fun teaching them about nature on this great little hike.

Miles and Directions

0.0 Start from the Wildcat Walk trailhead and head north. The trail is narrow and very enclosed as you walk through a thick tunnel of vegetation. In 50 feet pass a bench on the right. You are now entering the cypress forest.

0.2 Come to the end of the Wildcat Walk at the park road. There is a bench here. Cross the road to the northeast and pick up the West-We-Go Trail (it's clearly marked). There is a bird feeder and bench at the entrance.

0.4 Pass some impressive cypress trees and a bench on the left.

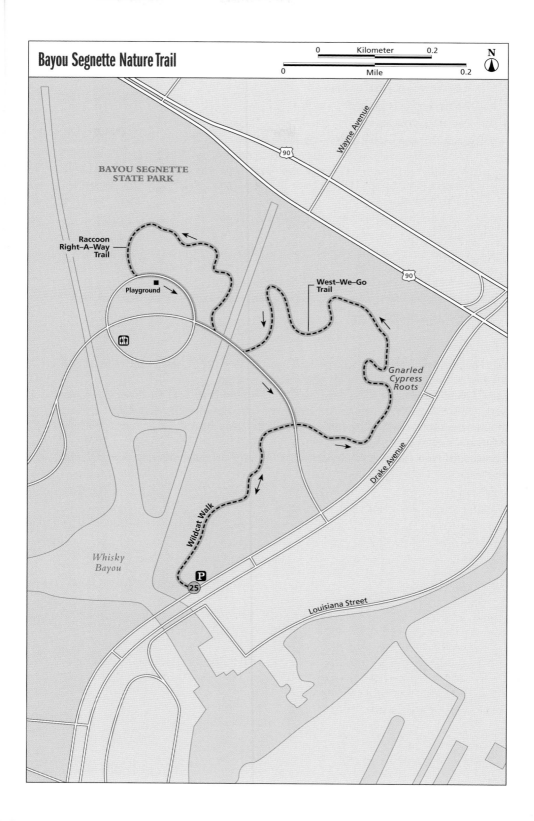

0.5 As the trail turns to the north, pass a bench on the right and walk alongside a chain-link fence on your right. US 90 is on the opposite side of the fence. In the early morning you'll come across many rabbits here.

0.6 Pass a bench on the right.

0.7 Pass a bench on the left.

0.8 Come to the end of the West-We-Go Trail at the park road. Cross the road on a diagonal to the northwest and cross a bayou over a pedestrian bridge. After crossing the bridge, in less than 0.1 mile cross the road again on a diagonal to the north and pick up the Raccoon Right-A-Way Trail to the north. There is a bench at the entrance and the trail is clearly marked.

0.9 Pass a bench on the right and small patches of palmetto.

1.0 Pass a bench on the left.

1.1 Come to the end of the Raccoon Right-A-Way Trail at the park road. There is a playground and restrooms across the road. Cross the road here to the southeast and follow the road back to mile 0.2 and the entrance of the Wildcat Walk.

1.3 Turn right (southwest) onto the Wildcat Walk and retrace your steps back to the trailhead.

1.5 Arrive back at the trailhead.

Hike Information

Local Information: Jefferson Convention and Visitors Bureau, 1221 Elmwood Blvd., Ste. 411, New Orleans, LA 70123; (877) 572-7474; experiencejefferson.com

Local Events/Attractions: Bayou Segnette State Park Wave Pool, 7777 Westbank Expwy., Westwego; (888) 677-2296; crt.state.la.us/louisiana-state-parks/parks/bayou-segnette-state-park. Hit the waves in Bayou Segnette State Park's wave pool. The pool can accommodate up to 400 people. Admission is charged.

Restaurants: Perino's Boiling Pot Restaurant, 3754 West Bank Expwy., Harvey; (504) 340-5560; perinosboilingpot.com

26 Fontainebleau Hiking Trail

Head on down to the bayou on the Fontainebleau Hiking Trail. This wide, grassy path leads to the grassy marsh of Cane Bayou, with white-tailed deer and gopher tortoises making an occasional appearance on your journey. The path is lined with plenty of wildflowers to keep the botanist, or artist, in you satisfied. Long, flowing Spanish moss drapes the trees along the bayou's banks, giving the trail that quintessential Southern feel.

Start: Trailhead north of parking lot on Group Camp Road
Distance: 5.2-mile double loop
Hiking time: About 2 to 2.5 hours
Difficulty: Moderate on main loop, easy if only doing the nature trail section
Trail surface: Grass, gravel, dirt
Best seasons: Sept to May
Other trail users: Cyclists
Canine compatibility: Leashed dogs permitted
Land status: State park
Nearest town: Mandeville

Fees and permits: Admission fee (seniors 62 and over and children under 3 free as of publication)
Schedule: Year-round; 6 a.m.–9 p.m. Sun–Thurs; 6 a.m.–10 p.m. Fri, Sat, and the day preceding holidays
Maps: USGS Mandeville, LA; maps available at entrance station
Trail contact: Fontainebleau State Park, 62883 LA 1089, Mandeville, LA 70448; (888) 677-3668; crt.state.la.us/louisiana-state-parks/parks/fontainebleau-state-park

Finding the trailhead: From the intersection of US 190 and LA 22 in Mandeville, take US 190 south 5.5 miles. Turn right onto LA 1089. Drive 0.3 mile and arrive at the entrance station. After paying your fee, continue straight ahead 0.8 mile. A small parking area will be on your right, next to the ruins of the old sugar mill. The trailhead is 300 feet north of the parking lot, on the opposite side of the road. It is easily identifiable with an information kiosk. GPS: N30 20.214' / W90 02.271'

The Hike

If you're looking to find the quintessential image of the Southern outdoors, then look no further than Fontainebleau State Park in Mandeville, Louisiana. It's everything you would expect in the Deep South—dark green bayous, expansive salt marshes, flowing Spanish moss, and lots of hospitality.

You might be saying to yourself, "Isn't Fontainebleau in Paris or a hotel in Miami?" Well, yes, but this park wasn't named for the hotel. Fontainebleau is an area in France that is known for its fortified castles that date back to 1137 and was the "Riviera," as it were, for French kings.

In 1829 a man by the name of Bernard de Marigny de Mandeville, the person who established the town of Mandeville, built and ran a sugar mill here on the banks

A couple enjoys a stroll along the wide grass path.

of Lake Pontchartrain just north of New Orleans. It was a booming business and afforded him a lavish lifestyle, much like the kings of France, hence the name of the plantation, Fontainebleau. The remains of the sugar mill still stand in the park a quarter mile from the park entrance and near the trailhead for this hike.

This hike uses two different trails, the Bayou Cane Hiking Trail and Sugar Mill Nature Trail. There used to be a third trail here and one of the most popular in the park, the Alligator Marsh Trail that extended out into the marsh for an exciting mile walk among the gators and throngs of birds. Sadly the devastating hurricane seasons of the past decade obliterated the boardwalk. All that remains are scattered pieces in the brush along the sides of the Sugar Mill Nature Trail.

There are two parking areas near the trailhead. One is at the trailhead, a gravel lot with room for maybe three cars. The other parking area is just a few yards southwest of the trail head, next to the ruins of the old sugar mill. Again it is a gravel lot, with room for four regular cars and one handicap spot.

We start the hike on the Sugar Mill Nature Trail. From the trailhead the path is a 6-foot-wide gravel path. French mulberry, wild grape, and yaupon line the path. It won't be long before you come to the intersection with the Bayou Cane Hiking Trail. At this point don't continue straight on Sugar Mill. We'll come back to this spot later. Right now turn left to the north and continue on the Bayou Cane Hiking Trail.

> **For decades Lake Pontchartrain in Louisiana had the distinction of being the site of the world's longest bridge over water—the Lake Pontchartrain Causeway. The bridge connects the town of Metairie with St. Tammany Parish and is 23 miles long. In 2011 the Jiaozhou Bay Bridge in China beat the record at 25.84 miles.**

Considering its length, this trail is a very easy walk. The trail is flat throughout and wide, a good 10 feet in spots, and for just about the entire length, it is an all-grass footing that is meticulously mowed. There is a great canopy to help shield you from the hot sun. Cicadas serenade you as you walk, and white-tailed deer dart out in front of you. A few side trails lead to the edges of the marsh, where tall live oaks draped in Spanish moss invite you to sit down at a picnic table, eat lunch, and reflect.

At the far end of the hike, you will come to a kiosk where the trail loops around to head back, but before you do, turn south down a side trail for a short, 0.3-mile walk to the banks of the beautiful, wide Cane Bayou. This section of the trail can be quite muddy after a good rain.

After visiting the bayou, head back to the intersection with the nature trail and continue straight to the west to finish the hike. On this trail you'll see plenty of blackberry, holly, sweet gum, bamboo, and cattails, and where the trail nears where the Alligator Marsh Trail used to begin, a nice view of the marsh and some of the over 400 species of birds that call the park home.

Miles and Directions

0.0 Start from the Sugar Mill trailhead across the main park road and about 300 feet northeast of the parking lot at the sugar mill ruins. Two trails leave from here—the Sugar Mill Nature Trail and Bayou Cane Hiking Trail. Head out on the wide gravel and dirt path to the east.

0.2 Cross two separate short bridges over a runoff.

0.3 Cross a short, 10-foot puncheon bridge. In less than 0.1 mile, come to the intersection where the Bayou Cane Hiking and Sugar Mill Nature Trails split. You will take the right fork on the return trip, but right now turn left (east) onto the Bayou Cane Hiking Trail. The trail varies from 4 to 10 feet wide with some dirt footing but mostly it's nicely mowed grass. **Option:** If you have smaller children or just want a shorter hike, turn to the right (west) onto the Sugar Mill Nature Trail and pick up the directions from mile 4.2 of this text. This shorter trip is 0.9 mile long.

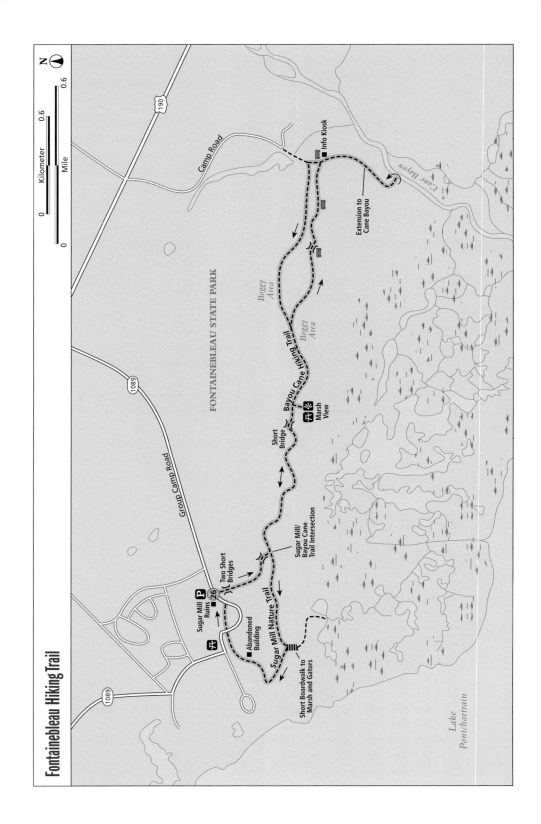

Fontainebleau Hiking Trail

N

Kilometer
0   0.6

Mile
0   0.6

190

Camp Road

Info Kiosk

Extension to
Cane Bayou

Cane Bayou

FONTAINEBLEAU STATE PARK

Boggy
Area

Boggy
Area

Bayou Cane Hiking Trail

Marsh
View

Short
Bridge

1089

Group Camp Road

Sugar Mill/
Bayou Cane
Trail Intersection

Two Short
Bridges

Sugar Mill
Ruins

P

26

Abandoned
Building

Sugar Mill Nature Trail

Short Boardwalk to
Marsh and Gators

1089

Lake
Pontchartrain

0.8 Pass a short path to the right (southwest).

0.9 Cross a short bridge over a runoff.

1.0 Pass another short side trail to the right (south). Through the trees and brush you can see the marsh on your right. In a few feet come to a short side trail on the right (south). This is a beautiful spot with a picnic table. Spanish moss is draped like curtains from the oaks around you. There used to be a boardwalk into the marsh here, but it was destroyed by hurricanes. If you can stretch far enough, you can see the marsh over the brush. It's impressive. When done, turn around and head back to the main trail. Turn to the right (east).

1.1 Pass a bench on the left (north).

1.2 The trail splits around a rutted boggy area. An old dilapidated bridge is on the left side. Take the right to walk around the area.

1.3 Come to a Y. A sign here reads "Hiking Trail Loop" and points to the right fork, and "Nature Trail" pointing back the way you came. A "Do Not Enter" sign is posted on the left fork. That will be the return route from the main loop. Take the right fork and head east. You will start seeing more bamboo along this section and hear the sound of cicada.

1.6 Pass a bench on the right and in a few feet a short bridge.

1.7 Pass a bench on the right.

1.9 Come to a T intersection. There is a bench and an information kiosk here that has posters about plants, early Native Americans, and a trail map. Turn to the right (south) and down another wide trail that connects to the bayou.

2.2 Come to a Y in the path. You can take either fork. In less than 0.1 mile, come to the banks of Cane Bayou for a beautiful panoramic view of the marsh. When done, turn around and retrace your steps back to mile 1.9.

2.5 Back on the main trail, continue straight to the north past the kiosk. In less than 0.1 mile, come to another Y. The right fork leads to the campground and a sign here reads "Wrong Way." Take the left fork to the west.

3.0 Come to another split in the trail around a rutted, boggy area. Take the left side.

3.6 Arrive back at the intersection at mile 1.3. Retrace your steps to the southwest.

4.2 Arrive back at the intersection at mile 0.3. Turn left (southeast) onto the Sugar Mill Nature Trail. The trail is a 3-foot-wide gravel path. Along this section you will see remnants of the old Alligator Marsh boardwalk that was washed away by past hurricanes. The marsh is next to you on the left (south).

4.6 Cross a short boardwalk. In less than 0.1 mile, come to a T intersection. A right turn is the Sugar Mill Nature Trail. Turn left (south) and head toward the Alligator Marsh boardwalk. Unfortunately the boardwalk, as I mentioned, has been destroyed by hurricanes, but it's still worth a walk to where it once began. In a few yards you have gone as far as you can go. Turn around and head back to the main trail. Turn left (northwest).

4.8 Pass a short bridge that leads to the main park road on the left (west). Continue straight to the northeast.

4.9 Pass an old abandoned brick building on the right (south). In a few yards cross a short wooden bridge over a runoff. After crossing, turn right and walk under the huge Spanish moss–draped oak trees next to the park road.

5.2 Arrive back at the parking area.

Hike Information

Local Information: St. Tammany Parish Tourist and Convention Commission, 68099 LA 59, Mandeville, LA 70471; (800) 634-9443; louisiananorthshore.com

Local Events/Attractions: Mandeville City Seafood Festival, Fontainebleau State Park, 62883 LA 1089, Mandeville; (985) 966-4623; mandevillecityseafoodfest.com. Held annually on the Fourth of July, this seafood fest does it up right with music from big-name stars, arts and crafts, food, and fireworks.

Lodging: Fontainebleau State Park Campground, 62883 LA 1089, Mandeville; (888) 677-3668; crt.state.la.us/louisiana-state-parks/parks/fontainebleau-state-park. The park has 103 improved campsites with water and electricity and 37 primitive sites.

Restaurants: Liz's Where Y'at Diner, 2500 Florida St., Mandeville; (985) 626-8477; lizswhereyat diner.com

27 River / Bottomland Hardwood Trail

Take a walk on a meandering trail through a mixed pine and hardwood forest along the banks of the Tickfaw River and along an elevated boardwalk above an impressive cypress-tupelo swamp. On your journey you may catch a glimpse of beaver, raccoon, American alligator, or white-tailed deer or see egrets and herons.

Start: Trailhead on southwest side of parking lot
Distance: 2.4-mile loop
Hiking time: About 1.5 hours
Difficulty: Easy over flat terrain, boardwalk section ADA-accessible
Trail surface: Boardwalk, gravel path
Best seasons: Sept to May
Other trail users: Cyclists
Canine compatibility: Leashed dogs permitted
Land status: State park
Nearest town: Springfield

Fees and permits: Admission fee (seniors 62 and over and children under 3 free)
Schedule: Year-round; 7 a.m.–9 p.m. Sun–Thurs; 7 a.m.–10 p.m. Fri, Sat, and the day preceding holidays
Maps: USGS Frost, LA; maps available at entrance station
Trail contact: Tickfaw State Park, 27225 Paterson Rd., Springfield, LA 70462-8906; (888) 981-2020; crt.state.la.us/louisiana-state-parks/parks/tickfaw-state-park

Finding the trailhead: From the intersection of LA 1037 and LA 22 in Springfield, take LA 1037 south 5.1 miles and make a right turn to continue on LA 1037. Travel 1.1 miles and turn left onto Paterson Road. Drive 1.1 miles and come to the entrance station. After paying your fee, continue straight on what is now called Canoe Launch Road 1.1 miles to the parking lot. The trailhead is on the southwest side of the parking area. GPS: N30 22.932' / W90 38.904'

The Hike

An aptly named trail if ever there was one, the River / Bottomland Hardwood Trail (RBHT) is located in Tickfaw State Park along the banks of the Tickfaw River. Just east of the state's capital, Baton Rouge, the park and trail offer respite to the residents of the bustling city and is a wonderful place for visitors to just slow down and relax.

The 1,200-acre park has four separate ecosystems: cypress and tupelo swamp, bottomland hardwood forest, mixed pine and hardwood forest, and the park's namesake, the Tickfaw River. There is a wonderful nature center here that I encourage you to visit that has exhibits, a gift shop, and an 8-minute documentary video on the history of the region and the park. There is also an 800-gallon aquarium stocked with the fish you would find in the river.

Tickfaw State Park is unique in that they encourage you to do some hiking at night, a perfect time to walk the swamps and river and hear frog song or catch a glimpse of the creatures of the night, like owls.

A suspension bridge hangs across the Tickfaw River.

We begin the hike at the well-marked trailhead next to one of the park's pavilions. The trail starts off using a cement sidewalk for a few yards, then continues onto an elevated boardwalk. The boardwalk ranges anywhere from a few feet to 30 feet above a fabulous cypress and tupelo swamp. The walkway is wide with high rails and mesh barricades to keep the kids safe and is completely ADA-accessible. The best view comes as you cross the river over a suspension bridge. Being originally from New Jersey, I could make jokes about paying a toll here; my wife strongly urged me not to do that, but I just did anyway.

But seriously, it is an impressive bridge and boardwalk system and is one of the best ADA-accessible walkways I have seen. In all you could walk about a mile on the boardwalks alone.

After crossing the bridge, the trail temporarily turns to a dirt path and dead-ends with a view of the river. Turn around here and retrace your steps back across the bridge. When you get to the other side, you will see a sign that reads "River Trail 2.5 Mile Loop" and a set of stairs that lead down to the banks of the river. This is the beginning of the River Trail section of the hike. Climb down the steps and follow the trail that hugs the banks of the river.

You will have nice views of the river all along this stretch, as you're only an arm's length away from it. The trail is intermittently marked with blue diamond blazes with arrows pointing the direction. Being in such close proximity to the river, you will walk through stands of tall bamboo and some saw palmettos.

Odds are as you walk you will run into a white-tailed deer or two, raccoons, and plenty of squirrels. Beavers call this area home as well, and snowy egrets and great blue herons make themselves at home along the water's edge. And maybe, just maybe, you might see an American alligator silently lurking beneath the water, with only its eyes and nose breaching the surface.

As the trail makes its return, it swings to the north where there is a small kayak launch next to a small but picturesque bayou. The trail here becomes a wide gravel road that will take you through another pretty little cypress and tupelo swamp.

The trail finally comes out on the north side of the parking lot. You can either cut straight across the parking loop through a small patch of trees or follow the road around to the northwest/west to arrive back at the trailhead.

Miles and Directions

0.0 Start from the trailhead to the south. The trail starts off as a wide gravel path for only a few feet, then becomes a wide ADA-accessible boardwalk. Along the boardwalk there are magnificent views of the river and swamps. The boardwalk is a few feet to 30 feet above the river/swamp.

0.1 Come to a T intersection. There is a sign here pointing left (east) for the short way, right (west) for the long way. Turn left and continue on the boardwalk.

0.2 At another T in the boardwalk, make a right turn to the southwest. The left leads to a nice overlook of the river. It's worth a stop. In a few yards come to a suspension bridge. Continue straight over the bridge for views of the river. On the other side of the bridge, the trail becomes dirt and takes you to the banks of the river. After spending some time there, turn around and head back across the bridge the way you came.

0.3 Just after recrossing the bridge, there is set of stairs heading down to the river on your left to the southwest. Turn left here and head down the stairs. The trail is now a gravel path and heads west as it begins to follow the banks of the river. You will have many chances to see the river along this section via short side trails or the trail itself as it meanders to the riverbank. There is plenty of bamboo through here.

0.8 Pass a fire ring next to the river on your left.

0.9 Walk through a very boggy area from runoff, especially after a heavy rain.

1.2 Pass another fire ring next to the river. The trail moves away from the river and is more of an old service road that can be thick in mud or deep in water after a good rain.

1.3 Cross two metal culverts over a runoff stream.

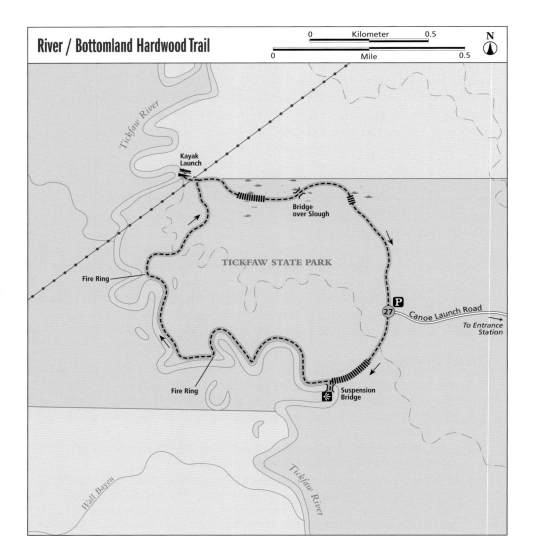

River / Bottomland Hardwood Trail

Kilometer
0   0.5
Mile
0   0.5

N

Kayak
Launch

Bridge
over Slough

TICKFAW STATE PARK

Fire Ring

P
27
Canoe Launch Road

To Entrance
Station

Fire Ring

Suspension
Bridge

Tickfaw River

Wall Bayou

Tickfaw River

1.5 Pass a sign warning that this is an unimproved trail that could flood and that hikers shouldn't start it after 4 p.m. In a few feet come to a T intersection. A short side trail under some power lines to the left (west) takes you to a kayak launch and a pretty bayou. Back on the main trail, continue straight to the east.

1.7 Walk through a swamp area. The trail actually has brick pavers here for 30 or 40 feet.

1.8 Cross a long 8-foot-wide boardwalk over a swamp. Following the boardwalk, the trail becomes a gravel road.

1.9 Cross a short bridge over a slough.

2.0 Cross another boardwalk over a swamp. In less than 0.1 mile, come to the end of the boardwalk. This is a very pretty section, especially in the morning, with very tall trees and the sun streaming through.

2.3 Come out to the road on the opposite side of the parking area. Turn right (southwest) and follow the road around to your vehicle.

2.4 Arrive back at the trailhead.

Hike Information

Local Information: Town of Springfield, 27378 LA 42, Springfield, LA 70462; (225) 294-3150; townofspringfield.org

Local Events/Attractions: Collinswood School Museum, East Pine Street, Ponchatoula; (985) 386-2221. Built in 1874 as a schoolhouse, the Collinswood School Museum traces the history of the region with displays of Native American and Civil War artifacts and items from the town's growth around the railroad. Open Fri–Sat 10 a.m.–4 p.m., Tues–Thurs flexible times. Admission is free.

Lodging: Tickfaw State Park, 27225 Paterson Rd., Springfield; (888) 981-2020; crt.state.la.us/louisiana-state-parks/parks/tickfaw-state-park. Tickfaw State Park has 30 improved campsites with water and electricity and 20 primitive sites.

Restaurants: Lagniappe Restaurant, 30161 LA 22, Springfield; (225) 414-0258; lagniappe restaurant.com

28 Port Hudson State Historic Site

We move just a few miles north of I-10 to Baton Rouge and Port Hudson State Historic Site with this fascinating hike back in time to the Civil War battle that was fought here. Port Hudson was one of a series of fortifications designed to protect New Orleans during the war. This trail will take you to the redoubts, breastworks, and Fort Desperate, the only fortification that the Union army couldn't take in the battle.

Start: Back of Port Hudson State Historic Site visitor center
Distance: 2.9-mile loop
Hiking time: About 2 hours
Difficulty: Easy over flat trail, moderate up short hills
Trail surface: Gravel, dirt, boardwalk, cement sidewalk
Best seasons: Year-round
Other trail users: None
Canine compatibility: Leashed dogs permitted
Land status: State historic site
Nearest town: Jackson

Fees and permits: Admission fee (seniors 62 and over and children 12 and under free, as of publication)
Schedule: Year-round, 9 a.m.–5 p.m. Tues–Sat; closed Thanksgiving, Christmas, and New Year's Day
Maps: USGS Port Hudson, LA; maps available at visitor center
Trail contact: Port Hudson State Historic Site, 236 US 61, Jackson, LA 70748; (888) 677-3400; crt.state.la.us/louisiana-state-parks/historic-sites/port-hudson-state-historic-site

Finding the trailhead: From the intersection of LA 952 and LA 10 / Charter Street in Jackson, take LA 10 east 1.7 miles. Turn right onto LA 68 West. Travel 11.3 miles and turn left onto US 61 South. Travel 1.1 miles, turn right onto Park Road, and drive to the park's visitor center. Pay entry fee and begin the hike behind the building at the observation tower. GPS: N30 41.587' / W91 16.550'

The Hike

We move away from the Gulf to just north of Baton Rouge to the town of Jackson, where we find another wonderful hike to the past through a Civil War battlefield. This time it's at the Port Hudson State Historic Site.

Following the fall of New Orleans during the war, the Confederacy knew they needed to fortify the banks of the Mississippi River in order to keep the waterway out of Union control. Their response was to build a series of forts along the river, including Port Hudson.

The battle that took place here began on May 23, 1863, and ended forty-eight days later. It was one of the bloodiest battles of the war and the longest battle in American military history. One of the interesting side notes to the battle at Port Hudson is that the Union army pressed into action two African-American regiments,

One of two observation towers at Port Hudson to get a bird's-eye view of the historic battlefield

which had a stellar performance in the Union victory. Following the battle the fort became a recruiting station for African-American soldiers.

There are several different paths you can follow, 6 miles in all, through the woods here at Port Hudson. All are interconnected, making an intricate network that allows you to pick and choose the route you want to take. The hike described here is a basic 2.9-mile loop that will take you to the main points of interest in the park.

The trails are not blazed but are easy to follow. They are wide gravel footpaths with the exception of Fort Desperate, which I'll talk about in a minute. The trails are lettered A through P, and the intersections are well-marked with wooden signs that have the trail name engraved on them, directional arrows when necessary, and a copy of the trail map. The trails we will be using on this hike are A, B, C, D, F, G, H, and O.

The hike begins behind the Port Hudson State Historic Site visitor center. It's a marvelous facility with exhibits depicting the events that led to the battle and the battle itself. An audiovisual presentation is available on request, which may be a good idea to view before you head out so you can get a grasp on what you will be seeing on the trail. The center also has a gift shop and very knowledgeable and friendly staff who are eager to answer your questions.

The trail is strewn with informative signs pointing out the vegetation that you'll see during this hike. The signs include very descriptive text that will give even the most amateur of botanist a good idea of what they are looking at. This is also one of the best-labeled battlefields I have been to on the coast. Instead of simply having numbered signs and brochures to go by, descriptive signs tell you the story of what occurred in that location.

We are far removed from the marsh and scrub pines of the Gulf of Mexico and will be traveling through a hardwood forest. With the exception of the very end of the hike, when the trail crosses an open field, the canopy is thick thanks to the many pignut hickory, American beech, hackberry, and black ironwood trees that line the path. You will see some saw palmettos along the route near wetlands and, of course, beautiful magnolias that bloom with big fragrant white flowers in the spring.

As you would expect, some of the roots of these trees are exposed on the trail. To help prevent tripping, the staff has painted many orange so they can easily be seen. And while this isn't a mountain hike, you will have a few considerable hills to climb as the trail makes its way up and down ravines.

Immediately after leaving the visitor center, you come to a four-story observation tower where you can look out over the surrounding area. This is the junction of the loop, and you will begin by taking the trail to the right (south). From there the trail winds through the forest to such sites as Fort Babcock, the nearest point seized by the Union army during the battle, and the Alabama-Arkansas Redoubt.

The highlight of the journey is Fort Desperate. The state historic commission did an excellent job of preserving this piece of history. A long winding boardwalk leads to a gigantic wooden deck high above the ground. There is a small, three-sided

FORTRESSES OF THE GULF COAST

One thing you will find when traveling the Gulf Coast, especially on the Florida panhandle and coastal Alabama and Mississippi, is that there are many forts, most of which date back to before the Civil War. These brick and cement fortresses would become important pieces in the battle to preserve the Union.

Following the War of 1812, it was quite obvious that coastal defenses, namely the country's earthen forts, were inadequate for the weapons and tactics of the period. They were already becoming obsolete.

In 1816 President James Monroe commissioned a board to study how best to fortify the US coastline from invasions. The final report was released in 1821; in it the commission recommended that Atlantic, Gulf, and Pacific coastlines be fortified with new stone fortresses. The report went on to say that to be completely secure, the country would need 200 of the structures. The plan was called the Third System of Fortification. By the start of the Civil War in 1864, only thirty of the forts had been completed.

Most of the coastal forts were built by slaves brought in from nearby cities who were skilled carpenters and masons. The wages they earned were sent directly back to their owners.

Some of the forts you will visit as you travel the Gulf Coast are Fort Pickens (hike 9) and Fort Barrancas in Florida, Fort Morgan and Fort Gaines in Alabama, Fort Massachusetts in Mississippi, and Fort Jackson in Louisiana.

building here with information about the battle and a place where programs and discussions are often held.

The deck winds around with many signs pointing out the Confederate Tunnel, a series of tunnels dug underground that allowed Confederate soldiers to travel undetected from the heart of the fort to the outer ditch, where they could shoot downhill into a ravine where the advancing Union army was. Signs also depict how the Rebels planted cannon shell with friction fuses in their earthworks that when stepped on would explode. There is also another four-story observation tower here.

From here the trail is a cement sidewalk until it reaches a utility easement just before a parking lot. You will turn here and follow the easement to a field and back to the visitor center. For persons with disabilities, the trail is ADA-accessible from this parking lot to Fort Desperate so you, too, can experience the history.

Miles and Directions

0.0 Start from the back of the Port Hudson State Historic Site visitor center at the observation tower. The trail Ys here. The left fork is the return route. Take the right fork to the south. In a few feet pass the Peace Monument on your left. The path is wide and mostly gravel. Cross a short wooden bridge over a runoff.

0.2 Come to a T intersection with a sign pointing left (south) to the F trail and right (west) to the C trail. Take the right fork onto the C trail. In less than 0.1 mile, pass a maintenance shed on the right. A deep ravine is on your left.

0.4 At the bottom of a moderate hill, cross another bridge then scamper up the other side using tree roots for handholds and steps.

0.5 Come to a T intersection with a bench. A service road heads off to the right (a sign here reads "Trail Ends"); turn left (southwest).

0.6 Come to a T intersection. To the left is a short trail that dead-ends. Turn right (west) onto Trail D. The thick canopy opens up somewhat here, with lush green grass surrounding the trees.

0.7 Come to a T intersection with Trails E and F at an informational sign about Artillery Ridge. Turn left (south) onto Trail F.

0.9 Cross a bridge over a runoff.

1.0 Cross another short bridge. Some palmettos line the sides of the trail.

1.1 Come to a Y. A sign here shows that the museum and Trail B are off to the left (north). Take the right fork (south) onto Trail F. In less than 0.1 mile, turn right onto Trail G. Immediately after making the turn, cross a 0.1-mile-long boardwalk anywhere from 10 to 20 feet over Foster Creek.

1.2 Climb a moderate grade uphill. Creosote poles are used as water bars . . . and steps. Come to a wide field with a thin canopy. Trail I heads to the left (south). Turn right (north) on Trail H.

1.5 Arrive at Fort Babcock. When done reading the informational sign, turn around and head back to the intersection at mile 1.2.

1.6 Back at the intersection, continue straight and in less than 0.1 mile you will have a good look at the Alabama-Arkansas Redoubt. When done viewing, retrace your steps to Trail F at mile 1.1.

1.9 Back at the main trail, turn right (southeast). This is now Trail O. In less than 0.1 mile, come to a Y. Take the right fork to the southeast. In a few hundred feet, cross a bridge over a runoff.

2.0 Come to a Y. You can take either fork. They rejoin in just a few yards and the trail crosses a bridge.

2.2 Come to a long boardwalk and elevated platform. This is Fort Desperate. There is plenty of information here along the platform deck and a sheltered pavilion with more info.

2.4 When finished, walk down the ramp to the northwest. The trail is now a cement sidewalk. There is a tall observation tower here.

2.5 Pass a bench on the left.

2.7 Come to a utility line. Turn left (north) onto the wide cut-grass path.

2.8 Turn left (west). You will be walking across a large field next to a re-creation of breastworks.

2.9 Arrive back at the visitor center.

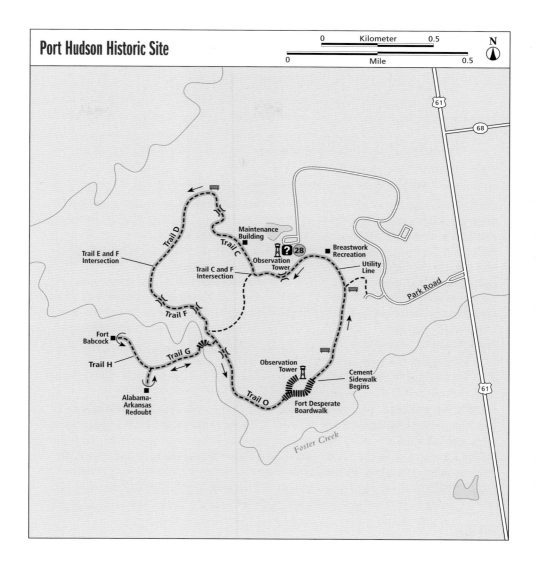

Port Hudson Historic Site

0 Kilometer 0.5

0 Mile 0.5

N

Maintenance Building

Trail D

Trail C

Trail E and F Intersection

Observation Tower

? 28

Breastwork Recreation

Utility Line

Trail C and F Intersection

Park Road

61

68

Trail F

Fort Babcock

Trail H

Trail G

Observation Tower

Cement Sidewalk Begins

Alabama-Arkansas Redoubt

Trail O

Fort Desperate Boardwalk

61

Foster Creek

Hike Information

Local Information: East Feliciana Parish Tourist Commission, PO Box 667, Jackson, LA 70748; (225) 634-7155; felicianatourism.org

Local Events/Attractions: Republic of West Florida Historical Museum, 3317 College St., Jackson; (225) 634-7444; jacksonlamuseum.com. An extensive collection of Civil War artifacts, antique cars and carriages, musical instruments, and more. Open Sat 10 a.m.–4 p.m. and Sun 1:30–4:30 p.m. A small admission fee is charged.

Restaurants: Bobby's Drive Inn, LA 10, Jackson; (225) 634-7190. A great little hamburger joint.

29 Trail C

Louisiana is known for its swamps, and there is no better place to get up close and personal with these green, murky waters than walking Trail C at Lake Fausse Pointe State Park. The trail winds its way over a magnificent cypress swamp via boardwalks and climbs up and down ravines along the wide banks, sloughs, and bayous of Lake Fausse Pointe. Make this into a real adventure by backpacking into one of the trail's eight primitive campsites.

Start: Trailhead kiosk
Distance: 3.6-mile loop
Hiking time: About 2 to 2.5 hours
Difficulty: Moderate over rolling hills
Trail surface: Dirt foot path, boardwalk
Best seasons: Sept to May
Other trail users: None
Canine compatibility: Leashed dogs permitted
Land status: State park
Nearest town: St. Martinville
Fees and permits: Admission fee (seniors 62 and older and children under 3 free)

Schedule: Year-round; 6 a.m.–9 p.m. Sun–Thurs; 6 a.m.–10 p.m. Fri, Sat, and the day preceding holidays
Maps: USGS Jackass Bay, LA; maps available at entrance station
Trail contact: Lake Fausse Pointe State Park, 5400 Levee Rd., St. Martinville, LA 70582; (888) 677-7200; crt.state.la .us/louisiana-state-parks/parks/lake-fausse -pointe-state-park

Finding the trailhead: From the intersection of LA 31 and LA 96 in St. Martinville, take LA 96 east 3.4 miles. Turn right onto LA 679 and travel 4.2 miles. Turn left onto LA 3083. In 0.7 mile turn left to stay on LA 3083. Drive 3.2 miles and turn right onto Bayou Benoit Levee Road / Par Road 169. In 7.6 miles turn right into Lake Fausse Pointe State Park. Travel 0.2 mile and arrive at the entrance station. After paying your fee, continue straight another 0.2 mile and arrive at the parking area. The trailhead is well-marked across the road to the west. GPS: N30 03.615' / W91 36.586'

The Hike

When people think of Louisiana, they of course think of New Orleans and Mardi Gras but they also think about marshes, swamps, and bayous. A visit to Lake Fausse Pointe State Park in St. Martinville will take you right into the heart of this beautiful landscape, and this hike along what is called Trail C is the perfect path to take you there.

The park is located on an island at the edge of Atchafalaya Bay, right in the middle of an intricate network of bayous that snake their way around this vast swampland that was created by natural levees. You really need to visit Google Earth to get an aerial view of this swamp. It's amazing. The park encompasses over 6,000 acres of the swamp.

The park itself is beautiful and very well-maintained. There is plenty to do for everyone, including swimming, picnicking, playgrounds, canoeing, and camping. Don't be surprised to see how many people flock to Lake Fausse year-round. It can

Meandering through a beautiful pea-green swamp along Trail C

get crowded. Fortunately this hike will take you away from the maddening crowds and deep into the heart of nature.

There are three main trails in the park, each designated with a letter from A to C. Trail A is a short, 0.7-mile, white-blazed trail; Trail B is a 1.6-mile, blue-blazed path; and this trail, Trail C, is an orange-blazed, 3.6-mile loop. The distance and the lightly rolling hills along the far end of this loop make it a moderate-rated hike.

All of the trails here are well-marked with engraved signs showing trail directions and mileages at intersections, and 2-by-2-inch diamond markers with the color of the trail you're on pointing the way. There are small mileage signs along the way that show how far you've gone on the trail, but don't forget those are just for Trail C and do not include the other trails you use to get to the main path.

The trail starts near the park's interpretive center. A big sign proclaims where the trail system begins. There is a nice restroom here and water fountains so you can fill up before heading out.

The trail follows a cement sidewalk for a few yards, then crosses one of the fingers of a wide bayou called Bird Island Chute via a nice big bridge. The waters are picturesque with their green color and families of canoeists and kayakers paddling by. By the way, the park has canoes, kayaks, and flat-bottom boats to rent by the hour or day.

Paddlers serenely float beneath the bridge on Trail C.

After the bridge the trail is a boardwalk where all three trails run together. Since Trail A is a very short boardwalk loop trail near the parking lot, you can expect heavy traffic on this section. Many families and people out for an afternoon stroll walk this path.

It won't be long, though, before Trail A drops off, then Trail B, and you find yourself on the orange-blazed Trail C. Here we leave the boardwalk and are on a more traditional dirt footpath.

The trail winds around the banks of Bird Island Chute across Old Bird Island with great views throughout. Almost immediately after setting foot on the trail, you're walking through a cypress and water tupelo swamp with its classic pea-green water and cypress knees. You are in the middle of a swamp, so it goes without saying, slather on the insect repellant.

Keep your eyes to the sky and treetops and you may see barred owls, red-bellied woodpeckers, and bald eagles. Carolina chickadees playfully dart from the brush in front of you.

On sections away from the swamp, the path is lined with beautiful sycamore, eastern cottonwood, and black walnut trees. Muscadine vines hang about you and, of course, there are those majestic southern oaks with Spanish moss–draped branches.

Several small boardwalks take you across this Louisiana swamp where there are alligators. I can't stress enough that gators are naturally afraid of humans—just don't get in their space.

As you walk, you may run up on an armadillo rustling through the underbrush or a raccoon, or find yourself sharing the trail with white-tailed deer. And near the water's edge, be careful where you sit or put your hand. There are many varieties of snakes that call this swamp and bayou home, including cottonmouth.

If you're looking to do a little backcountry camping and backpacking, this is the place to do it. There are eight primitive backpacking campsites along the trail that are available on a first-come, first-served basis for downright cheap. And the sites are all in beautiful locations and well off the trail.

Miles and Directions

0.0 Start from the trailhead across from the parking lot and playground. In 100 feet cross a big bridge over a bayou. The scene is very picturesque, with kayaks and canoes often seen paddling beneath. Just after the bridge the path turns into a 3-foot-wide paved walkway that leads to a kiosk that tells about the trail system. At this point Trail A turns off to the right (north). Trail B and Trail C head straight to the west. Continue straight on Trail B (blue-blazed).

0.2 Pass a sign that shows Trail B continues straight to the west; the white-blazed Trail A comes in from the right (north). Turn left here onto the orange-blazed Trail C. In less than 0.1 mile, come to a short boardwalk that leads to an observation deck with binoculars overlooking the river on your right (southwest). When done viewing, turn around and head back to the main trail. Once there turn right (southeast). There is a sign here showing the direction to the backpacking and canoeing campsites. In a few yards cross a long boardwalk.

0.3 Come to a Y. The blue Trail B turns off to the right (southwest). Take the left fork southeast on the orange Trail C. The trail is no longer paved. It is a dirt footpath about 2 to 3 feet wide. You'll be walking alongside a very pretty swamp lined with a small fern forest.

0.5 Pass backpacking campsite #1 on the right (west). In less than 0.1 mile, come to a Y. The left fork is a blue-blazed trail that leads to backpacking campsite #2. Take the right fork to the south. Just after the fork there is a nice view of the bayou.

0.6 Come to a Y. The right fork to the south leads to backpacking campsite #3. Take the left fork to the east. In a few yards cross a 100-foot bridge over a boggy area, then soon after pass another blue-blazed trail to a backpacking campsite on the left (north) and cross a short footbridge.

0.7 Pass a backpacking campsite on the right.

0.8 Cross a long boardwalk over a beautiful swamp. A sign in the swamp tells you this is the Barred Owl Trek.

0.9 Reach the end of the boardwalk.

1.1 Pass a 1-mile marker.

1.2 Pass backpacking campsite #4 on the right (southwest). Cross a short bridge over a creek.

1.3 Pass a large downed tree with big roots. A sign reminds you to watch for snakes, especially cottonmouth, living in those roots. You are right next to the swamp.

Trail C

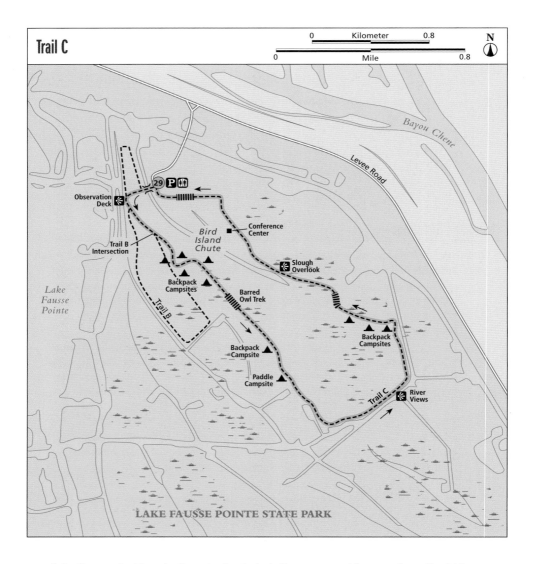

0   Kilometer   0.8

0   Mile   0.8

N

Bayou Chene

Levee Road

Observation Deck

Trail B Intersection

Bird Island Chute

Conference Center

Slough Overlook

Backpack Campsites

Barred Owl Trek

Backpack Campsites

Lake Fausse Pointe

Trail B

Backpack Campsite

Paddle Campsite

Trail C

River Views

LAKE FAUSSE POINTE STATE PARK

1.4 Cross a short boardwalk over a slough. Just after, pass a paddle campsite on the right (south) along the river. The campsite is above a bayou with a little wooden deck atop a bluff. The trail moves uphill a bit and now follows a bluff about 20 feet above the river, which is on your right (south).

1.6 Cross a boardwalk over a back bay. In less than 0.1, mile cross a bridge. There are nice views of the river here. You'll see the blue markers for the canoe trail along the banks.

1.8 Pass a "Halfway Point" sign on the right.

1.9 Great views of the river to your right (east). A fern forest lines the path, as well as large palmettos.

2.1 Pass a 2-mile marker.

2.2 Pass backpacking campsites #6 and #7 on the left (west).

2.3 It looks like the trail continues straight but it actually turns to the left (west). Look for the sign pointing the way and the orange blazes. In less than 0.1 mile, pass backpacking campsite #8 on the left (south) and soon after pass a very pretty watery swamp to the left (south).

2.5 Cross a boardwalk.

2.6 Come to the end of the boardwalk and a T intersection. A sign points the way to the conference center and the trail route to the left (north) and the park's cabins to the right. Turn left. In less than 0.1 mile, pass a 2.5-mile marker. You are paralleling a road on your right.

2.7 Pass a handwritten "Deer Watch" sign.

2.8 Pass a metal fire ring with benches used for nature talks on the right. In about 20 feet arrive at the Slough Lookout, a long boardwalk with an observation deck at the end that stretches into a wetland with some really nice views.

2.9 Arrive at the end of the lookout. When done viewing, turn around and head back to the main trail, and turn left (northwest).

3.1 Pass a 3-mile marker and cross another boardwalk over a swamp.

3.2 Come to the end of the boardwalk, and the trail comes out to a road. Follow the road straight ahead to the north, passing the conference center on your left.

3.3 Come to a T intersection with another paved road. Cross the road to the north and pick up the orange blazes on the opposite side, then cross a bridge over a runoff. In less than 0.1 mile, pass a side trail coming in from the right (north). A sign shows directions to the interpretive center. Continue straight to the west. You are walking parallel to the conference center road on your left.

3.5 Cross another boardwalk.

3.6 Come out to Levee Road at the interpretive center. Turn right (northwest) onto the paved road. Cross the road and follow the sidewalk back to the trailhead.

Hike Information

Local Information: St. Martin Parish Tourist Commission, 314 East Bridge St., Breaux Bridge, LA 70517; (337) 442-1597; cajuncountry.org

Local Events/Attractions: Acadian Memorial, 121 S. New Market St., St. Martinville; (337) 394-2258; acadianmemorial.org. The Acadian Memorial is a museum dedicated to preserving the history of the 3,000 men, women, and children who found refuge in this area after the British forced them from their home of Acadia. The memorial is open 7 days a week, except major holidays, from 10 a.m. to 4:30 p.m.

Lodging: Houseboat Adventures at Cypress Cove Landing, Cypress Cove Landing, Henderson; (800) 491-4662; houseboat-adventures.com. Ok, this is unique. You can stay in a houseboat tucked away in a remote cove of the Atchafalaya Basin, which is described as one of the last great river swamps in the country.

Restaurants: Café Des Amis, 140 East Bridge St., Breaux Bridge; (337) 332-5273; cafedesamis .com. You know you're in Cajun country when you visit Café Des Amis, especially on Sunday with their Zydeco Breakfast.

30 River Walk Trail

Another beautiful Southern black–water river is the centerpiece of this 2.6-mile loop trail. But not only will you be walking the banks of the wide and deep Calcasieu River, but also an impressive cypress swamp with its quintessential thick covering of Spanish moss and wildflower glades bursting with color.

Start: Trailhead on west side of parking lot
Distance: 2.6-mile loop
Hiking time: About 1.5 hours
Difficulty: Easy
Trail surface: Dirt, sand, boardwalk
Best seasons: Oct to Apr
Other trail users: Cyclists
Canine compatibility: Leashed pets permitted
Land status: State park
Nearest town: Lake Charles
Fees and permits: Admission fee (seniors 62 and older and children 3 and under free)

Schedule: Year-round; 6 a.m.–9 p.m. Sun–Thurs; 6 .a.m.–10 p.m. Fri, Sat, and the day preceding holidays
Maps: USGS DeQuincy, LA; maps available at entrance station
Trail contact: Sam Houston Jones State Park, 107 Sutherland Rd., Lake Charles, LA 70611; (888) 677-7264; crt.state .la.us/louisiana-state-parks/parks/ sam-houston-jones-state-park

Finding the trailhead: From the intersection of LA 379 / Sulphur Avenue and LA 378 in Lake Charles, take LA 378 north 2.9 miles. Turn right to stay on LA 378 North. Travel 1.7 miles and turn left onto LA 38 Spur West / Sam Houston Jones Parkway. Travel 0.9 mile and turn left onto Sutherland Road (Sutherland Road will become Gahagan Lane in 0.2 mile). Continue 0.2 mile and come to the entrance station. After paying your fee, continue south on Sam Houston Jones State Park Road 0.2 mile and take the left fork. Arrive at the parking lot and trailhead in 0.4 mile. GPS: N30 17.524' / W93 15.519'

The Hike

We get another chance to visit one of the South's amazing black–water rivers, tinted a darker color by the tannin of shoreline trees, this time along a beautiful 2.6-mile loop trail, the River Walk Trail. The trail meanders along the banks of the wide and deep West Fork of the Calcasieu River and weaves its way through an impressive cypress swamp with its classic thick blanket of Spanish moss and wildflower glades bursting with color.

This hike actually uses two trails: the River Walk Trail and the Cypress Tupelo Trail. Together these two trails give you a good feel for this wonderful park and the land and water features it holds.

The River Walk Trail begins at one of the many parking areas that line the shoulder of Sam Houston Jones State Park Road. In fact, just about the entire road has parking spaces marked off. The trail is a 5- to 6-foot-wide gravel path at the start that

The River Walk Trail parallels a beautiful cedar swamp with plenty of wildflowers.

quickly narrows to a more traditional 2-foot-wide sand and dirt trail. The path is not blazed except at the beginning of the hike and at the end, where an orange blaze shows which path you're getting ready to hike. Both blazes are on the trailhead kiosks. The path then meanders through a forest filled with longleaf pine, southern magnolia, mockernut hickory, dogwood, and yaupon.

Needless to say, the trail gets its name from the fact that you will be walking alongside a river. You will be hiking along the banks where the West Fork of the Calcasieu River makes a big U, or oxbow. This is a wide, deep, green river. Don't worry about missing the river views. The trail is directly on its banks, so you'll have a great view around every turn.

As the trail makes its way halfway around the bend, you will see across the river some really nice, and expensive, houses with families frolicking in the water and on boats. At this point you will start to notice a watery pond and wetland to your left, and soon you will be walking next to a beautiful cypress swamp with long, flowing

Spanish moss hanging from the branches. Ducks, egrets, herons, and pileated wood-peckers will frequently be seen.

By the way, the hard-packed dirt of this trail makes it an excellent bike riding path. Families bring their children here to get their first "off-road" biking experience, so keep your eyes open for them as they round the bends.

The River Walk Trail finally moves away from the river to the west and arrives back at the park road near a very nice restroom. Cross the road here to the west into a picnic area. Keep walking straight, and as you near the brush on the far side, you will see the trailhead for the red-blazed Cypress Tupelo Trail. This is a very narrow dirt footpath along the eastern and northern edge of a magnificent cypress and tupelo swamp.

The blazes on the trees were faded when I hiked the trail, but it is still pretty easy to follow. Numerous signs warn you that a mother alligator lives in the brush along the banks and nests here, so if hiking with small children or a dog, keep them close by.

At about 0.3 mile from the end of the hike, you will come to a big, wide observation deck with great views of the swamps and the many birds that call the park home.

Soon you will arrive back at the road and will follow it to the south and east, but before you make it back to your car, you will have two more views of the swamp from a steel and cement bridge and an observation deck next to the road.

Miles and Directions

0.0 Start from the trailhead on the east side of the parking lot.

0.1 A short side trail to the right (northwest) takes you to the banks of the river for a nice view.

0.2 Another good view of the river is on your right (northwest). From here on, you are walking right along the banks of the river. In less than 0.1 mile, pass a bench on the left.

0.3 Pass an orange marker on a 4-by-4-inch post on the left and a bench on the right. Along this section you will see many beautiful houses lining the banks of the river on the opposite side (south).

0.4 A cedar swamp begins on your left (north) side, with the river to your right. Along this section you will have some excellent views of the swamp and many varieties of birds and reptiles.

0.5 Pass a bench on the left.

0.6 The best view of the swamp is to your left, along with some towering longleaf pines.

1.1 A side trail to the right (east) leads to the banks of the river. The trail becomes more enclosed through here.

1.2 The trail crosses a large culvert with a runoff to the river. It's very pretty through here, with lots of Spanish moss and cedar knees in the swamp.

1.4 Cross another culvert and the prettiest view of the swamp to your left, with Spanish moss and wildflower glades. In less than 0.1 mile, cross a third culvert. The canopy opens up to reveal a wide view of the river to the right (east).

1.5 As the trail turns to the west away from the river, you will see some old fishing/swimming piers and you will be walking next to a chain-link fence to your right. The trail widens out again.

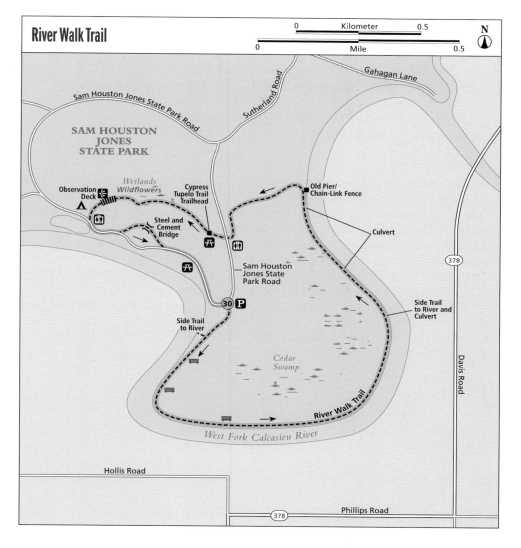

0   Kilometer   0.5

0   Mile   0.5

N

River Walk Trail

Gahagan Lane

Sam Houston Jones State Park Road

Sutherland Road

SAM HOUSTON JONES STATE PARK

Wetlands Wildflowers

Observation Deck

Cypress Tupelo Trail Trailhead

Old Pier/ Chain-Link Fence

Steel and Cement Bridge

Culvert

Sam Houston Jones State Park Road

30 P

Side Trail to River and Culvert

Side Trail to River

Cedar Swamp

378

River Walk Trail

Davis Road

West Fork Calcasieu River

Hollis Road

378

Phillips Road

1.6 Come to an intersection at a power line. Straight (west) takes you to the second trailhead for the River Walk Trail. Turn left (south) under a power line.

1.7 Come to a restroom. Turn to your right (west) and cross the road, then walk straight into the picnic area. (***Option:*** You can continue straight at this point and follow the road 0.1 mile back to your car, skipping the red-blazed Cypress Tupelo Trail.)

1.8 Come to the Cypress Tupelo Trail trailhead. The trail is a narrow 2-foot-wide sandy path and is blazed in red. A swamp is to your left (southeast). Heed the warnings about the alligators! There is a mama here that protects her nest.

1.9 Come to a Y. Take the left fork to the south.

2.0 Cross over a pretty wetland with wildflowers over a long composite boardwalk. There is a large observation deck in the middle and your best chance to see an alligator.

2.1 Come to one of the park's campgrounds. Turn left (southwest). In less than 0.1 mile, pass a restroom on your left and follow the park road to the southeast.

2.2 Turn to the left (north) off the road onto a dirt and sand footpath. There is a picnic area here, and you'll be walking along a cypress swamp with more wildflowers.

2.3 Cross a slough over a steel and cement bridge. On the opposite side come to a parking lot. Continue straight to the southeast and come to the park road again. Follow the road to your left (southeast). In less than 0.1 mile, pass an observation deck on your left.

2.6 Arrive back at the trailhead.

Hike Information

Local Information: Lake Charles Visitors Bureau, 1205 N. Lakeshore Drive, Lake Charles, LA 70601; (337) 436-9588; visitlakecharles.org

Local Events/Attractions: Contraband Days, 900 Lake Shore Dr., Lake Charles; (337) 436-5508; contrabanddays.com. I could lay on a bunch of pirate clichés, but I'll leave that to the experts as the city of Lake Charles celebrates its pirate heritage during this annual festival held the last weekend of April. There is plenty of history, entertainment, and food. Arrggh! Sorry.

Lodging: Sam Houston Jones State Park Campground, 107 Sutherland Rd., Lake Charles; (888) 677-7264; crt.state.la.us/louisiana-state-parks/parks/sam-houston-jones-state-park. Sam Houston Jones State Park has many lodging options, including 6 cabins that sleep 6 each and 58 improved campsites.

Restaurants: Steamboat Bill's on the Lake, 1004 N. Lakeshore Dr., Lake Charles; (337) 494-1070; steamboatbills.com. Cajun and Creole cooking.

31 Sabine Wetland Walkway

Tucked away in the far southwestern corner of Louisiana, almost directly on the Texas-Louisiana border, in the middle of nowhere (or as close as you can get), you will find the Sabine Wetland Walkway. Despite its location, this 1.4-mile cement and boardwalk path is a popular tourist destination, as people come from all over the country to this magnificent expansive marsh with its tall bullwhip grass and Roseau cane blowing in the breeze to view the many varieties of animals that live here, including northern shoveler, blue-winged teal, marsh rabbit, and maybe a glimpse of an alligator.

Start: Trailhead on north side of parking lot
Distance: 1.4-mile loop
Hiking time: About 1 hour
Difficulty: Easy over cement walkway and boardwalk
Trail surface: Cement sidewalk, boardwalk
Best seasons: Oct to Apr
Other trail users: None
Canine compatibility: Leashed dogs permitted but not recommended due to alligators

Land status: National wildlife refuge
Nearest town: Cameron Parish
Fees and permits: None
Schedule: Year-round, sunrise to sunset
Maps: USGS Browns Lake, LA
Trail contact: Sabine National Wildlife Refuge, 3000 Holly Beach Hwy., Hackberry, LA 70645; (337) 762-3816; fws.gov/refuges/profiles/index.cfm?id=43640

Finding the trailhead: From the intersection of Gallegos Road and LA 27 in Hackberry, take LA 27 south 13.3 miles. Turn right into the parking lot. The trailhead is on the north side of the parking lot. GPS: N29 51.982'/W93 27.344'

The Hike

Despite it being in the middle of nowhere at the very southern end of Cameron Parish, Sabine National Wildlife Refuge is one popular destination. In fact, over 280,000 people venture out to this wetland to view the many birds and species of wildlife that inhabit the area.

The refuge encompasses over 120,000 acres of brackish and freshwater marsh land and is one of the largest estuarine-dependent marine nurseries in Louisiana. It was established in 1939 with a mission to preserve and protect the water and vegetation of this region, which is so important for the survival of the 300 species of birds, 26 species of mammals, 41 species of reptiles, and 132 species of fish and invertebrates that call this area home. The refuge also protects an important wintering area for waterfowl that migrate south through the Mississippi and Central Flyways.

Before heading out on this hike, I would suggest you stop by the Sabine National Wildlife Refuge Visitor Center. Located on LA 27, 7 miles north of the Sabine

Expect amazing panoramic vistas along the popular Sabine Wetland Walkway.

Wetland Walkway trailhead, the center features exhibits about the inhabitants of the region, videos, and a diorama of the wetlands with your animatronic Cajun hosts, T'Maurice and Tante Marie.

Marsh grasses and plants can be seen for miles to the horizon from the trail's observation deck. The tall, round-stemmed bullwhip grass that you will see can be used to determine where the deeper water is. The predominate plant you will see on the hike is Roseau cane, which is thick along the path. The cane acts as nesting areas for birds and wildlife and also as cover for protection from predators.

Bring your binoculars and walk quietly, and you are guaranteed to see many of those 300 species of birds that have been cataloged here. Chances are you will glimpse great blue heron, red-winged blackbird, white ibis, roseate spoonbill, kingfisher, and yellowthroat. As for wildlife, the most common critter you will come across is the eastern cottontail rabbit—they are everywhere!

And, of course, there is the most popular attraction of this hike: the American alligator. The best time to see gators is in the spring or fall. Male alligators can be as much as 11 to 12 feet long, while female gators average 8 to 10 feet in length; just about half of that length is their tail. The tail is mostly used for propulsion in the water but can be a lethal weapon out of the water. Their average weight is 800 pounds, with some granddaddies coming in at over 1,000 pounds.

▶ **When the Acadians were exiled from what is now Nova Scotia in the nineteenth century and moved to Louisiana, Americans couldn't pronounce "Acadian" so the name was Americanized to "Cajun." Cajuns are fun-loving people with joie de vivre, "love of life" (and food).**

Alligators can stay underwater for up to seven hours if they are not actively swimming or hunting. They are incredibly fast in the water and, of course, much slower on land, but don't let that fool you. They can run with a burst of amazing speed for a short distance. And they eat anything that comes near the water's edge—deer, raccoon, nutria, and dogs. While dogs are permitted on the trail, you may want to leave them behind for this hike. At least keep them on a short leash. Children should also be kept under close supervision. You may be one of the fortunate ones who get to see a gator sunning itself on the walkway or crossing it. Just remember to keep your distance from them, and if they don't move out of your path, turn around and head back.

Gator "courtship" begins in late May through June, with nesting soon afterwards. It is believed that there are over 1,000 alligators living in the refuge, not bad for a species of wildlife that was on the endangered species list thirty years ago but has since been removed.

The trail begins at the trailhead on the north side of the parking lot on LA 27. The path is mostly a cement sidewalk about 4 feet wide, with the exception of a 0.3-mile boardwalk that takes you to an expansive view of this coastal prairie on an observation deck and connects the overlook to the return segment. The entire length of the trail is ADA-accessible. There are several benches under shelters along the route, a must in the sweltering Southern sun.

The trailhead has some very informative posters, and advice about alligators, that you should read over before heading out. There is also a nice men's and women's restroom here and a water fountain.

Oh, and just a friendly little reminder: No matter what time of year you visit, even in the dead of winter when it is still pretty warm on the Gulf Coast, bring your insect repellant! When I was there, it was interesting to watch other visitors start the path at a nice, leisurely pace as they disappeared around the bend, then return moments later in full gallop covered by mosquitoes.

Miles and Directions

0.0 Start from the trailhead at the parking lot. Take the cement sidewalk to the right (north-east). You will be paralleling LA 27 on your right, buffered by a narrow bayou lined with Roseau cane and bamboo. Marsh rabbits dart across the path in front of you, and pinkish-red roseate spoonbills wade in the water.

0.2 Pass a trail shelter on your right as the trail bends to the northwest.

0.3 Pass a bench on the left.

0.5 Cross a short wooden bridge over a slough.

0.6 Pass a bench on the left. The boardwalk splits off to the left (west) and straight to the north. Continue straight.

0.7 Come to a composite observation deck with magnificent views of the marsh (there are binoculars here). When done viewing, turn around and head back to the intersection at mile 0.6.

Sabine Wetland Walkway

0.9 Back at the intersection, turn right (west) onto the side boardwalk.

1.0 Cross a bridge over a slough and arrive at a shelter with a bench. Turn left (southeast) onto the cement sidewalk. A bayou runs alongside the trail on the left.

1.2 Pass an observation deck overlooking the bayou on the right.

1.4 Arrive back at the trailhead.

Hike Information

Local Information: Cameron Parish Tourist Commission, PO Box 388, Cameron, LA 70631; (337) 775-5718; cameronparishtouristcommission.org

Local Events/Attractions: Marshland Festival, Lake Charles Civic Center, 900 Lakeshore Dr., Lake Charles; (337) 540-3182; marshlandfestival.com. Celebrate Louisiana's beautiful marshes, music, and Cajun cuisine at the annual Marshland Festival, which is held the last weekend of July.

Lodging: Sam Houston Jones State Park Campground, 107 Sutherland Rd., Lake Charles; (888) 677-7264; crt.state.la.us/louisiana-state-parks/parks/sam-houston-jones-state-park. Sam Houston Jones State Park has many lodging options, including 6 cabins that sleep 6 each and 58 improved campsites.

Restaurants: Mr. A's Deli, 905 Main St., Hackberry; (337) 762-4150

Louisiana Honorable Mentions

That's not the end of the hiking adventure in Louisiana. There are many more treks you should check out. Here are a few to get you started. Pay a visit and let us know what you think. Maybe the hike should be upgraded, or maybe you know of a little-known hike that would make a good honorable mention.

L Boy Scout Trail

As you drive south off I-10 toward Fontainebleau State Park, you'll see a sign for Big Branch Marsh National Wildlife Refuge. Don't pass it! Stop by and pay a visit to the visitor center and then hike the Boy Scout Trail. The visitor center used to be a Redemptorist seminary. The enormous building was once the chapel and now it is an amazing natural science center with exhibits depicting scenes and wildlife from the eight refuges in the area, videos, and an interactive cabin. There are also some nice walks through the camellia and bayou garden around the center. The visitor center is open Thursday through Saturday from 9 a.m. to 4 p.m. For a good long hike, try the 4.5-mile Boy Scout Trail. The trailhead is only a short 7 miles from the visitor center off Bayou Paquet Road. The first half mile is a boardwalk around a pine flatwood forest with an oddity: A single live oak estimated to be 700 years old sticks out like a sore thumb. From there the trail is a 2-mile gravel path to the banks of Bayou Lacombe. An observation platform gives you a chance to get a good high-level look at the marsh and the pine forest directly behind you. You will see old clay bricks here. At one time this was a loading dock for the locally made brick that built much of New Orleans French Quarter. For more information contact Big Branch Marsh at (985) 882-2000 or visit fws.gov/bigbranchmarsh.

M Barataria Preserve

Earlier in this guide we explored the amazing bayous and marshes of the National Park Service's Barataria Preserve (hike 24). The preserve is within the shadows of the Big Easy but a truly fantastic natural wonder to hike through. After you've finished that hike, don't rush off for beignets quite yet. Almost directly across from the trailhead on the opposite side of LA 45 is another series of trails, almost 8 miles in all! Trails with names like Plantation, Christmas, Ring Levee, Wood Duck, and Old Barataria all interconnect, giving you ample opportunity to pick your own route through several vegetation zones. Wood ducks nest in the cavities of trees near the ponds, and crawfish mounds protrude from the trail bed. For more information contact the Jean Lafitte National Historical Park and Preserve at (504) 689-3690 or visit nps.gov/jela/barataria-preserve.htm.

N Bonnie Carre Spillway

The Bonnie Carre Spillway is located off the banks of the mighty Mississippi in Norco, Louisiana. It is used for flood control, diverting rising waters of the Mississippi into Lake Pontchartrain. The spillway is a US Army Corps of Engineers property, and with the help of volunteers and nonprofit organizations like the New Orleans Area Mountain Bike Organization (NOAMBO), there are 5.5 miles of hiking trail to explore. This is a loop trail with plenty of excellent views of the waterway but be careful. This is also a mountain biking course so keep your eyes open. For more information contact the US Army Corps of Engineers at (985) 764-7484 or visit mvn.usace.army.mil/Missions/Recreation/BonnetCarreSpillway.aspx.

O Acadiana Park Nature Station

Back in 1971 the City of Lafayette realized that it was growing rapidly, and something needed to be done to help protect some of the natural beauty of the area. The city purchased a 42-acre tract of land and called it Acadiana Park Nature Station. The park has a single mission—to "reacclimatize people to their natural surroundings"—and does this by providing a wide range of educational programs for all ages most any day of the week (visit their website for a schedule). The park is literally just off I-10 at exit 100. There are 4 miles of trails at the park. These are dirt footpaths lined with resurrection fern and dwarf palmetto that weave through the landscape, with the newer sections skirting the banks of the Vermillion River with views from atop 20-foot bluffs. Virginia opossum, short-tail shrew, cottontail rabbit, and nine-banded armadillo are commonly seen on the trails. The trails are open 7 days a week from dawn to dusk. The nature station is open Monday through Friday 8 a.m. to 5 p.m. and Saturday and Sunday from 11 a.m. to 5 p.m. For more information contact Acadiana Park Nature Station at (337) 291-8448 or visit naturestation.org.

Texas

Amazing hiking adventures await you along the Texas Gulf Coast. Endless barrier islands and wildlife refuges provide countless opportunities to get out and explore this amazing landscape.

Our adventure begins near the Louisiana state line, where we continue hiking through salt marsh. On the Oak Bayou Loop (hike 33) at Galveston Island State Park, you will have the opportunity to explore this world up close as the trail meanders through the marsh to the beautiful wide banks of Oak Bayou and over an impressive long boardwalk across Butterowe Bayou. On the Egret Loop and Heron's Walk section of the trail, you can wander about watching the roseate spoonbills, great blue herons, and snowy and reddish egrets as they search the grounds for food, then see the state's effort to restore the marsh.

Moving away from the coast a little to just south of Houston, the action of the flow of Big Creek creates a stunning hike called the Lake Loop (hike 34). The creek has formed two separate horseshoes in the past few decades, attracting an unbelievable array of birds to the site, like egrets and terns and the marsh duck. Wildflowers such as Indian blanket and water primrose zap the banks of the lakes with brilliant colors.

Then there are the wildlife refuges that stretch almost the entire length of the state's Big Bend. These refuges are protected as part of the Central Flyway, where hundreds of species of birds migrate to and from each year. One of those, the endangered whooping crane, can be found exclusively at the Aransas National Wildlife Refuge (hike 38, Heron Flats Loop).

Then we wrap up our journeys just north of Mexico at Corpus Christi, where one of my favorite hikes is located—the Salt Island Marsh Trail (hike 40). This hike is a 2.2-mile out-and-back almost entirely on a boardwalk through a spectacular salt marsh to a single, lone island. The variety of birds you will spy on the hike is amazing, as well as the plants like the glasswort.

As you would expect, the weather is very pleasant all along the coast. At the far southwest side in Corpus Christi, temperatures run from an average high of 67°F and low of 47°F in January to 94°F and 75°F in July. Unlike other areas along the Gulf Coast, rainfall is lighter here, with the wettest month being 4.5 inches in August. On the opposite side, near the Louisiana border, the temperatures range from a winter high of 62°F and low of 50°F to a summer high of 87°F and low of 76°F.

Also, as you would expect, hurricanes do hit the Texas coast (see the sidebar "The Hurricane of 1900" in hike 33, Oak Bayou Loop). Just be sure to keep vigilant during your visit when it's hurricane season (generally June to November) and listen to the warnings posted by local EMA officials.

32 Gambusia Marsh Nature Trail

A short but oh-so-satisfying boardwalk hike through the marshes of Texas's northern Gulf Coast. This is especially so if you hike in the early morning when egrets, ibis, and flocks of ducks take flight in the mist and river otters laze on the boardwalk, while the bubbles of alligators swimming beneath your feet add an element of excitement to the hike.

Start: Trailhead on north side of parking lot
Distance: 0.9-mile lollipop
Hiking time: About 1 hour
Difficulty: Easy over a narrow boardwalk inches above the marsh
Trail surface: Boardwalk
Best seasons: Sept to Apr
Other trail users: None
Canine compatibility: Leashed dogs permitted but not recommended due to alligators
Land status: State park
Nearest town: Sabine Pass
Fees and permits: Admission fee (children 12 and under free)

Schedule: Year-round; 8 a.m.–9 p.m. Sun–Thurs, 8 a.m.–10 p.m. Fri–Sat
Maps: USGS Sabine Pass, TX; maps available at entrance station
Trail contact: Sea Rim State Park, 19335 S. Gulfway Dr., Sabine Pass, TX 77655; (409) 971-2559; tpwd.state.tx.us/state-parks/sea-rim
Special considerations: Hunting is allowed in the park on certain days in the fall and winter. Visit the park's website for information on dates and restrictions.

Finding the trailhead: From the intersection of Dowling Road and TX 87 in Sabine Pass, take TX 87 south 10.1 miles. Turn left onto Park Road and in a few yards come to the entrance station. After paying your fee, continue south on Park Road and in a few yards come to a Y; take the left fork. Follow Park Road 0.4 mile and arrive at the parking lot. The trailhead is on the north side of the parking area. GPS: N29 40.600' / W94 02.345'

The Hike

The Gambusia Marsh Nature Trail at Sea Rim State Park is a short one, coming in at just under 1 mile long, but it is oh so satisfying. The trail is entirely made up of a 4-foot-wide boardwalk that is only inches above the watery marsh. Long, tall bamboo stalks line the path, as do marsh grasses like cordgrass, marsh salt grass, and alligator weed.

Sea Rim State Park has a total of 5.2 miles of Gulf coastal shoreline and over 4,000 acres of marshland. Here you can swim in the surf of the Gulf, play on the beach, or do a little bird and wildlife watching. If you're a paddler as well as a hiker, there is a 10-mile- and 5-mile-long blue trail through the marsh.

The park has had its share of troubles in the recent past and they both had names—Ike and Rita. In 2005 Hurricane Rita came ashore and ravaged the park, taking out

A river otter does a little cleanup on the boardwalk at Sea Rim State Park.

much of its infrastructure. With only two weeks before the scheduled reopening of the park in 2008, Hurricane Ike blasted in and destroyed it once again. It wasn't until the summer of 2014 that the park reopened, this time bigger, better, and ready for the next storm.

The Gambusia Marsh Nature Trail is named for the fish found in these marsh waters: the gambusia, or mosquito fish. These fish are native to the Texas marshes and people love them because they eat mosquitoes. With their unique upturned mouth, they can easily snatch mosquito larvae from the surface water. The problem is that people bring them to their local ponds and lakes where they are not a native species, and they soon become invasive and threaten local fish.

The best time to hike this trail is either early morning or late evening, when the birds are either waking up or calling it a day. Catching a flock of ducks taking flight in an early morning mist is an inspiring sight. Do remember that you are hiking directly over a marsh, and even though the gambusia fish love mosquitoes, they can still be formidable foes if you walk this trail during those hours.

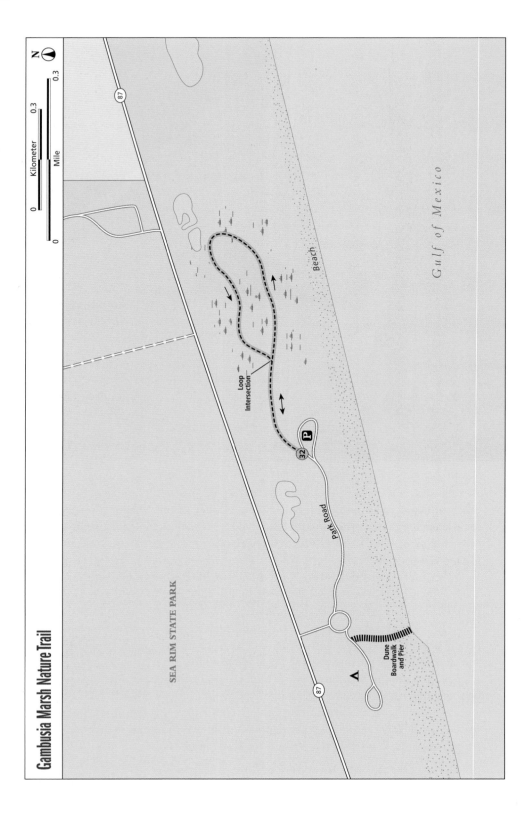

Gambusia Marsh Nature Trail

SEA RIM STATE PARK

87

Park Road

Dune
Boardwalk
and Pier

Loop
Intersection

32
P

Beach

Gulf of Mexico

87

N

Kilometer
0   0.3   0.3

Mile
0   0.3

The wildlife here is spectacular, especially the birds. This location is a resting spot for migrating birds as they fly the Central Flyway to and from Mexico. Several species of heron live here, including the great blue, Louisiana green, and yellow-crowned night heron. The beautiful red hues of the roseate spoonbill will be seen here, along with the snowy and cattle egret. And the waters are filled with ducks, including wood, mottled, American black, and mallard.

There are mammals here, too, and I was quite surprised when rounding a bend to see a river otter sitting on the boardwalk cleaning up. The otter can grow to 11 inches long and weigh as much as 30 pounds. They love to dine on fish but will sometimes partake in crayfish, small rodents, or turtles. Raccoons also like to use the boardwalk to move between ponds, and you may spot a bobcat, coyote, or even nutria, a large rodent-like animal akin to the muskrat.

The deepest part of the marsh appears to be around the area where the loop reconnects to itself. As I stood there taking in a flock of coot in the early morning light, I was surprised to hear something bubbling underneath me. Looking over, I saw an alligator swimming underwater beneath the boardwalk. There are plenty of warning signs about the gators. Heed them and keep your children close by and your dog on a short leash. Don't allow anyone in the water.

Miles and Directions

0.0 Start from the trailhead on the north side of the parking lot and head to the northeast on the wooden boardwalk.

0.2 Pass the junction of the loop on your left. Continue straight to the east.

0.7 Arrive back at the end of the loop (the junction at mile 0.2). Turn right (west) and continue on the boardwalk.

0.9 Arrive back at the trailhead.

Hike Information

Local Information: Ben J. Rogers Regional Visitor Center, 5055 IH-10 South, Beaumont, TX 77705; (866) 432-8951; co.jefferson.tx.us/VisitorCenter/brrvc.htm

Local Events/Attractions: Sabine Pass Battleground, 6100 Dick Dowling Rd., Port Arthur; (512) 463-7948; visitsabinepassbattleground.com. Sabine Pass Battleground is the site of a significant battle of the Civil War. Here in 1863 the Confederate army defeated four Union gunboats and prevented the Union army from moving into Texas. Open daily 8 a.m.–5 p.m. Sept–Apr, 8 a.m.–8 p.m. May–Aug.

Lodging: Sea Rim State Park Campground, 19335 S. Gulfway Dr., Sabine Pass; (409) 971-2559; tpwd.state.tx.us/state-parks/sea-rim/fees-facilities/campsites. Sea Rim has 8 primitive campsites and 15 improved sites with water and electricity, plus 6 cabins with all amenities and canal views.

Restaurants: Olde Time Diner, 5405 S. Gulfway Dr., Sabine Pass; (409) 971-2573. A good old-time diner serving up breakfast, lunch, and dinner.

33 Oak Bayou Loop

Take a walk along the bayous and tidal flats of Galveston on the Oak Bayou Loop. This loop uses three trails—the Clapper Rail Trail, Heron's Walk, and Egret Loop—to take you over some beautiful wide bayous, through the salt marsh, and to an area where a wetland restoration project is under way.

Start: Trailhead on north side of parking lot
Distance: 1.7-mile loop trail with out and backs
Hiking time: About 1.5 hours
Difficulty: Easy over flat, level terrain
Trail surface: Boardwalk, grass, dirt
Best seasons: Year-round
Other trail users: None
Canine compatibility: Leashed pets permitted
Land status: State park

Nearest town: Galveston
Fees and permits: Admission fee (children 12 and under free)
Schedule: Year-round, 8 a.m.–10 p.m.
Maps: USGS Lake Como, TX; maps available at entrance station
Trail contact: Galveston Island State Park, 14901 FM 3005, Galveston, TX 77554; (409) 737-1222; tpwd.state.tx.us/state-parks/galveston-island

Finding the trailhead: From the intersection of TX 3005 and 8 Mile Road in Galveston, take TX 3005 southwest 5.3 miles. Turn left onto Park Road 66. Travel 0.2 mile and come to the entrance station and park headquarters. After paying your fee, turn around and head back to TX 3005. Go straight across TX 3005 and take the unnamed road to the northwest. Follow this road for 0.5 mile and take the first left. Travel 0.4 mile and turn right into the parking lot. The trailhead is on the north side of the parking area. GPS: N29 12.041' / W94 57.735'

The Hike

As I pulled up to Galveston Island State Park, the Glen Campbell song kept playing in my head incessantly, "Galveston, oh, Galveston." I had been told about the marvelous hikes here and was excited to get going, but unlike Glen's song, you won't hear sea waves crashing here, at least not on this fabulous hike along the bayous and wetlands of the northern coast of the island.

The trail is strewn with wildflowers of all types. Indian blanket, or firewheels, with their distinctive red petals with yellow tips brighten up the greens and browns of the marsh. There are also many prickly pear cactuses along the trail bed adorned with big purple bulbs on their pads, waiting to explode into colorful flowers in the summer.

Of course, being on a wetland you can expect a good variety of birds. The reddish egret with its auburn head and slate gray body calls the wetland home. They are called "active foragers" and you may see them run, jump, and spin to catch food. Roseate spoonbills are easily recognizable with their light pink and red color and

A view of this trail's namesake

their namesake spoon-shaped bills. Great blue herons and snowy egrets share the feeding grounds, too.

This hike uses three trails: the Clapper Rail Trail, Egret Loop, and Heron's Walk. It is an easy walker over dirt, grass, and sand footpaths. You will cross three boardwalks, two of which cross beautiful wide bayous and one of those is about 0.1 mile long.

Just after heading out from the trailhead, you will come to an elevated observation deck maybe 20 feet up. Here in the wetlands of the Gulf Coast, that's high enough to give you a sweeping view of the landscape, and it's the best place to do a little birding. From here the trail meanders off to the northeast along the grass and dirt path, crossing two boardwalks over narrow bayous and then a third over the wide Butterowe Bayou. The view is simply amazing from the center of the walkway.

Continuing straight, you will pass the Heron's Walk Trail, which will be our return route for this leg, and come to the Egret Loop Trail. The trail comes in from

THE HURRICANE OF 1900

On September 8, 1900, Galveston's population of 40,000 residents swelled with vacationers as the summer was winding down. The "Oleander City" had been a popular resort destination for Americans since the town was incorporated in 1839.

A week before, National Weather Service meteorologists knew that a storm was brewing in the Caribbean. The storm hit Cuba on September 4, then moved to just north of Key West on September 6. Back in 1900 there was no way to track storms and no radio communications from ships to report the hurricane's position. The best guess anyone had was that the hurricane would track to the northeast and head out into the Atlantic. That is, everyone except for one meteorologist, Isaac Cline, who on the evening of September 7 noticed that swells of "unusual heights were coming in from the southeast." Concerned about what he saw, Cline ordered hurricane warning flags be raised.

The next morning he hitched up his horses to a carriage and rode to the beach, where he warned everyone to get to higher ground, which on the island was only 9 feet above sea level. What happened next was truly a day, and night, of terror for the residents of Galveston. The wind increased exponentially to 100 miles per hour, then 120, then an estimated 140 mph, what today would be classified as a category 4 hurricane.

The ocean whipped into a white frenzy and inundated the tiny island with a 15.7-foot storm surge. Every structure was destroyed, and it is estimated that up to 8,000 people died. To this day the Galveston Hurricane of 1900 is the deadliest storm in US history.

the north and continues straight to the east. You'll want to continue straight for 0.1 mile for a good look at Oak Bayou from its banks.

After checking out the bayou, you'll retrace your steps and head back to the where the Egret Loop heads north. This trail takes you directly into the marsh as it connects with the Heron's Walk Trail. Now, I said that the total length of this loop is 1.7 miles, but remember that you are free to roam about and explore, and this is the perfect place to do just that.

When you're done exploring, head south on the Heron's Walk Trail for more great views of birds and Butterowe Bayou. Retrace your steps back across the water, but at the end of the boardwalk instead of heading back to the trailhead, turn right to the northwest on the Clapper Rail Trail.

This section of the hike is right in the middle of the park's wetland restoration project. Wetlands filter impurities from the water and soak up excess storm water. This helps protect the surrounding environment and habitat for all of the wetland creatures. Over time wave erosion threatened the Galveston wetlands, so in 2000 to stop their destruction, the state built marsh terraces. These are large, hollow fabric cylinders that are about 2 feet above the surface of the water. They are filled with sand and then planted with native wetland plants and grasses. The elevated terraces prevent erosion, and the native plants are then replanted elsewhere. You will see their work to the northwest and west of this section of the trail.

From here simply follow the loop back around to the trailhead, then head to the other side of the park and hit the beach.

Miles and Directions

0.0 Start at the trailhead on the north side of the parking area. The trail starts wide (about 4 feet) and grassy. In less than 0.1 mile, come to an observation deck at a Y in the trail with excellent views of the marsh. After viewing from the deck, take the right fork to the north onto the Clapper Rail Trail.

0.1 Come to a bench and cross a beautiful wide bayou over a boardwalk.

0.2 Come to a Y. The left fork to the northwest will be the second loop of this hike. Right now take the right fork to the northeast and cross Butterowe Bayou over a long boardwalk with beautiful views of the bayou.

0.3 Come to the end of the boardwalk. There is a bench here. Continue straight to the northeast on the dirt path and in a few yards come to a Y. The left fork is the Heron's Walk Trail and will be your return route for the hike. Take the right fork to the north onto the connector trail between the Egret Loop and Heron's Walk Trails.

0.4 Come to the intersection with the Egret Loop Trail. The trail comes in from the left (northwest) and goes to the right (northeast). Continue straight to the northeast on the Egret Loop Trail.

0.5 Come to the banks of Oak Bayou and some wonderful views. Turn around and retrace your steps to the intersection at mile 0.4.

0.6 Back at the intersection at mile 0.4, turn right (northwest) to continue on the Egret Loop Trail. In less than 0.1 mile, the Egret Loop joins with the Heron's Walk Trail, which comes in from the south. Continue straight to the northwest.

0.7 Come to three benches. Feel free to explore the area. When done, return to the intersection at mile 0.6.

0.9 Come to an intersection with the Heron's Walk and Egret Loop Trails. Take the right fork to the south onto the Heron's Walk Trail. In less than 0.1 mile, pass a bench with excellent bayou views.

1.0 Arrive back at the intersection with the boardwalk at mile 0.2. Turn right (southwest) and follow the boardwalk back across the bayou.

1.2 After crossing the boardwalk, do not retrace your steps back to the trailhead. Turn right (northwest) onto the Clapper Rail Trail. The trail opens up for expansive views of the marsh through here.

1.4 Pass a bench on the left. In the distance to the south, you can see the observation deck where you started the trip. The trail is muddy and slippery along this final stretch.

1.7 Arrive back at the observation deck. Turn right (southeast) onto the approach trail that started the trek. In less than 0.1 mile, arrive back at the trailhead.

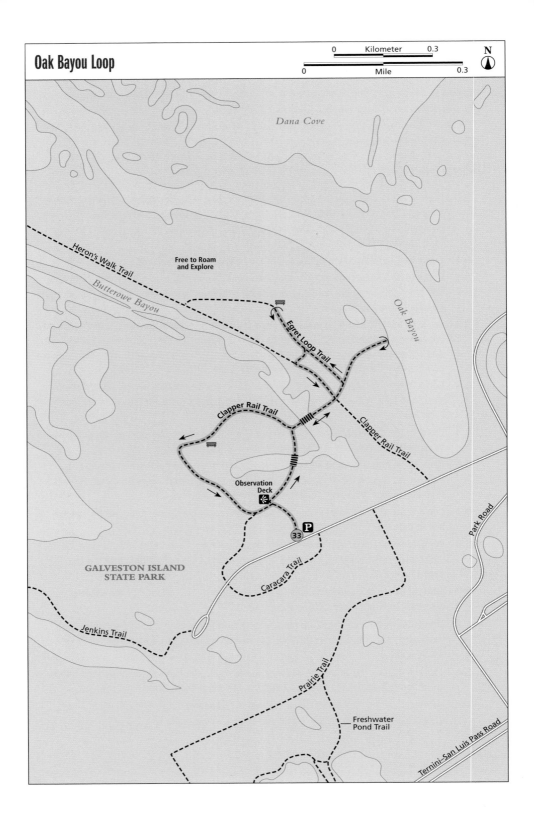

Oak Bayou Loop

0   Kilometer   0.3

0   Mile   0.3

N

Dana Cove

Heron's Walk Trail

Free to Roam
and Explore

Butterowe Bayou

Oak Bayou

Egret Loop Trail

Clapper Rail Trail

Clapper Rail Trail

Observation
Deck

P
(33)

Caracara Trail

GALVESTON ISLAND
STATE PARK

Jenkins Trail

Park Road

Prairie Trail

Freshwater
Pond Trail

Termini–San Luis Pass Road

Hike Information

Local Information: Galveston Island Tourism and Marketing, 2328 Broadway, Galveston, TX 77550; (888) 425-4753; galveston.com

Local Events/Attractions: Moody Gardens, 1 Hope Blvd., Galveston; (800) 582-4673; moody gardens.com. A fascinating adventure awaits you and your family at Moody Gardens. Explore the oceans at the Aquarium Pyramid, roam a rain forest with free-roaming monkeys and macaws in the Rainforest Pyramid, or enjoy a ride down a lazy river on the Colonel Paddlewheel Boat cruise—and there's much more. Open daily 10 a.m.–8 p.m. You can purchase one-day admission to everything (including rides) or individual attraction tickets at the gate.

Lodging: Galveston Island State Park Campground, 14901 FM 3005, Galveston; (409) 737-1222; tpwd.state.tx.us/state-parks/galveston-island/fees-facilities/campsites. Beach camping at its best, with 36 improved campsites along the Gulf with power and water (used by both RVs and tents) and non-improved tent sites with water and picnic table.

Restaurants: Mosquito Cafe, 628 14th St., Galveston; (409) 763-1010; mosquitocafe.com. Casual eating in an 1870s building.

Tours: Friends of Galveston Island State Park conducts tours of the park on a regular basis (see contact information below).

Organizations: Friends of Galveston Island State Park, PO Box 5428, Galveston, TX 77554; (409) 737-1222; fogisp.wordpress.com

34 Lake Loop

Not one, not two, but three stunning lakes are in store for you on this 3.1-mile double loop hike at Brazos Bend State Park. The first two lakes are horseshoe, or oxbow, lakes formed by the changing route of Big Creek over time, and then the trail takes you past Elm Lake. The banks of each of these lakes are lined with exquisite wildflowers and birds, and you will undoubtedly come across white-tailed deer and rabbits.

Start: Trailhead at end of Park Road 76 East
Distance: 3.1-mile double loop
Hiking time: About 2 hours
Difficulty: Easy to moderate due to length
Trail surface: Gravel
Best seasons: Year-round
Other trail users: Cyclists
Canine compatibility: Leashed pets permitted
Land status: State park
Nearest town: Needville
Fees and permits: Admission fee (children 12 and under free, as of publication date)

Schedule: Year-round; 8 a.m.–9 p.m. Sun–Thurs, 8 a.m.–10 p.m. Fri–Sat
Maps: USGS Thompsons, TX, and Otey, TX; maps available at entrance station
Trail contact: Brazos Bend State Park, 21901 FM 762, Needville, TX 77461; (979) 553-5102; tpwd.state.tx.us/state-parks/brazos-bend
Special considerations: Deer hunting is allowed in the park in winter and during that time the park is closed. Visit the Texas Parks and Wildlife website for dates at tpwd.texas.gov/state-parks/brazos-bend/park-hunts.

Finding the trailhead: From the intersection of FM 360 / Main Street and TX 36 West in Needville, take TX 36 southeast 9.1 miles. Turn left onto FM 1462 East and travel 7.1 miles. Turn left onto FM 762 and travel 1.4 miles, then turn right onto Park Road. In 0.5 mile arrive at the entrance station. After paying your fee, continue straight on Park Road 3.6 miles until you come to the end of the road at a loop with parking. The trailhead is on the north side of the parking lot. GPS: N29 22.761' / W95 36.456'

The Hike

Get ready for a Kodak moment on this hike, the Lake Loop at Brazos Bend State Park. This double loop takes hikers around three separate lakes with dozens of species of birds, wildlife, and wildflowers creating dazzling photo opportunities.

The entire path is a 6- to 10-foot-wide gravel road that virtually forms a figure eight. The trail is lined with majestic oak trees covered in Spanish moss. Benches and picnic tables are strategically located for optimum views of the lakes, birds, wildlife, and wildflowers that you will encounter.

The trail is not blazed, as far as I could see, except for a single orange marker at the trailhead, but the route is quite obvious and easy to follow. This is an easy trail and even smaller children or parents who have strollers can walk it. Of course, length will determine how far your children can walk. By having the two loops interconnect

A great blue heron takes up a striking pose along the banks of New Horseshoe Lake.

only 0.3 mile from the trailhead, you can easily cut the trip down to a single loop of either 1.5 or 1.9 miles.

The first of the loops takes you around the banks of the park's two horseshoe lakes, Old Horseshoe and New Horseshoe. These lakes are remnants of earlier paths of Big Creek years ago. As rivers flow, they tend to meander, snaking their way across the landscape looking for the path of least resistance. Often a river will bend into a U shape, looking almost like an old ox collar, or oxbow, hence the name.

Eventually the river erodes its banks, creating a newer, straighter channel. This leaves the original curve detached from the main river, and this is called a horseshoe lake. Big Creek has had two such changes in its life at this location, the earliest being what is now called Old Horseshoe and the latest New Horseshoe. Old Horseshoe Lake is now a shell of its former self, with lower water levels; however, the park has the ability to adjust the level of New Horseshoe Lake in case of flooding by diverting water to the former.

When walking this trail in late summer and early fall, the scene is sheer beauty, with the deep blue Southern sky and puffy white clouds reflecting off the water and the banks of the lakes ablaze with color from water primrose, Indian blanket, cone-flower, cucumber flower, and groundsel.

The second loop takes you around Elm Lake. This is a man-made lake formed by levees and is a birder's paradise. Be on the lookout for marsh duck, diving duck, coot, great blue heron, and an amazing variety of egrets and terns. A brochure on the birds of Brazos Bend State Park is available on the park's website.

On the south end of this loop, there are several observation platforms that extend into the lake for your viewing enjoyment. There is also a "his and hers" composting toilet with hand cleaner and a doggie watering station so your pet won't go thirsty. The station is open spring through summer.

While the lakes look inviting, do not go swimming! The park is adamant about the alligator population and keeping visitors safe from them. They even have a brochure, "Alligator Etiquette," available to teach you about these ancient reptiles and how to stay safe when you encounter one. Remember to keep dogs and children away from the banks and the brush.

You may encounter some white-tailed deer along the route. Remember, hunting is allowed in the park and it will be closed to recreational use during hunting season. Please refer to the "Special considerations" section for more information.

Miles and Directions

0.0 Start from the parking lot trailhead. There is an information kiosk, bench, and water spigot here. The path is lined with oak trees draped in Spanish moss.

0.1 Pass a bench on the left. In less than 0.1 mile, pass a bench on the right with beautiful views of New Horseshoe Lake.

0.2 Pass a U-shaped bench on the left.

0.3 Come to a Y. The left fork to the southwest will be the section around Elm Lake. Right now take the right fork to the northwest to loop around the horseshoe lakes. In less than 0.1 mile, come to another Y. The left fork is the return route for the Horseshoe Lake Loop. Take the right fork to the north. There is a bench here.

0.4 Cross a culvert that joins the two horseshoe lakes. There is a picnic table on the left under a big oak tree. This is a good spot for watching white-tailed deer. In less than 0.1 mile, pass a bench on the right.

0.6 Pass a bench on the right.

0.8 A short side trail to the left (south) leads to an observation deck overlooking the lake. After viewing, continue straight on the main trail to the west.

0.9 Come to a T intersection. The Big Creek Loop Trail heads off to the right (north). Turn left (southwest) to continue on the Horseshoe Lake Loop.

1.0 Pass a bench on the left.

1.1 Cross a culvert over a runoff.

1.2 Pass a bench on the left.

1.3 Pass a deer stand on the right, a reminder that hunting is allowed here.

1.4 Arrive back at the Y at mile 0.3. Turn to the right (south).

1.5 Arrive back at the Y with the Elm Lake Loop. Turn to the right (south) onto the Elm Lake Loop.

1.6 Pass a bench on the right. You are now walking between the lake on your left and a nice cedar pond on your right.

1.8 Pass a bench on the right.

Lake Loop

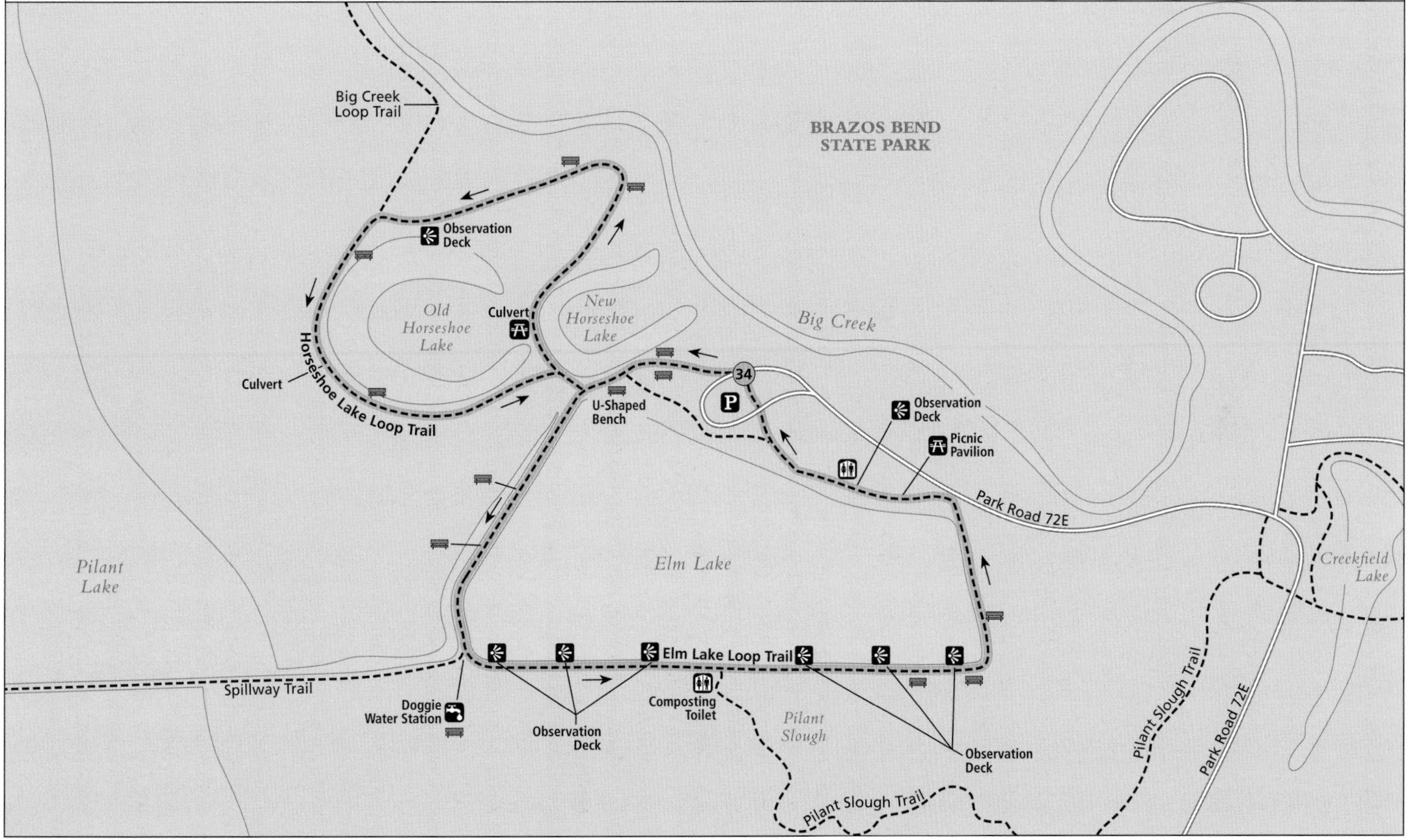

Lake Loop map — Brazos Bend State Park

N

Kilometer
0   0.4

Mile
0   0.4

BRAZOS BEND
STATE PARK

Big Creek

Park Road 72E

Observation Deck

Picnic Pavilion

34

P

U-Shaped Bench

New Horseshoe Lake

Old Horseshoe Lake

Culvert

Observation Deck

Big Creek Loop Trail

Culvert

Horseshoe Lake Loop Trail

Elm Lake

Elm Lake Loop Trail

Observation Deck

Composting Toilet

Pilant Slough

Pilant Slough Trail

Park Road 72E

Creekfield Lake

Observation Deck

Doggie Water Station

Pilant Lake

Spillway Trail

1.9 Come to a Y with three benches, one with a shelter, trash cans, and a doggie watering station that is open April through October. Take the left fork to the east. You're walking atop a levee with Elm Lake to your left and a cedar pond to your right. In less than 0.1 mile, pass a bench on the right and an observation deck on the left.

2.0 Pass an observation deck on your left.

2.1 Pass another observation deck on your left.

2.2 Pass a short side trail for a view of the cedar swamp on your right. There is a men's and women's composting toilet here and a lake observation deck on your left. In less than 0.1 mile, pass an observation deck on your left and the intersection with the Pilant Slough Trail on the right.

2.3 Pass an observation deck on your left.

2.4 Pass another observation deck on your left.

2.5 Pass a bench on the right. In less than 0.1 mile pass, an observation deck on your left and a bench on the right.

2.6 Pass a bench on the right.

2.7 Come up to the Park Road 72 East. Turn left (west) and walk through the picnic area on the north side of Elm Lake on a pea-sized–gravel footpath.

2.8 Pass a picnic pavilion on the right.

2.9 A short trail goes to the left (south) to an observation deck overlooking Elm Lake. A cement sidewalk leads to a restroom on the right. Continue straight to the west.

3.0 Turn right (north) and cross through a parking lot and grassy median, and head back to your car and the trailhead.

3.1 Arrive back at the trailhead.

Hike Information

Local Information: City of Rosenberg, 2110 4th St., Rosenberg, TX 77471; (832) 595-3300; ci .rosenberg.tx.us

Local Events/Attractions: George Observatory, 21901 FM 762, Needville; (281) 242-3055; hmns .org/index.php?option=com_content&view=article&id=108&Itemid=116. Explore the stars at this fantastic observatory located within Brazos Bend State Park. Far away from light pollution, visitors can marvel at the night sky through one of the observatory's many telescopes or check out the planetarium shows (a different one runs every half hour). Open Sat, 3:30–9 p.m. Admission to the planetarium is charged in addition to the park's entrance fee. Telescopes are available for a fee (weather permitting) beginning at 5 p.m.

Lodging: Brazos Bend State Park Campground, 21901 FM 762, Needville; (979) 553-5102; tpwd .state.tx.us/state-parks/brazos-bend/fees-facilities/campsites. The park has 15 primitive campsites and 73 improved campsites.

Restaurants: Another Time Soda Fountain, 800 3rd St., Rosenberg; (281) 232-2999; anothertime sodafountain.com. Soda jerks take you back in time to a good old-fashioned soda fountain. Another Time has hamburgers, blue-plate specials, and, of course, fountain treats including their famous 1-pound banana split.

Tours: The Brazos Bend State Park Volunteer Organization conducts tours of the park on a regular basis (see contact information below).

Organizations: Brazos Bend State Park Volunteer Organization, 21901 FM 762, Needville; (979) 553-5101; brazosbend.org

35 White Oak-Red Buckeye Loop

What would a trip to Brazos Bend State Park be without a visit to the famous Brazos River? The White Oak-Red Buckeye Loop trail gives you that opportunity to view the wide river made famous in many Western songs, as well as a feeder to the river, Big Creek, with its fast-running shoals.

Start: White Oak Trail trailhead on south side of parking lot

Distance: 2.8-mile loop

Hiking time: About 2 hours

Difficulty: Easy on gravel road portions, moderate with some short climbs on Big Creek and Brazos River sections

Trail surface: Dirt, gravel

Best seasons: Sept to May

Other trail users: None

Canine compatibility: Leashed pets permitted

Land status: State park

Nearest town: Needville

Fees and permits: Admission fee (children 12 and under free)

Schedule: Year-round; 8 a.m.–9 p.m. Sun-Thurs, 8 a.m.–10 p.m. Fri-Sat

Maps: USGS Thompsons, TX, and Otey, TX; maps available at entrance station

Trail contact: Brazos Bend State Park, 21901 FM 762, Needville, TX 77461; (979) 553-5102; tpwd.state.tx.us/state-parks/brazos-bend

Special considerations: Deer hunting is allowed in the park in winter and during that time the park is closed. Visit the Texas Parks and Wildlife website for dates at tpwd.texas.gov/state-parks/brazos-bend/park-hunts.

Finding the trailhead: From the intersection of FM 360 / Main Street and TX 36 West in Needville, take TX 36 southeast 9.1 miles. Turn left onto FM 1462 East and travel 7.1 miles. Turn left onto FM 762 and travel 1.4 miles, then turn right onto Park Road. In 0.5 mile reach the entrance station. After paying your fee, continue straight on Park Road 2.7 miles and turn right to continue on Park Road 72 East. In a few yards turn right and follow this unnamed road 1.3 miles to where it ends at a loop. Park here on the south end of the parking area. The trailhead is on the south side. GPS: N29 22.508' / W95 34.939'

The Hike

As I drove to Brazos Bend State Park just southwest of Houston, the old Marty Robbins song kept popping into my head, "Cross the Brazos at Waco . . ." Well, this wasn't Waco, but I was determined to see the famed Brazos River before I left Texas. On my last day in the Lone Star State, I made plans to hike a loop that would take me along the banks of a feeder to the Brazos, Big Creek, then along the Brazos itself. I cleverly called this loop the White Oak–Red Buckeye Loop since it uses two separate trails, coincidentally enough the White Oak and Red Buckeye Trails.

The intersection of the Red Buckeye and White Oak Trails is demarcated with this wooden gate.

The Brazos River flows some 840 miles from its headwaters at the confluence of Double Mountain and Salt Forks in Lubbock at an elevation of 1,500 feet to the Gulf of Mexico. Native Americans called the river *Tokonohono*. Historians believe that early European settlers to the region actually referred to what is now the Colorado River as the Brazos, but other explorers confused the two rivers, calling this one the Brazos and the other the Colorado. Well, the name Brazos stuck.

There are several accounts of how the river actually got its name. One of those involves a Spanish ship that was lost in the Gulf after a ferocious storm. The ship sailed aimlessly for days until the crew finally ran out of fresh drinking water. The situation seemed hopeless when they spotted a streak of mud flowing into the Gulf. They followed it to the mouth of a wide river, sailed up the channel, and finally arrived at a point where the brackish water became drinkable. The crew was saved and they named the river Brazos de Dios, "the arms of God."

Brazos Bend State Park is a beautiful facility with a well-stocked store for those items you might have forgotten or in case you need a souvenir. There are 25 miles of well-maintained trail here that crisscross the park, allowing you to create your own special adventure.

For this trip we'll start at the White Oak Trail trailhead just east of Hale Lake. The trail here is a good 5-foot-wide gravel path that takes you through some nice live oaks draped in Spanish moss. This section of the trail is part of an orienteering course. At the trailhead kiosk there is information about orienteering and how to test yourself on the course. The course was an Eagle Scout project of local Boy Scout Troop 220.

At 0.2 mile you will come to the intersection with the Red Buckeye Trail. The trail is unmistakable, with a wooden gate that is used to shut it down during hunting season. The trail is a traditional, narrow dirt footpath that is marked with flat fiberglass field marker posts with red reflective markers on top and the international hiker logo. Take this path to the south.

Along this trail there are several short side paths that take you to the tops of bluffs for some great views of Big Creek. The creek cuts across the park diagonally and has many rocky shoals where the water rushes through. The best views will be in late fall and winter when the leaves are down. Be careful on the bluffs; they are slippery and it's a long way down. The trail is very shady, with a thick canopy provided by pecan, elm, sugar, and live oak trees.

At mile 0.5 you will come to an intersection with a side trail to your left (east). This is a shortcut in case you don't want to do the entire hike around Big Creek. This trail cuts off over a half mile from the trip and brings you out to just south of where the trail meets up once again with the White Oak Trail but just before the view of the Brazos River. Another shortcut trail is available less than 0.1 mile south of the first one.

At mile 1.2 you will come to the first of a series of either short side trails or benches that overlook the Brazos River. The view is beautiful in the fall when the hardwoods are changing color, but heavy vegetation obscures your view during the summer. The best time to see it would be late fall and winter. The path through here is lined with sycamore and black willow.

Soon you will leave the Red Buckeye Trail and return to the White Oak Trail. This section is just a nice stroll along a gravel path through the hardwoods. At the 2-mile mark the White Oak Trail splits to the north and west. Turn to the left (west). You are now on the White Oak / Bluestem Trail, which is marked with purple markers. This section is your best chance to see wildlife. White-tailed deer—lots of them—forage through the brush. Bobcats, raccoons, coyotes, and foxes also patrol the area.

Don't forget that hunting is allowed in the park. During hunting season the park will be closed to recreational users. Please visit the website listed under "Special considerations" to learn about closing dates.

Miles and Directions

0.0 Start from the trailhead kiosk on the south side of the parking lot. The hike starts on the White Oak Trail. Just a few yards after starting, pass a deer stand on the left, evidence of hunting here in the fall and winter.

0.2 The White Oak Trail splits off to the east. Turn right (south) onto the Red Buckeye Trail, passing through a wooden gate used to close the trail at certain times like during hunting season. The trail is more of a traditional, 2- to 3-foot-wide dirt footpath here. In less than 0.1 mile, cross a short bridge over a runoff.

0.3 A very short side trail takes you to a bluff high above Big Creek. In the fall and winter when leaves are down, you can see the creek and its shoals.

0.5 Come to a Y. A sign points the way to the left (east) for a short route to Big Creek. Take the right fork to the south for the longer loop. There is a bench here. (**Options:** In less than 0.1 mile, a side trail comes in from the left [east] with a sign that reads "Shortcut to Creek." Turn left to take 0.3 mile off the hike. Another sign points the way to Big Creek straight ahead to the south. Keep going straight to take another 0.5 mile off the hike.)

0.7 Another side trail to the right takes you to a bluff overlooking the creek. In less than 0.1 mile, pass a bench on the right. In about 20 yards you will see a red blaze on a short (2-foot-tall) 4-by-4-inch post on the right.

0.8 A side trail comes in from the left (north). This is the second shortcut trail passed at mile 0.5. A sign shows the way back. Right now, continue straight to the east.

1.0 Come to an intersection. A short trail to the right (southeast) goes to Big Creek. Take the trail to the right to view the creek. Be careful! It's rather steep and can be slippery. When done, turn around and return to the main trail.

1.1 Back on the main trail, turn right (northeast).

1.2 A trail intersects from the right (east). A 6-inch creosote pole painted half white, half red is in the center of the Y and a sign here reads "Brazos River—Do Not Enter Water." Take the trail to the right and in a few yards come to a bench with a view of the Brazos River. When done, return to the main trail and turn to the right (north).

1.5 Pass a bench on the right next to a sign that reads "Brazos River" with a view down the bluff of the river. Continue straight ahead to the north (a sign in front of you reads "Red Buckeye Trail"). In less than 0.1 mile arrive at the end of the Red Buckeye Trail at an intersection with the White Oak Trail. Turn right (north) onto the wide shell road.

1.7 Pass Franky's Dam Trail on the right (east). Continue straight to the north on the White Oak Trail.

2.0 The White Oak Trail splits to the left (west) and straight (north). Turn left here to continue on the White Oak Trail.

2.3 Pass a deer stand on the right.

2.6 Come to the park road and walk straight across to the west, picking up the trail on the other side.

2.7 Come to the parking area and turn left (southwest). Follow the road around to the south.

2.8 Pass a restroom on the right. In less than 0.1 mile, arrive back at the trailhead.

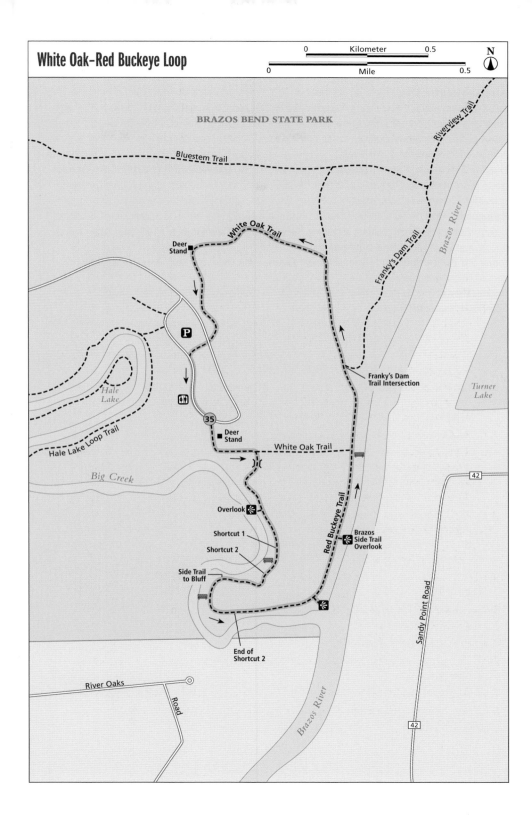

White Oak-Red Buckeye Loop

Kilometer
0   0.5

Mile
0   0.5

N

BRAZOS BEND STATE PARK

Bluestem Trail

Riverview Trail

Brazos River

White Oak Trail

Deer Stand

Franky's Dam Trail

P

Hale Lake

Franky's Dam Trail Intersection

Turner Lake

35

Deer Stand

White Oak Trail

Hale Lake Loop Trail

42

Big Creek

Overlook

Shortcut 1

Shortcut 2

Red Buckeye Trail

Brazos Side Trail Overlook

Side Trail to Bluff

End of Shortcut 2

River Oaks

Road

Sandy Point Road

Brazos River

42

Hike Information

Local Information: City of Rosenberg, 2110 4th St., Rosenberg, TX 77471; (832) 595-3300; ci
.rosenberg.tx.us

Local Events/Attractions: George Ranch, 10215 FM 762, Richmond; (281) 343-0218; george
ranch.org. Travel back through over a hundred years of history on this 20,000-acre working ranch
where costumed interpreters bring to life how it was back in the day. Open 9 a.m.–5 p.m. Tues–Sat.
Admission fee (children under 5 free).

Lodging: Brazos Bend State Park Campground, 21901 FM 762, Needville; (979) 553-5102; tpwd
.state.tx.us/state-parks/brazos-bend/fees-facilities/campsites. The park has 15 primitive campsites and 73 improved campsites.

Restaurants: Ol' Railroad Cafe, 819 2nd St., Rosenberg; (832) 595-0995; facebook.com/OlRailRoad
Cafe. Down-home Texas cooking, including the Big Nasty, a humungous hamburger with cheese,
bacon, barbecue sauce, and onion strings.

Tours: The Brazos Bend State Park Volunteer Organization conducts tours on a regular basis (see
contact information below).

Organizations: Brazos Bend State Park Volunteer Organization, 21901 FM 762, Needville; (979)
553-5101; brazosbend.org

36 Bobcat Woods Trail

Another important stop for migrating birds along the Central Flyway, San Bernard National Wildlife Refuge plays hosts to hundreds of them each year. This walk along the levee system that forms long reservoirs offers birders and hikers a chance to view them up close and personal.

Start: Parking lot trailhead
Distance: 1-mile out-and-back, longer if you walk farther on the levees
Hiking time: About 1 hour
Difficulty: Easy over flat terrain
Trail surface: Boardwalk, gravel
Best seasons: Sept to May
Other trail users: None
Canine compatibility: Leashed pets allowed

Land status: National wildlife refuge
Nearest town: Brazoria
Fees and permits: None
Schedule: Year-round, sunrise–sunset
Maps: USGS Freeport, TX
Trail contact: San Bernard National Wildlife Refuge, 6801 CR 306, Brazoria, TX 77422; (979) 964-4011; fws.gov/refuges/profiles/index.cfm?id=21541

Finding the trailhead: From the intersection of TX 36 West and TX 332 in Brazoria, take TX 36 West 5.6 miles. Turn right onto FM 2611. Travel 4.3 miles and turn left onto FM 2918. In 1.2 miles turn right onto CR 306. Drive 2.1 miles and turn left into San Bernard National Wildlife Refuge. Follow the road 1.9 miles and the parking lot and trailhead will be on your right. GPS: N28 52.966' / W95 35.045'

The Hike

Look at a map of the Texas Gulf Coast, and you'll notice one thing: From Freeport to the Louisiana state line, the coast is wall-to-wall national wildlife refuges, all established with one thing in mind, to provide a stopover for the hundreds of species of migrating birds that fly through the area on what is called the Central Flyway. The Flyway is an area generally from the Rocky Mountains to the Great Plains and the western Gulf of Mexico. This region sees birds that are migrating to places as far south as Patagonia in South America and as far north as the Arctic Circle.

The farthest south of these refuges is the San Bernard National Wildlife Refuge. The refuge was established in 1969 and encompasses 54,000 acres of land from the beaches of the Gulf of Mexico to bottomland forests and marshes further inland. Over 340 species of birds stop here each year, which garnered the refuge the distinction of being named an "Internationally Significant Shorebird Site" by the Western Hemisphere Shorebird Reserve Network.

The refuge is dotted with hiking trails like the 2.5-mile Cow Trap Marsh Trail and this one, the Bobcat Woods Trail. Needless to say, the trail was named for the fact that there is bobcat in the area. Whether you are fortunate enough to see one or not, that's a different story.

A dramatic sign marks the beginning of the Bobcat Woods Trail.

The first part of the trail is a narrow boardwalk that runs along the banks of Cocklebur Slough. You will have several views of the slough as you walk. The trail has plenty of shade, with a thick canopy courtesy of the live oaks with Spanish moss dripping from their branches. You will also see hackberry. Clay-colored sparrows and black-capped chickadees dart across the path before you.

In 0.1 mile you'll come to a new little observation deck overlooking the slough and wetland. At mile 0.2 you'll come to the northern end of the boardwalk. Refuge maps show that a dirt footpath with a loop should head northeast from here, but during my visit there was no sign of it. The path was completely blocked and overgrown, so I turned around and headed back the way I came, passing the short side trail to the trailhead on the way.

At just about the half-mile mark, the boardwalk ends again to the southwest, this time at a parking lot. This is a moderate-size gravel parking lot that is used by people who come here to picnic (there is a picnic pavilion just a few yards away near the levee) or where persons with disabilities can park for easy access to either the trail that follows or the boardwalk we just left. By turning to the right (northwest) here, you will begin a hike over levees in an area known as the Wolfweed Wetlands. This is an area over 700 acres in size with large, long reservoirs that provide a rest stop and feeding grounds for the migrating birds. According to rangers, reservoirs here are kept full of water which is used to help maintain moist soil units nearby to grow food for waterfowl.

In the distance you may notice some telephone poles. These were erected by US Fish and Wildlife to create a wading bird rookery, keeping birds high and away from alligators and predators like raccoon.

Just after arriving at the levees, you will make a left turn and arrive at an observation deck that takes you 10 to 15 feet above ground level for a good expansive view of the marsh reservoirs. If you didn't bring your binoculars, don't worry. The post is outfitted with a set for you to use. It is in this area that the skull of a woman was found that was dated to be 5,000 to 6,000 years old, evidence that early man also found this bountiful land.

I turned around at about the 0.6-mile mark of the trip, but you can stroll along the tops of the levees for hours on end watching sandhill cranes or dowitchers. The bird of prey population skyrockets in the fall, with peregrine falcons, kestrels, and bald eagles calling the refuge home.

▶ **Don't be surprised if you see a large number of white-tailed deer while hiking the trails of Texas's Gulf Coast. Texas has the largest herd of white-tailed deer in the country. The Texas Parks and Wildlife Department estimates the herd is 1,555,000 strong.**

Miles and Directions

0.0 Start from the trailhead on the northwest side of the parking lot and take the boardwalk to the west-northwest. In less than 0.1 mile, come to a T intersection at the sign warning of mosquitoes. Turn right (north) and continue on the boardwalk. The trail is very enclosed with thick brush, trees, and vines.

0.1 A short side trail to the left (west) leads to a small observation deck overlooking Cocklebur Slough.

0.2 The boardwalk ends and turns into a grassy path. At the time of this writing, the trail was not passable any further. Turn around and retrace your steps back to mile 0.1.

0.3 Back at the intersection, the trailhead is to your left (south). Continue straight to the southwest on the boardwalk. In a few feet pass a bench. You are walking along Cocklebur Slough on your right (northwest).

0.4 Come to a T intersection with a dirt service road. Turn to the right (northwest) onto the grassy road, walking around a gate that stops vehicles from riding the levee. In less than 0.1 mile, pass a picnic pavilion on the right (north) with an accessible parking area.

0.5 The levee system begins with one heading straight (northwest) and one to the right (southwest). Turn right and in a few yards arrive at an observation deck. When done viewing the marsh, turn around and head back to the main trail. Once at the main path, turn left (northwest) onto the levee. *Option:* You can spend a lot of time meandering along the myriad levees here. One option is to continue straight to the southwest.

0.6 Arriving at a secondary pond, I chose to turn around and retrace my steps to the trailhead. There are miles of levees to walk and explore here, and you're invited to do so.

1.0 Arrive back at the trailhead.

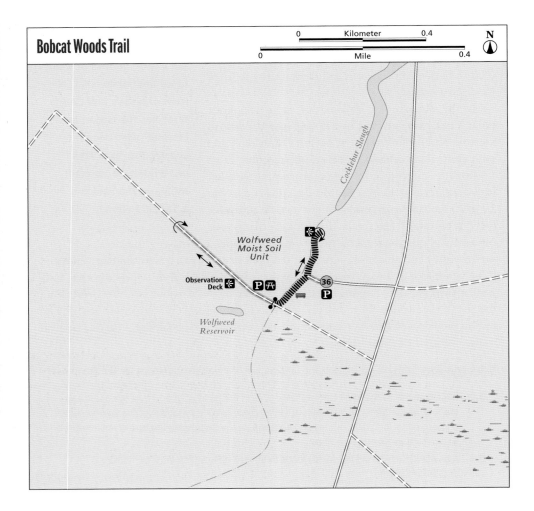

Hike Information

Local Information: Brazosport Convention & Visitors Bureau, 300 Abner Jackson Pkwy., Lake Jackson, TX 77566; (979) 285-2501; visitbrazosport.com

Local Events/Attractions: Brazosport Museum of Natural Science, 400 College Blvd., Clute; (979) 265-7831; bcfas.org/museum2014. The museum is the home of the largest seashell collection in the South as well as mammoth and dinosaur bones, fossils, and more. Open 10 a.m.–4 p.m. Tues–Sat and 2–5 p.m. Sun. Admission is free.

Lodging: Quintana Beach County Park Campground, 330 5th St., Quintana; (800) 872-7578; brazoria-county.com/parks/quintana/rv_tent.html. Fifty-five improved and primitive campsites are available, located only 200 yards from the Gulf beach. Cabins are also available.

Restaurants: Kitty's Purple Cow, 323 Ocean Ave., Surfside Beach; (979) 233-9161; kittyspurple cow.com. Great burgers and seafood. You can't miss the big purple building.

Organizations: Friends of Brazoria Wildlife Refuges, PO Box 505, Lake Jackson; (866) 403-5829; refugefriends.org

37 Matagorda Bay Nature Trail

An important stop for migrating birds and home to many other "permanent" residents, the Matagorda Bay Nature Trail is the perfect example of big corporations doing right by preserving this valuable habitat while at the same time providing recreational opportunities to the public. This trail is short, only 0.6 mile (one way), but the birder in you will love the 200-plus species that make themselves at home here.

Start: Trailhead on left (north) side of pavilion
Distance: 1.3-mile out-and-back
Hiking time: About 1 hour
Difficulty: Easy over flat terrain
Trail surface: Dirt, gravel path
Best seasons: Year-round
Other trail users: None
Canine compatibility: Leashed pets permitted
Land status: LCRA nature park

Nearest town: Matagorda
Fees and permits: None
Schedule: Year-round, sunrise–sunset
Maps: USGS Matagorda SW, TX
Trail contact: Lower Colorado River Authority (LCRA), 6430 FM 2031, Matagorda, TX 77457; (979) 863-7120; lcra.org/parks/developed -parks/Pages/matagorda-bay-nature-park.aspx

Finding the trailhead: From the intersection of CR 60 / Fisher Street and FM 2031 in Matagorda, take FM 2031 south 6.6 miles. The road ends in the preserve's parking lot. The group pavilion is on the east side of the parking lot. The trailhead is on the left (north) side of the pavilion. GPS: N28 35.876' / W95 58.668'

The Hike

The Matagorda Bay Nature Park is a 1,600-acre facility owned by the Lower Colorado River Authority (LCRA). The LCRA is a regional power company that purchased this property in 2001 as part of its commitment to preserve the area's wetlands and provide recreational opportunities for the community.

The park is located on the southern tip of a long and mostly barren barrier island, Matagorda Island. The preserve is bordered by the Colorado River (no, not that one—the one in Texas) to the west, East Matagorda Bay to the north, and the Gulf of Mexico to the south and east. The park has canoe and kayak rentals, so you can paddle its blue trails, and a natural science center with exhibits focusing on the natural habitat of the island. Nature programs with titles like "Adventures in Beachcombing" or "Wings Over the Wetlands" are also offered on a regular basis. See the "Hike Information" section for contact information.

Apart from walking the beach, there is only one hike at the park: the Matagorda Bay Nature Trail. This 1.3-mile out-and-back is a wetland walk over a dirt and gravel path. Once again the star of the show is the birds. Beautiful reddish and snowy egrets, roseate spoonbill, willet, white-faced ibis, and great blue heron are only a few of the

Prickly pear cactuses sit center stage before the marsh at Matagorda Bay.

many species you may see as you hike the trail. Monarch butterflies also make a stop here during their migration.

A variety of wetland grasses and plants can be seen along the hike, including glasswort. Some call this plant pickleweed or the "poor man's asparagus" because it looks like small asparagus stalks. It is a fascinating little plant that is related to cactus. The stems are green in the spring and summer and bright red in the fall. The plant has adapted to survive in a saltwater environment by extracting freshwater from the salty water and then storing it in its stems. You will also see beautiful Indian blanket, or firewheel, flowers with their distinctive red petals with yellow tips, and prickly pear cactuses with big, bulbous purple growths on their pads that bloom into beautiful flowers in late spring and summer.

No matter the time of year you take this hike, you will find that it tends to be windy since it's on the tip of this barrier island. That's a good thing. It helps to keep the number of mosquitoes down, but always carry that bug spray just in case. You are walking through a wetland after all.

A showdown at Matagorda Bay Nature Park

As you walk the trail you will hear a distinctive roar off in the distance. It's the sound of the Gulf of Mexico only about 1,000 feet away, just past the wetland and over dunes to the southeast. After your hike it's worth your time to head down to the beach for a swim or to just enjoy the surf. An access trail is available on the left side of the pavilion where this hike starts.

You will never be out of sight of the main road into the park, FM 2031, on this hike but it's far enough away where it isn't a nuisance. The only other sign of civilization is at the very beginning of the hike, when you cross a road that leads into the Sterling Shores Community, a small subdivision just a short distance away.

About halfway into the hike, you will pass an old cattle pen. No one I talked with could tell me the last time this wooden stockade was used, but from the looks of it, it has been a long time.

The turnaround for the trip is at an observation deck that provides the best view of the wetland and the birds that call the park home.

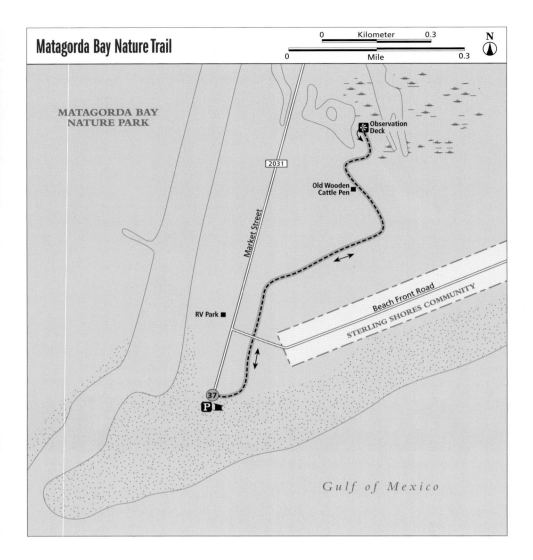

Matagorda Bay Nature Trail

MATAGORDA BAY
NATURE PARK

2031

Observation
Deck

Old Wooden
Cattle Pen

Market Street

RV Park ■

Beach Front Road

STERLING SHORES COMMUNITY

37

P

Gulf of Mexico

N

0   Kilometer   0.3
0   Mile   0.3

Miles and Directions

0.0   Start from the trailhead to the left (north) of the park pavilion. A metal gate blocks off vehicle traffic to the beach. The trail is a wide gravel road.

0.1   Cross a paved road to the north. To the right is the Sterling Shores Community.

0.4   Pass a wooden cattle pen to your left (north).

0.5   Closest approach to that cattle pen.

0.6   Come to the end of the trail at the observation deck. When done viewing, turn around and retrace your steps to the trailhead.

1.3   Arrive back at the trailhead.

Hike Information

Local Information: Matagorda County Convention and Visitors Bureau, 201 7th St., Bay City, TX 77414; (877) 878-5386

Local Events/Attractions: Matagorda County Museum, 2100 Avenue F, Bay City; (979) 245-7502. Matagorda County is famous for the discovery and recovery of artifacts from the shipwreck *La Belle*. The ship went down in 1685 during a failed attempt to colonize the area by the French. The Matagorda County Museum takes you through the steps archeologists followed to uncover the wreck. The museum also highlights the history of the Karankawa Indians and early western cowboys. Open Wed–Sat, 1–5 p.m. A small admission fee is charged.

Lodging: Matagorda Bay Nature Park Campground, 6272 FM 2031, Matagorda; (979) 863-7120. The park has cabins plus 24 improved campsites and 19 waterfront sites. Prices range greatly depending on site selection. Make reservations through Reserve America, reserveamerica.com.

Restaurants: The Hotel Blessing Coffee Shop, 128 10th St., Blessing; (361) 588-9579. Great down-home Texas cooking in a former hotel built in 1906 and now listed on the National Register of Historic Places.

Tours: Matagorda Bay Nature Park, 6420 FM 2031, Matagorda; (979) 863-2603; lcra.org/parks/outdoor-programs/matagorda-bay-nature-park

38 Heron Flats Loop

Four hundred species of birds, beautiful views of wetlands and San Antonio Bay, and home to the endangered whooping crane, that's what you'll find at Aransas National Wildlife Refuge, and the perfect trail to take it all in is the Heron Flats Loop. This 1.4-mile loop is the longest in the park and gives you a good overview of what makes Aransas so special.

Start: Trailhead on FM 2040
Distance: 1.4-mile loop
Hiking time: About 1 hour
Difficulty: Easy over relatively flat, level terrain
Trail surface: Dirt, grass, boardwalk
Best seasons: Year-round
Other trail users: None
Canine compatibility: Leashed pets permitted
Land status: National wildlife refuge
Nearest town: Tivoli

Fees and permits: Admission fee (18 years of age and younger free, as of publication)
Schedule: Year-round, 30 minutes before sunrise–30 minutes after sunset; Claude F. Lard Visitor Center, 8:30 a.m.–4:30 p.m. Thurs–Sun, closed Thanksgiving and Christmas
Maps: USGS Tivoli SE, TX; maps available at visitor center
Trail contact: Aransas National Wildlife Refuge, 1 Wildlife Circle, Austwell, TX 77950; (361) 286-3559; fws.gov/refuge/Aransas

Finding the trailhead: From the intersection of TX 239 and TX 35 in Tivoli, take TX 35 south 1.6 miles. Take the left fork onto TX 239 East and travel 4.3 miles. Turn right onto FM 774. In 0.3 mile turn right to stay on FM 774. In 0.4 mile turn left onto FM 2040 East. Travel 6.7 miles and arrive at the Claude F. Lard Visitor Center. After paying your entrance fee, continue south 0.5 mile. The parking lot and the trailhead are on the left. GPS: N28 18.093' / W96 48.385'

The Hike

The brochure on the counter at the Claude F. Lard Visitor Center at Aransas National Wildlife Refuge said it all: "Welcome! Whooping Crane Stronghold!" Of course, I had to ask what that meant. The volunteer on duty was very cordial and chuckled, "You're not from here, are you?"

I knew of Aransas National Wildlife Refuge and that it was a haven for birds, but had no idea how important this facility was. Over 400 species of birds either call this place home or migrate in. Naturally, the next question was why do all of those birds come here.

The answer is the smorgasbord that is laid out before them. The rangers and volunteers call it a banquet table. The strong Gulf winds here push bay water over low-lying shoreline, which forms a fertile feeding ground in the brackish water.

A sticky situation along the Heron Flats Loop—a prickly pear cactus and Spanish dagger plant

You will definitely need to pick up a scorecard, the birding checklist, from the visitor center when you arrive to keep track of all you will see. Of course, species are dependent on the season, but no matter when you arrive, you will see a show.

The one bird that everyone wants to see and the one that Aransas is the most noted for is the whooping crane. With its distinctive cry of "whoop," the crane was near complete extinction in the 1940s with only fifteen known birds surviving. Today the number is up to just over 500, but the species is still on the brink. Aransas plays host to the largest population of these birds, with 250 arriving between late October and mid-April before making their 2,400-mile-long journey back to Wood Buffalo National Park in Canada.

There are just too many bird species to name here, and the list of other wildlife you may see is equally as impressive. On any given day you could see everything from orange sulphur, southern dogface, and sleepy orange butterflies to bottlenose dolphin, cottontail rabbit, raccoon, armadillo, and least shrew. There is also an abundance of white-tailed deer and, of course, American alligators.

There are seven hiking trails in the refuge, most 0.7 mile or less in length. The Heron Flats Loop is the longest at 1.4 miles and one of the most popular because of the wide variety of plants and wildlife you will see along its length.

The trail begins at a small parking lot just off the main preserve road. For the most part the trail is a wide mowed path with some dirt footing and a boardwalk. The path has numbered markers identifying plants and interesting features along the route, so be sure to pick up a brochure at the visitor center.

Just as you start the hike, you will come to an observation deck that juts out a short distance into the marsh, with San Antonio Bay on the horizon. Your outbound walk and the return on the loop are separated by a small pond that is known to have alligators from time to time and snakes. Again, I know I'm overstating it, but keep small children close by and dogs on a short leash.

There are some amazing wildflowers and plants growing here, including some beautiful prickly pear cactuses that bloom with purple flowers and Spanish dagger

THE WONDROUS WHOOPING CRANE

There are fifteen species of crane in the world, only two in North America, and of those two the whooping crane is the rarer. The whooping crane is named for its distinctive "whoop" calls. Standing at over 5 feet tall, this white bird with black wingtips and red crown is the tallest bird in North America. Its wingspan can be over 7 feet wide.

Scientists believe the whooping crane is one of the few species of bird that survived the Pleistocene-era extinction of animals some sixty million years ago. They might have survived that extinction but now face their biggest enemy—humans.

According to Operation Migration, one of several nonprofit groups working to bring back the whooping crane, there were over 1,400 cranes in existence in 1860. Through hunting, loss of wetland habitat, and pollution, the number dwindled to only fifteen in 1941. Through the efforts of organizations like Operation Migration and the Whooping Crane Eastern Partnership, the crane is making a slow but tenuous comeback so that today the wintering flocks number just over 500.

The flocks winter in and around Aransas National Wildlife Refuge in Texas (see hike 38, Heron Flats Loop), then fly to Canada in the spring and nest at Wood Buffalo National Park.

To learn more about this majestic bird, efforts to save them, and how you can help, go to the web and visit Operation Migration at operationmigration.org and Whooping Crane Eastern Partnership at bringbackthecranes.org.

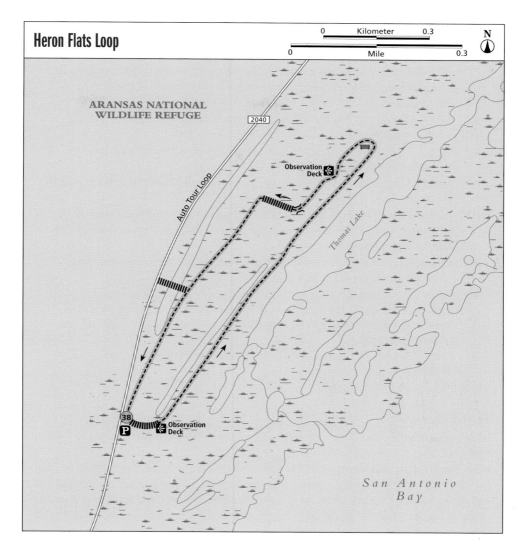

plants. This plant is a succulent that has very, and I mean *very*, sharp branches. There is also a plant called Turk's cap here, easily recognizable by the small apple-like fruit it bears.

As the trail loops around and heads south, you do a short uphill climb and come to an observation deck with binoculars to take in the marsh and bay. Soon after the deck you will cross the pond with a very picturesque view of the water feature as you cross over a bridge and begin the trek back to the trailhead on the opposite side of the pond.

Miles and Directions

0.0 Start from the trailhead at the parking lot and head east on a short boardwalk. In a few yards come to an intersection. The trail turns to the left (north) but a short side trail leads to an observation deck with beautiful views of San Antonio Bay and is a perfect spot for bird watching. When done viewing, return to the main trail.

0.1 Back at the main trail, take the dirt and grass path to the right (north). There is also a bench at this intersection.

0.3 The trail continues on a levee above a nice narrow wetland on the left (west) and San Antonio Bay on your right to the east.

0.6 Across the wetland to your left, you will see the second observation deck of the hike, which you will be coming to soon.

0.7 The trail arrives at the north end of the pond and wetland and loops to the west before heading southwest. This section is very enclosed with thick brush, vines, and trees. In less than 0.1 mile, pass a bench on the left.

0.8 Arrive at the second observation deck, which is equipped with binoculars. After viewing, continue southwest on the trail.

0.9 Pass a bench on the right. In less than 0.1 mile, cross a boardwalk over the slough. At the time of this writing, the bridge was out but you were still able to cross by wading through the bayou. A sign here read "Cross at Your Own Risk." There are alligators and snakes in the bayou.

1.1 Pass a boardwalk on your right (northwest) that leads back to the road. Continue straight to the southwest.

1.4 Arrive back at the trailhead.

Hike Information

Local Information: Rockport-Fulton Chamber of Commerce, 319 Broadway, Rockport, TX 78382; (800) 242-0071; rockport-fulton.org

Local Events/Attractions: Rockport Birding and Kayak Adventures, 202 N. Fulton Beach Rd., Fulton; (866) 277-3468; whoppingcranetours.com. There isn't a better way to see the beautiful and endangered whooping crane than to take to the water. Rockport Birding and Kayak Adventures not only offer whooping crane tours, but also kayak tours of the marshes, sunset cruises, and dolphin tours. Prices and times vary depending on the tour. Contact them for information.

Lodging: Goose Island State Park Campground, 202 S. Palmetto St., Rockport; (361) 729-2858; tpwd.state.tx.us/state-parks/goose-island. Goose Island State Park has 25 primitive campsites and 57 improved sites with water, electricity, picnic table, grill, and fire ring.

Restaurants: Daily Grind, 302 S. Austin St., Rockport; (361) 790-8745. Sandwiches and subs.

Organizations: Friends of Aransas National Wildlife Refuge, PO Box 74, Austwell, TX 77950; (361) 286-3559; friendsofaransas.org

39 Turk's Cap Loop

What makes this hike special are the trees—big, gnarled-limbed live oak trees that line the path, their tenuous fingers stretching out over the trail, creating an eerie yet beautiful canopy. In the underbrush warblers and hummingbirds flitter about their business while cottontail rabbits hop alongside.

Start: Trailhead on west side of parking lot
Distance: 1.3-mile loop
Hiking time: About 1 hour
Difficulty: Easy over a flat dirt footpath
Trail surface: Crushed shell, dirt, short road walk
Best seasons: Year-round
Other trail users: Cyclists
Canine compatibility: Leashed pets permitted
Land status: State park

Nearest town: Rockport
Fees and permits: Admission fee (children 12 and under free, as of publication)
Schedule: Year-round, 8 a.m.–10 p.m.
Maps: USGS Beeville, TX; maps available at entrance station
Trail contact: Goose Island State Park, 202 S. Palmetto St., Rockport, TX 78382; (361) 729-2858; tpwd.state.tx.us/state-parks/ goose-island

Finding the trailhead: From the intersection of Traylor Boulevard and TX 35 in Rockport, take TX 35 north 5.9 miles. Turn right onto E. Main Street / State Park Road 13 and travel 1.4 miles. Turn right onto Palmetto Street / State Park Road 13. Travel 0.4 mile to the entrance station. After paying your fee, continue straight 200 feet and turn right onto Lantana Loop; in 0.1 mile turn right (north) again. Continue toward the north/northwest on Lantana Loop counterclockwise around the campground loop another 0.4 mile. Just past campsite #157, turn right into the parking lot on Warbler Way. The trailhead is on the west side of the parking lot. GPS: N28 08.278' / W96 59.321'

The Hike

There are two pieces to Goose Island State Park. One piece, the main park itself, is on the tip of the Lamar Peninsula that separates Copano and St. Charles Bay, and the other, smaller piece is on the short, narrow island that is just south of the peninsula called Goose Island.

As with many state parks across the country, Goose Island was a product of the Civilian Conservation Corps (CCC). The first park facilities, which included a concession building and picnic area, were built over two six-month periods in 1934 and 1935. The concession building was made of what is called "shell crete," blocks cast of crushed oyster shells, much like cement blocks. The building is currently used as the park's recreation hall. The picnic area was made up of shelters that had palmetto leaf–thatched roofs.

There are two trails here at Goose Island, the Nature Trail and the Turk's Cap Trail. For purposes of this hike, I have combined the two to form a loop. The live oak trees line the path creating an eerie archway through the forest.

Long, sinuous, gnarled branches of live oak trees hang across the Turk's Cap Loop.

The path is also lined with yaupon holly. You will most likely notice the female of the species, with its ever-present bright red berries running up the branches. The leaves contain caffeine, and Native Americans used the plant to make a ceremonial tea which they would drink and then—skip the next line if you have a sensitive stomach—vomit back up. It wasn't the plant that caused the vomiting, though. That was self-induced as part of the ceremony, but it did give the plant the alternate name vomitoria. You will also see the trail's namesake plant along the hike, Turk's cap, which can be identified by the very small apple-like berries it sprouts.

Another tree that grows here and Native Americans found medicinal uses for is the red bay. Some of you cooks may have used red bay leaf at one time or another. You will also see American beautyberry along the trail, with its distinctive clusters of glossy, iridescent purple berries hugging its branches; wax myrtle; and coralbean, or what is better known as red cardinal, with its long, red-purple, tubular-looking flowers.

You may be treated to the knocking of red-headed or yellow-bellied woodpeckers as they flitter from tree to tree looking for their daily meal, scare up a wild turkey or two, or see one of five different species of hummingbirds that return here each year.

This is a very easy walking trail over a wide path with ground shell footing. It's an excellent trail for you to bring your children on or to just take a nice, quiet walk in the woods. The path is also used by cyclists, so keep your eyes and ears open for them coming around bends. And don't be surprised if a white-tailed deer or two share the trail with you. As for the quiet, you will hear the hushed din of traffic from nearby Front Street along a short section, but it's nothing that will disturb your walk.

▶ Separating the Gulf of Mexico from Laguna Madres is Padre Island. This island just off the coast of Corpus Christi is the longest stretch of undeveloped barrier island in the world, measuring over 70 miles long. The largest native mammal on the island is the coyote.

The hike begins at the Turk's Cap Trail trailhead on the west side of the parking lot just north of the Lantana (campground) Loop. Immediately you will come to your first big live oak with sprawling branches. You will notice that there is thick underbrush around the oaks. The park intentionally leaves it like this as habitat for warblers and hummingbirds. By the way, if you love hummers, this is the place to be in September when the annual Hummingbird Festival is held in the town of Rockport. Goose Island State Park is one of the venues for the celebration (see "Hike Information" for details).

The Turk's Cap Trail is an out-and-back trail, but as I said, I have joined it with the park's Nature Trail to create a loop. When you arrive at the opposite end of the trail along the park's main road, turn left (northwest) and walk up the road a short distance, then turn right (northeast) onto the paved Warbler's Way, which leads into the campground. Directly across from campsite 131 you will see a sign and the entrance to the Nature Trail.

This is a short, narrow dirt path that wraps around just inside the campground. There are lots of white-tailed deer and cottontail rabbits through here, along with a nice view of a very pretty little wetland. Follow the trail around, passing a restroom, to where it comes back out on Warbler's Way and walk the road back to the trailhead.

Miles and Directions

0.0 Start from the trailhead on the west side of the parking lot. There is a kiosk at the trailhead that includes information and an invitation to visit the park's "Big Tree," one of the largest live oaks in the nation. (**FYI:** The Big Tree is located northeast of the hiking trail, a short drive up Palmetto Street.) In less than 0.1 mile, pass a big, old, gnarled oak tree (but not the Big Tree), then pass a wetland on the left and a bench. The path is lined with gnarled oaks.

0.1 Cross a runoff over a short bridge. You are running parallel to E. Main Street on your right (you can hear it through the trees and brush but it's not too disturbing).

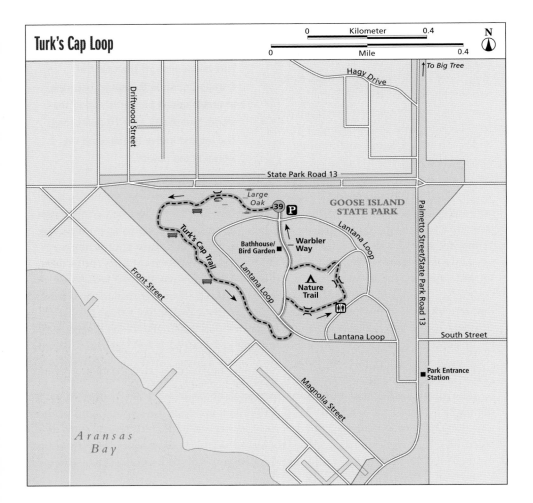

Turk's Cap Loop

0   Kilometer   0.4

0   Mile   0.4

N

To Big Tree

Hagy Drive

Driftwood Street

State Park Road 13

Large Oak

39 P

GOOSE ISLAND STATE PARK

Lantana Loop

Palmetto Street/State Park Road 13

Turk's Cap Trail

Bathhouse/ Bird Garden

Warbler Way

Lantana Loop

Nature Trail

Front Street

Lantana Loop

South Street

Magnolia Street

Park Entrance Station

Aransas Bay

0.2   Pass a bench on the right.

0.3   Pass a dirt service road to the left (south) and in a few yards another one to the right (west). Continue straight to the southwest. In less than 0.1 mile, pass a bench on the left.

0.5   Pass a bench on the right.

0.7   Arrive at a second parking area and the south end of the Turk's Cap Trail. Turn left (north) onto the paved Lantana Loop Road. In less than 0.1 mile, turn right (north) onto the paved Warbler's Way and head toward the campground.

0.8   Directly across from campsite 131 you will see a sign that reads "Nature Trail." Turn right (southeast) onto the dirt nature trail. In less than 0.1 mile, cross a short bridge over a runoff.

0.9   As you walk along the far end of the campground, pass a restroom on the right. Just past the restroom turn left (northeast) onto the dirt path. In less than 0.1 mile, cross a runoff over a short bridge.

1.0 Come to a paved road and turn to the left (northwest). Cut across the campground loop to the west toward campsite 222. On the left side of the campsite, the trail reenters the woods. The route is very enclosed with thick vines, giving it a cavelike feel for a short distance.

1.1 Back on the paved Warbler's Way, turn right (north) and follow the road through the campground. In less than 0.1 mile, pass a bathhouse and a bird garden on the left. Beautiful song fills the air early mornings. Keep going straight to the north.

1.3 Arrive back at the trailhead.

Hike Information

Local Information: Rockport-Fulton Chamber of Commerce, 319 Broadway, Rockport, TX 78382; (800) 242-0071; rockport-fulton.org

Local Events/Attractions: Texas Maritime Museum, 1202 Navigation Circle, Rockport, TX 78382; (866) 729-2469; texasmaritimemuseum.org. Learn about the nautical history of the Texas Gulf Coast at the Texas Maritime Museum. With over 300 miles of coastline, and history that goes back as far, visitors will learn about the earliest sailors to the region when the French and Spanish ruled the waves, the oil boom, and more. Open Tues–Sat 10 a.m.–4 p.m. and Sun 1–4 p.m. Admission is charged.

Hummingbird Festival, 319 Broadway, Rockport; (800) 242-0071; rockporthummingbird .com. An annual event held throughout the Rockport area in the middle of September celebrating the hummingbird.

Lodging: Goose Island State Park Campground, 202 S. Palmetto St., Rockport; (361) 729-2858; tpwd.state.tx.us/state-parks/goose-island. Goose Island State Park has 25 primitive campsites and 57 improved sites with water, electricity, picnic table, grill, and fire ring.

Restaurants: Moondog Seaside Eatery, 100 N. Casterline Dr., Rockport; (361) 729-6200. Seafood and barbecue.

40 Salt Island Marsh Trail

A truly amazing hike can be found just north of Corpus Christi at the Port Aransas Nature Preserve at Charlie's Pasture. Once distressed farmland, the City of Port Aransas, nonprofit organizations, and volunteers worked to reclaim the salt marsh. The result is this fantastic 2.2-mile boardwalk hike through the salt marsh and salt and algal flats where roseate spoonbills, black-bellied whistling ducks, and reddish egrets greet you and you are treated to magnificent, beautiful, expansive views.

Start: Pavilion at end of Port Street
Distance: 2.2-mile out-and-back with short island loop
Hiking time: About 1.5 hours
Difficulty: Moderate
Trail surface: Boardwalk, gravel
Best seasons: Year-round
Other trail users: None
Canine compatibility: Dogs not permitted
Land status: City nature preserve

Nearest town: Port Aransas
Fees and permits: None
Schedule: Year-round, sunrise–sunset
Maps: USGS Port Aransas, TX; maps available at pavilion
Trail contact: City of Port Aransas Parks and Recreation, 739 W. Avenue A, Port Aransas, TX 78373; (361) 749-4158; cityofportaransas .org/nature_preserve.cfm

Finding the trailhead: From the intersection of TX 35 and W. Wheeler Avenue in Aransas Pass, take W. Wheeler Avenue south 2.5 miles. W. Wheeler Avenue turns into Harrison Boulevard. Continue south 0.6 mile and turn left onto W. Goodnight Avenue/TX 361. Travel 6.6 miles and come to the Aransas Pass–Port Aransas Ferry (there is no charge to ride the ferry). After exiting the ferry, travel 300 feet and turn right onto Port Street, then almost immediately make another right to stay on Port Street. Follow Port Street 1.2 miles to the trailhead. For ferry information such as running times and the number of ferries in operation, visit portaransas.org/about/shuttle-ferry. GPS: N27 50.038'/W97 05.188'

The Hike

Over half of the country's salt marshes are found along the Gulf Coast, and one of the most amazing hikes through one is found in the city of Port Aransas just north of Corpus Christi. It is here that you will find the Salt Marsh Island Trail.

A salt marsh is a coastal wetland with a network of snaking channels or tidal creeks that flood at least twice a day with saltwater from the ocean brought in by the tide, then just as quickly the water drains as the tide goes out. Low-lying areas in the marsh retain water for a time, and as the remaining water evaporates, a very high concentration of salt is left behind. This is called a salt panne and plants like the glasswort, also called pickleweed, thrive in this environment and provide habitat for small invertebrates and a food source for other animals. Some of the deeper depressions retain water all year. These are called pools and are home to green crabs and salt marsh snails.

Birds hunker down in the rain among the glasswort plants on the Salt Island Marsh Trail.

Some of the other plants that call a salt marsh home include the upland bayberry, marsh elder, black grass, salt marsh hay, sea lavender, and saltwater cordgrass.

The preserve itself is actually called the Port Aransas Nature Preserve at Charlie's Pasture. This land was once distressed farmland until the City of Port Aransas, several nonprofit organizations, and countless volunteers worked to reclaim the marsh. In the end they gave us this fantastic 2.2-mile boardwalk hike through the marsh and flats.

The Salt Island Marsh Trail begins behind the pavilion at the Port Aransas Nature Preserve to the northwest, then quickly swings to the south. The path will take you through all of these marsh environments along a boardwalk that is 0.7 mile (one way). The view is marvelous as you walk just inches from the top of the water and take in the expansiveness of the marsh. Along the way there are several shelters with benches to allow you to rest or just enjoy the views. The shelters are a blessing in the summer when the sun beats down on you mercilessly. There is absolutely no shade otherwise on this hike.

As you walk this trail, you will notice long flat expanses of mud. These are mud-flats where fiddler crabs, mussels, oysters, and clams can be found.

The marsh is filled with wonderful birds. Willets, least terns, white pelicans, Wilson and snowy plovers, roseate spoonbills, black-bellied whistling ducks, and reddish egrets are only a few that you will see. The preserve is rightfully serious about not bringing your pets on this hike. You may not see them, but many birds nest in the nearby brush and a disturbance by a pet—or you—could actually cause the eggs and chicks to die.

There are a few snakes in the drier areas of the marsh, including coachwhip and rat snakes. And as you pass the shelters, watch for small lizards like the green or brown anole.

As I said, the bulk of the hike is over a wooden, 4-foot-wide boardwalk. The rest of the route is a 4-foot-wide path with a brown gravel footing. These sections are found at the very beginning of the hike, a short 5-foot section in the middle of the marsh, and at the loop around the island.

On Salt Island you get another fantastic view from an observation deck looking out to the south. This is your turnaround as you ring the island and head back the way you came. By the way, mosquitoes are not usually a problem at the beginning of the hike, but during my visit the island was teeming with them. Slather on that bug repellant in the warmer months.

And another note, this is one place where you won't want to be caught out in a storm. You are literally standing out in nowhere where the winds can lash, and during a good Southern thunderstorm, it's a dangerous place to be. I visited on a fall morning just after a storm passed through, and as soon as I got to the island, a second squall came through and blew hard, making the return trip more difficult. Don't let that deter you from enjoying this amazing hike—just be aware of the elements when heading out.

WHERE HAVE ALL THE MONARCHS GONE?

Monarch butterflies are truly one of nature's wonders. These fragile creatures are able to migrate from Canada to Mexico then to the Gulf Coast, a trip of over 3,000 miles, but that trip may be coming to an end.

In a report issued by the Center for Biological Diversity, researchers have found that the monarch population has decreased 90 percent over the last twenty years. According to the study, that would be like losing every living person in the United States except those in Florida and Ohio.

The reason for the decline? Scientists say that the unprecedented record cold winters of the past few years followed by the droughts of 2012–2014 and the deforestation and destruction of the butterfly's habitat, especially milkweed, have combined to cause this decline.

So what would losing the monarch mean? As the US Department of Agriculture puts it, the monarch is the most recognized, studied, and loved butterfly in the country, but their importance goes far beyond aesthetics. The monarch is an important pollinator for our fruits and vegetables. The problem has become so critical that President Obama and the leaders of Canada and Mexico are looking at ways the governments can act to save them.

Learn more about the monarch butterfly and what is being done to help them make a comeback at monarchwatch.org.

There is only one route onto the island and that is by taking a ride on one of the famous free Texas ferries. The ferry leaves every 15 minutes, and if traffic warrants, other boats are pressed into service. Visit portaransas.org/about/shuttle-ferry for information on schedules and wait times.

Miles and Directions

0.0 Start from the parking lot and walk up to the guest pavilion to the south, which has brochures and maps. There is a short footpath to an observation deck and a trail that leads to the left and right. Take the gravel path to the right (northwest). In less than 0.1 mile, cross a bridge over a slough with nice views of the sound that links Corpus Christi Bay and Aransas Bay, wildflowers, and white pelicans. Sand dunes and a dune fence are on your left.

0.2 The main long boardwalk begins.

0.3 Pass a shelter on the left with a bench as you begin the boardwalk section of the hike. It's an amazing sight as the trail seemingly meanders and disappears on the horizon.

0.6 Pass a shelter with a bench on the right.

0.7 The boardwalk ends. You'll cross about 5 feet of gravel path and pick up the boardwalk again.

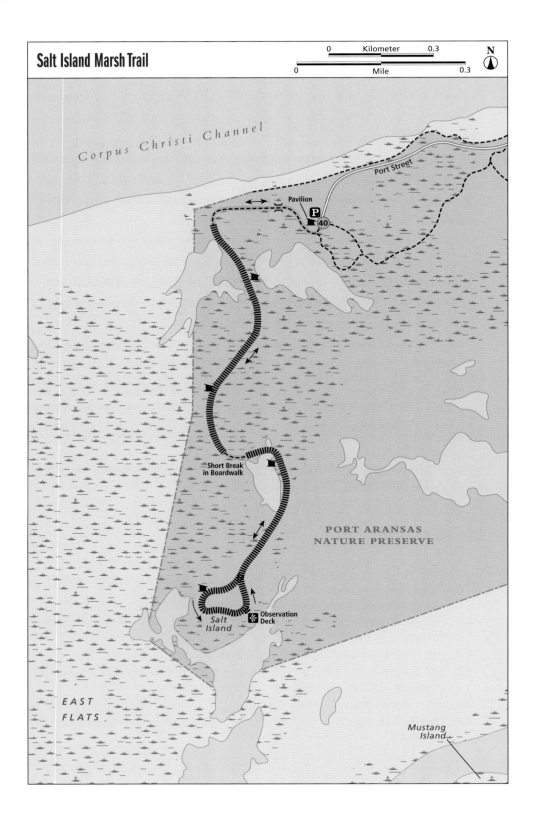

0.8 Pass another bench and shelter on your right. Many varieties of birds will be seen as the waters shallow to only a few inches and you can see the white sand under the ripples.

0.9 The boardwalk ends at Salt Island. The trail once again has a pea-sized gravel footing.

1.0 Come to a Y. This is the junction of the loop. Take the right fork to the southwest.

1.1 Pass another bench and shelter on the right with trash cans.

1.2 Come to a two-story observation deck that provides magnificent views of the marsh and Corpus Christi Bay. Pelone Island will be seen to the southwest. When done, climb down off the deck and turn right (north) to continue on the loop. In less than 0.1 mile, come to the Y from mile 1.0. Turn right (north) and retrace your steps back to the trailhead.

2.2 Arrive back at the trailhead.

Hike Information

Local Information: Port Aransas Chamber of Commerce & Tourism Bureau, 403 W. Cotter St., Port Aransas, TX 78373; (361) 749-5919; portaransas.org

Local Events/Attractions: Annual Whooping Crane Festival, 403 W. Cotter St., Port Aransas; (800) 452-6278; portaransas.org/play/whooping-crane-festival. Held each year the middle of February, the festival celebrates the beautiful and remarkable whooping crane, which can only be viewed close up on the Coastal Bend of Texas. The weekend has various nature tours, speakers, workshops on birding and photography, and more throughout the city of Port Aransas and Mustang Island. Contact the organizers or visit their website for event locations.

Lodging: Mustang Island State Park, 17047 TX 361, Port Aransas; (361) 749-5246; tpwd.state.tx .us/state-parks/mustang-island. There are plenty of camping options at Mustang Island State Park. The park has 300 primitive tent sites scattered over 1.5 miles of Gulf beach and 48 improved sites with water, electricity, picnic table, grills, and shade shelter.

Restaurants: Island Cafe and Smokehouse, 301 S. Alister St., Port Aransas; (361) 749-1741. Just good, old-fashioned home cooking.

Tours: City of Port Aransas, 403 W. Cotter St., Port Aransas; (361) 749-5919; portaransas.org/play/ birding. The City of Port Aransas and many local groups host birding and nature events at the Port Aransas Nature Preserve. Visit the city's website or call for dates and times.

Texas Honorable Mentions

But wait—there's more! Many more hiking trails on the Texas Gulf Coast. It would have been impossible to place them all on this guide's A list. So here's a few more I thought you should check out. Pay a visit and let us know what you think. Maybe the hike should be upgraded, or maybe you know of a little-known hike that would make a good honorable mention.

P Shoveler Pond Trail

Take a walk through the rice fields of Texas. No, seriously. At Anahuac National Wildlife Refuge there are rice fields growing, and because they hold large acres of shallow water, they make the perfect home for a magnificent lineup of birds, everything from dowitchers to western sandpipers, tanagers, and in the winter snow geese. Sometimes 80,000 of the geese migrate in and feed on the rice. There are also twenty-seven species of ducks here and alligators, lots of them. Rangers tell me that this is the best place in the United States to see gators, especially in spring. The best way to see all of this as well as the surrounding marshes is on the Shoveler Pond Trail, a 4.2-mile loop through this expansive scenery on the banks of Galveston and East Bays. The trail uses a combination of paved road walk, wide grassy paths, and boardwalks with several observation platforms to navigate around the landscape. There is no admission charged to visit the refuge, but remember, hunting is allowed so check with the refuge office for dates in the fall and winter. Contact Anahuac NWR at (409) 267-3337 or online at fws.gov/refuge/Anahuac for more information.

Q Armand Bayou Nature Center

Hidden away in the shadows of a major US city, Houston, is the amazing Armand Bayou Nature Center (ABNC). The center was established in 1974 with one mission in mind—to preserve the wetlands, prairie, forests, and marshes of Armand Bayou and to educate the public about the great outdoors, conservation, and preservation practices. The center encompasses 2,100 acres, making it the largest urban wildlife refuge in the United States. ABNC has 5 miles of trails with such names as Martyn, Karankawa, Marsh, and Lady Bird leading you to the big, beautiful, wide banks of the bayou and its marshes, a "Watersmart" pond, and one of the last vestiges of Texas prairie grass left in the state. White-tailed deer, armadillo, raccoon, and hundreds of songbirds escort you on your travels. Oh, and there's bison in the demonstration farm. The center holds regular nature programs like their monthly "Owl Prowl" where you can look for owls by the light of a full moon. Admission is charged (children under 4 are free). The center is open Wednesday through Saturday 9 a.m. to 5 p.m., Sunday noon to 5 p.m. For more information visit abnc.org or call (281) 474-2551.

R Mustang Island State Park

Ready for a beach walk? Just a nice, leisurely stroll down bright white beaches, the ocean waves roaring, the salt air reinvigorating your senses? We have the hike for you, the beaches of Mustang Island State Park. Located just south of the Port Aransas Nature Preserve (see hike 40, Salt Island Marsh Trail), the park offers you the chance to walk 5 miles along the beaches of the Gulf of Mexico, picking up seashells, watching the shorebirds, building sand castles, or maybe taking a swim. Just like the Salt Island Marsh hike, you will need to take one of the free Texas ferries to get to the island. The ferries run just about every 15 minutes. Admission is charged to the park (children 12 and under free). The gates are open from 7 a.m. to 10 p.m. daily. For more information call Mustang Island State Park at (512) 389-8900 or visit online at tpwd.texas.gov/state-parks/mustang-island.

S Grasslands Nature Trail

Padre Island is the largest undeveloped barrier island in the world. Encompassing 70 miles of coastland, the island is a prime nesting ground for the Kemp's ridley sea turtle and over 380 species of birds, making this area the "Birdiest Place in America." While short in length, only a 0.75-mile-long loop, the Grasslands Nature Trail gives you a glimpse behind the magic curtain at what makes the ecosystem of this major island so special. The trail starts just past the main entrance on South Padre Island Drive and winds its way through sand dunes and prairie grasses and past freshwater marshes. White-tailed deer, jackrabbits, and coyotes may be seen. Numbered posts line the trail, so pick up a brochure from the entrance station so you can learn more about this fascinating landscape. Contact the Padre Island National Seashore at (361) 949-8286 or visit online at nps.gov/pais for more information.

Appendix: Clubs and Trail Groups

Alabama Forever Wild, Alabama Department of Conservation and Natural Resources, 64 N. Union St., Montgomery, AL 36130; (334) 242-3484; alabamaforeverwild.com
Forever Wild is an arm of the Alabama Department of Conservation and Natural Resources, whose mission is to purchase and protect lands of historical and environmental significance and provide recreational opportunities.

Alabama Hiking Trail Society, PO Box 231164, Montgomery, AL 36123; hikealabama.org
AHTS is a statewide nonprofit organization with a mission to design, build, and maintain safe hiking trails across Alabama.

Brazos Bend State Park Volunteer Organization, 21901 FM 762, Needville, TX 77461; (979) 553-5101; brazosbend.org
The Brazos Bend State Park Volunteer Organization helps to educate the public about the beautiful park and its environment as well as assists in the projects and maintenance that make Brazos Bend one of the top parks in Texas.

Florida Trail Association, 5414 SW 13 St., Gainesville, FL 32608; (352) 378-8823; floridatrail.org
FTA develops, maintains, protects, and promotes a network of hiking trails throughout the state, including the Florida National Scenic Trail.

Friends of Aransas and Matagorda Island National Wildlife Refuges, PO Box 74, Austwell, TX 77950; (361) 286-3559; friendsofaransas.org
FAMI works to support and assist the Aransas and Matagorda Island National Wildlife Refuge Complex in its goal of enhancing habitat and wildlife and encouraging compatible wildlife-dependent public uses of the refuges through educational, interpretive, scientific, and other activities appropriate to the refuges' mission.

Friends of Bon Secour, 12295 AL 180, Gulf Shores, AL 36542; fws.gov/bonsecour/friends.htm
The Friends of Bon Secour is a group of citizens from all over the United States who have banded together to work primarily as an advocacy group, making telephone calls and writing letters as needed in support of the Bon Secour National Wildlife Refuge.

Friends of Brazoria Wildlife Refuges, PO Box 505, Lake Jackson, TX 77566; (866) 403-5829; refugefriends.org
The Friends of Brazoria Wildlife Refuges is a nonprofit organization dedicated to supporting the Brazoria, San Bernard, and Big Boggy National Wildlife Refuges by raising funds through donations, grants, and gifts to help fund wildlife refuge projects, educational programs, and other activities.

Friends of Galveston Island State Park, PO Box 5428, Galveston, TX 77554; (409) 737-1222; fogisp.wordpress.com
The mission of FoGISP is to promote the interests of Galveston Island State Park and its users through volunteer work, fund-raising, and stimulating community interest in the park.

Friends of the Lower Suwanee & Cedar Key National Wildlife Refuges, PO Box 532, Cedar Key, FL 32625; friendsofrefuges.org
The mission of the Friends is to provide active advocacy and physical support for the successful stewardship of the Lower Suwannee and Cedar Keys National Wildlife Refuges.

Hike Index

(HM) denotes an Honorable Mention hike.